SOCIAL REPRESENTATIONS
AND IDENTITY

SOCIAL REPRESENTATIONS AND IDENTITY

CONTENT, PROCESS, AND POWER

Edited by Gail Moloney and Iain Walker

SOCIAL REPRESENATIONS AND IDENTITY
Copyright © Gail Moloney and Iain Walker, 2007.

All rights reserved.

First published in hardcover in 2007 by PALGRAVE MACMILLAN®
in the United States—a division of St. Martin's Press LLC,
175 Fifth Avenue, New York, NY 10010.

Where this book is distributed in the UK, Europe and the rest of the world,
this is by Palgrave Macmillan, a division of Macmillan Publishers Limited,
registered in England, company number 785998, of Houndmills,
Basingstoke, Hampshire RG21 6XS.

Palgrave Macmillan is the global academic imprint of the above companies
and has companies and representatives throughout the world.

Palgrave® and Macmillan® are registered trademarks in the United States,
the United Kingdom, Europe and other countries.

ISBN: 978-1-137-27107-5

The Library of Congress has cataloged the hardcover edition as follows:

Social representations and identity : content, process, and power / edited by
    Gail Moloney & Iain Walker.
        p. cm.
    Includes bibliographical references and index.
    ISBN 1-4039-7971-5 (alk. paper)
    1. Group identity. 2. Intergroup relations. 3. Social psychology. 4. Social
perception. 5. Collective behavior. I. Moloney, Gail. II. Walker, Iain, 1960–
HM753.S628 2007
    305.01—dc22   2007009838

A catalogue record of the book is available from the British Library.

Design by Scribe Inc.

First PALGRAVE MACMILLAN paperback edition: October 2012

10 9 8 7 6 5 4 3 2 1

Printed and bound in Great Britain by
CPI Antony Rowe, Chippenham and Eastbourne

With love to
Con, Róisín, and Ciarán
and Jane, Alex, Joel, and Patrick

CONTENTS

LIST OF CONTRIBUTORS

Martha Augoustinos is a professor and codirector of the Discourse and Social Psychology Unit (DASP) in the School of Psychology, University of Adelaide. She has published widely in the areas of "race" and prejudice, social representations theory, and discursive psychology. She is coeditor with Kate Reynolds of *Understanding Prejudice, Racism and Social Conflict* (Sage, 2001) and coauthor of *Social Cognition: An Integrated Introduction* (2nd ed., Sage, 2006) with Iain Walker and Ngaire Donaghue.

Pia Broderick is an associate professor in the School of Psychology at Murdoch University in Western Australia. She is a developmental and clinical psychologist with research interests including psychosocial issues in infertility treatment and alternate family formation, parent-child attachment, and the optimal development of families and individuals. She also runs a private practice in clinical psychology, specializing in work with children, adolescents, and families.

Helen Correia is an associate lecturer in the School of Psychology at the University of Western Sydney. Her research interests include psychological and social issues relating to the use of technology. She is also a registered psychologist with particular experience in the areas of anxiety and depression.

Kay Deaux is a distinguished professor of psychology at the Graduate Center of the City University of New York. She has served as president of the American Psychological Society, the Society for the Psychological Study of Social Issues, and the Society of Personality and Social Psychology. Her books include *Representations of the Social: Bridging Theoretical Traditions* (with Gina Philogène, Blackwell, 2001) and *To Be an Immigrant* (Russell Sage, 2006).

Caroline Howarth is a lecturer in social psychology at the London School of Economics. Her research and teaching seeks to push social psychology in general and social representations theory in particular into a more critical direction by addressing questions of racism, power, exclusion, and resistance. Together with Derek Hook (London School of Economics), she is establishing a Research Network on Racism and Critical Social Psychology. She is also on the editorial boards of *Journal of Community and Applied Social Psychology* and *Papers in Social Representations*.

Hélène Joffe is senior lecturer in the Department of Psychology, University College, London. She works on social representations of emerging infectious diseases from both a media and lay perspective, with recent publications including P. Washer and H. Joffe, "The Hospital 'Superbug': Social Representations of MRSA," *Social Science & Medicine* 63, no. 8 (2006): 2142–52. She also works on wider theoretical issues, expressed in articles such as H. Joffe and C. Staerkle, "The Centrality of the Self-Control Ethos in Western Aspersions Regarding Outgroups: A Social Representational Analysis of Stereotype Content," *Culture & Psycholology (forthcoming)*.

Nicole Kronberger received her PhD in psychology from Vienna University, Austria; currently she is a university assistant at Johannes Kepler University, Linz. Her research interests include social and societal aspects of technological innovation, everyday moral reasoning, and research methodology.

János László is professor of psychology and director of the Institute of Psychology at the University of Pécs. His is also affiliated with the Hungarian Academy of Sciences, where he is scientific advisor. His main research topics include social representations theory, narrative psychology, and social psychology of history.

James H. Liu is an Associate Professor in psychology and Deputy Director of the Centre for Applied Cross-Cultural Research at Victoria University of Wellington. He specializes in social identity and intergroup relations, with a focus on the dynamics of identity and history. He has been an executive of the Asian Association of Social Psychology for almost a decade and a fellow of the Society for the Psychological Study of Social Issues (SPSSI), reflecting interests in both culture and action-oriented research. He lives in a house overlooking Wellington Harbour with his wife Belinda and daughter Brianna, and identifies himself as a "Chinese American New Zealander."

Ivana Marková is professor of psychology at the University of Stirling in Scotland. Her main research interests are the theory of social representations, language, and communication. Recent publications include *Dialogicality and Social Representations* (CUP, 2003) and, with S.

Moscovici, *The Making of Modern Social Psychology* (Polity, 2006). She is a Fellow of the Royal Society of Edinburgh and of the British Academy.

Gail Moloney is a lecturer at the Department of Psychology at the Coffs Harbour campus of Southern Cross University, NSW, Australia. Her primary research interests are in social representations theory and social identity, community and the resettlement of forced migrants, intergroup relations, and social understandings of organ donation and transplantation.

Emda Orr is a retired professor at Ben-Gurion University of Negev, Beer-sheva, Israel. Her academic interests include social identity, representations of minority groups within the Israeli society specifically those of Kibbutz members, religious settlers, immigrants, Palestinian students, political minorities, and black minorities from the Jewish and the Arab societies.

Gina Philogène is a professor of psychology at Sarah Lawrence College in Bronxville, New York. Her research interests are in social and cultural psychology, history of psychology, race, and social identity, cultural anthropology, and social representations. She is the author of *From Black to African American: A New Representation* and various articles in professional journals; coeditor of the forthcoming *Social Representations and Social Psychology in the United States*; and associate editor of the international journal *Representation and Society*.

Damien W. Riggs is an ARC postdoctoral fellow in the School of Psychology, University of Adelaide. He has published widely in the areas of lesbian and gay psychology and critical race and whiteness studies, and is the editor of two books: *Out in the Antipodes: Australian and New Zealand Perspectives on Gay and Lesbian Issues in Psychology*, and *Taking up the Challenge: Critical Race and Whiteness Studies in a Postcolonising Nation*. His new book, *Priscilla, (White) Queen of the Desert: Queer Rights/Race Privilege* (Peter Lang) was published in 2006, and he is completing work on a second book due in 2007 entitled *Becoming Parent: Lesbians, Gay Men, and Family*.

Wolfgang Wagner is a professor of social psychology at Johannes Kepler University of Linz, Austria. His current research interests are social and cultural knowledge, particularly everyday thinking about popularized science such as biotechnology, essentialist thinking in the context of natural kinds, ethnic groups and racism, historical processes and national identities, and social representation theory. He is coauthor of *Everyday Discourse and Common Sense—The Theory of Social Representations* (2005), coeditor of the book *Meaning in Action—Construction, Narratives and Representations* (forthcoming), associate editor of *Culture and Psychology,*

Public Understanding of Science, and founding editor of *Papers on Social Representations*.

Iain Walker is a professor of psychology at Murdoch University in Perth, Western Australia. His research interests are diffused across several areas, including relative deprivation theory, prejudice, social representations, and social identity. He coauthored *Social Cognition: An Integrated Introduction* (Sage, 2nd ed., 2006) with Martha Augoustinos and Ngaire Donaghue, and coedited *Relative Deprivation Theory: Specification, Development, Integration* (CUP, 2002) with Heather Smith.

Shaun Wiley is a doctoral student in social-personality psychology at the Graduate Center of the City University of New York. He is interested in immigration, collective identity, and intergroup relations.

Chapter 1

Introduction

Gail Moloney
Iain Walker

> We cannot prove that representations exist, we can only demonstrate the power of this concept through the interpretations we can offer of social phenomena. (Duveen 1994, 207)

ALL MAJOR CONTEMPORARY SOCIAL ISSUES INVOLVE QUESTIONS of power, social positioning, identity, and social knowledge construction. The complex interplay between these becomes apparent when one considers examples such as immigration, minority groups, biotechnology, and health. All these examples appear in the present book. The social sciences have researched these issues considerably, so one could reasonably ask what is different about the collection of papers presented here.

In bringing these research papers together, we argue that there is still much to be learned about the constitutive nature of the social, particularly when the nonindividualistic perspective of social representations theory is utilized. An under-researched area here is the nature of the relationships between social identity and social representations (Deaux 2001; Duveen 2001), and the implications these relationships have for understanding social phenomena.

How the representation-identity relationship manifests, if indeed it does, and the nature of this relationship across diverse research contexts are concerns of this book. Similarly, we do not yet know if the context of the relationship becomes the relationship, or whether generalities exist in the nature of the relationship across research contexts. These questions are, however, underpinned by the theoretical position that social identity is part of social knowledge and, thus, the *processes* and *content* of social identity are inseparable in understanding identity. Central to this is the premise that social knowledge is collectively constructed through interaction among individuals and between individuals and the institutionalized structures that define that society (Wagner, Valencia, and Elejabarrieta 1996). Consequently, social identity must always be forged and permeated by societal relationships and structures. Thus, the articulations of social identity presented here are embedded in social knowledge and are primarily about content, process, and power relations.

Understanding social identity as such, however, requires a shift in analytic gaze away from the individual as the point of reference to identity as a relationship between individuals and their society. Although the nature of this relationship is not clear, what we do propose is that the centrality of the individual in identity analyses is itself a product of our representational systems.

THE REPRESENTATION OF THE INDIVIDUAL AND IDENTITY

Individual agency and responsibility are central to the pervasive collective representation of the individual that has shaped the historical development of most psychological theorizing (Farr 1991). We suggest that a similar claim can be made in relation to much experimentally driven social psychological analyses of identity. In particular, many empirical investigations within the framework of Tajfel and Turner's (1979) social identity theory imply that identity is concentric from the individual through a focus on the individual's motivation to achieve a positive social identity and associated levels of identification, salience, and knowledge with in- and out-group memberships (see Augoustinos, Walker, and Donaghue 2006).

What it *means* to be identified as belonging to a particular group, in contrast to how one is identified, has been neglected in identity research, the lack of attention attributed to an interest in the ways in which social identity influences and is influenced by intergroup encounters (Deaux 2001) and how identity may be sustained or manipulated (Duveen 2001). We suggest also that the prescriptiveness of the individual as a collective representation, including the constructed dichotomy between the individual and the social (Duveen and Lloyd 1986), has been influential in a research focus on process rather than content. The notion of agency, particularly, dictates a concentric understanding of identity in which the individual is at the center of the constructive process. Here the locus of identity is individualistic and resonates with Ichheiser's (1943) view that ideology "leads us to believe that our fate in social space depend[s] exclusively, or at least predominately, on our individual qualities . . . [rather than] the prevailing social conditions" (cited in Farr 1991, 138).

In his paper *The Coming Era of Social Representations*, Moscovici (1982) pre-empts Farr's call to recognize the power of the representation of the individual by urging social psychological research to shift to a level of analysis where society is regarded not as a backdrop for the individual but rather as an entity with the individual *sui generis*. Thus, in advocating an end to the conceptual separation between the individual and society, the processes and content of social thinking are inevitably entwined.

The importance of this argument for understanding the constitutive nature of identity is twofold: first, by arguing that the social and the individual are a unity, identity must be inclusive of social forces; and second, the interdependence between process and content immediately reinstates the content of identity to the foreground in identity analyses, suggesting that content and process be deduced concurrently (Jovchelovitch 1996).

The influence of the collective representation of the individual has ramifications also for understanding the *social* nature of knowledge, and therein links to how Moscovici (1984; 2000) conceptualizes social knowledge. Never simply a description or duplication, knowledge is constructed through interaction, communication, and its significance to the individuals and groups who engage with it (Duveen 2000). Thus, knowledge can only ever be social, and the purpose of the theory of social representations is to elucidate how individuals and groups go beyond mere description to construe meaningful understandings about issues and objects in their social environment (Marková 1996), particularly those that are unfamiliar and threatening (see Moscovici 1984/2000).

The content of identity—or what it means to be socially identified—is constructed through social representation, although its constitutive nature is often obscured by the ontological reality that representations create. The commonsense and habitual nature of representation often occludes how the content of identity is forged and permeated by societal relationships. And, as argued by Marková (1996), it is only when we are called to *consciously* engage with this reality that this can be realized.

Thus, the aim of this book is to encourage a conscious engagement with the relationship of social representation to identity so as to foreground an understanding of identity that is both process and content. The chapters herein do not reach a conclusive answer; rather they interrogate, elaborate, and enunciate this relationship across widely diverse research contexts. The chapters do, however, cultivate a view of identity that is interdependent with representation.

In Chapter 2, Kay Deaux and Shaun Wiley present a macro-to-micro analysis of immigration and identification in the United States in which the shifting demographics of immigration, and concomitant policy responses, are shown to redefine existing meanings of identity categories while creating new ones. The relationship of representation to identity is highlighted through their analyses of how groups must come to understand the dominant representations of race and legality in order to negotiate and position themselves in relation to the meanings associated with their ethnic and national identity. The interdependence between identity and representation is further examined by the distinctions between hegemonic, polemic, and emancipated representations, and by reference to the theoretical distinctions between Abric's (2001) theory of the central core, and Clémence's (2001) concept of positioning.

Gina Philogène also addresses the construction of the immigrant identity in her analysis of the dual meaning of alterity in the United States, but she does so to articulate how immigrants as the *Cultural Other* are positioned in contradistinction to the *Social Other*: Americans of African descent. Although both identity categorizations are a function of the representations of the Other, Philogène explicates how cultural otherness implies unfamiliarity and is thus malleable, while social otherness implies exclusion, and thus immutable difference. Philogène's analysis of the social positioning of these groups to each other, and to the ideal white American identity, demonstrates that identity cannot be separated from the processes of constructing otherness.

In Chapter 4, Emda Orr locates group identity within the representational structures of society as identity representations—the social reality of a group's identity as constructed by a specific society and relevant spectators. Orr's analysis of three minority groups in Israel—immigrants, religious people, and educationally slow children—unravels the coexistence and function of seemingly incompatible hegemonic and emancipated representations in constructing and maintaining the identities of these groups.

In Chapter 5, Gail Moloney's analysis of the depiction of refugees and asylum-seekers in the editorial cartoon is used to exemplify how asymmetrical communication processes construct and maintain the identity of voiceless groups in society. Social identity here is shown to be a function of social knowledge. Moloney argues that when voiceless groups have little redress to how they are portrayed in the media, the dichotomy and thus contradiction between the intent of the cartoon and the visual portrayal of these people through caricature allows the continual reproduction of a negative identity.

James Liu and János László also address the incongruities in our social knowledge, but they do so by showing how the narratives of history make sense of the different realties we encounter. The focus here is on how static event-based historical narratives forge, maintain, and reflect social identity through mechanisms of privilege, empathy, perspective, and emotive templates. Liu and László's analysis of the identity-representation relationship elucidates how the content and sources of collectively shared systems of knowledge justify the distribution of value and the allocation of social roles and, thus, group identity.

In Chapter 7, Martha Augoustinos and Damien Riggs present an analysis of the politics of identity in Australia, drawing from the collective level of historical narratives of Indigenous peoples and the dominant white majority of Australia. Augoustinos and Riggs argue that essentialized representations of race have become reified and objectified ways of making sense of difference, and despite challenges to the contrary, remain entrenched and resilient in everyday understandings of the nature of social relations in Australia. However, these authors argue strongly that racism functions through racial categories in the representations of *both* "us" and "them," rather than either the former or latter, thus making clear the inextricable relationship between identity and representation.

The focus of Caroline Howarth's chapter is also the social representations of race, specifically how young children who experience or witness racism contest, negotiate, and navigate it in their everyday school lives in a white-majority primary school in England. Howarth argues for a dialectical view of the relationship between identity and representations. She presents discourse as evidence that identity and representations are different sides of the same coin, and as such there can be no possibility of understanding identity without representation.

The interplay between identity and representation is also a nascent theme in the chapter by Iain Walker, Pia Broderick, and Helen Correia on social representations and Medically Assisted Reproduction Technologies (MART). Summarizing three studies, they show how, historically, social scientists actively helped construct a stained identity for children born through the use of MART, how public debate and discussion about MART and who should have access to MART relies on representations of the natural order of things to anchor understandings of MART, and how violations of nature are used to justify excluding lesbians, gay men, and others from accessing MART.

The chapter by Nicole Kronberger and Wolfgang Wagner also examines the interplay between technology, identity, and social representations to propose that while identity may constrain the enactment of social representations, the emergence of new technologies necessitates the restructuring of existing identities. The research presented by Kronberger and Wagner on cross-species gene transfer and human reproductive cloning focuses on the role that identity plays in the context of resistance to technopolitical rationality, particularly those technologies that address life and nature. Drawing from their research, these authors argue that fixity cannot be assumed for even our most basic categories, thus identity is not only about being but also about becoming.

Hélène Joffe focuses on the entwined nature of process and content in identity construction in her chapter on identity, self control, and risk. Integrating psychodynamic and social representations theory, Joffe presents a clear argument for why group membership *cannot* be the sole feature of who one is and how one is defined. Social identity here is about self-other relations, the vestiges of which are constructed in early infantile representations, while the content of these identity-based representations of the *Other* are constructed around values that sustain a positive sense of identity through their devaluing properties.

The chapter by Ivana Marková concludes the book, with a historical commentary on the relationships theorized to exist between identity and social representation. Pivotal questions that underpin the articulation of this relationship are addressed, including the following: Which comes first—identity or representation? Which theory of social representations should be used to understand and articulate which social identities? What is the nature of social categorization and social representation? How do our understandings of similarity and interaction depend on who it is or what it is we are interacting with? What is the role of themata in the content of social representation? Marková concludes this chapter, and the book, by urging social psychologists to utilize the knowledge gained from investigations of social representation and identity to find real-life solutions that promote intergroup tolerance.

Together, these chapters represent a major collection of contributions analyzing the complex interplay between power, social positioning, identity, and social knowledge construction, all from a social representations perspective. They encapsulate exciting research being done around the globe, with the aim of better understanding these issues. With such understandings comes a greater ability, and responsibility, for social psychologists to engage with real issues of power, positioning, and identity.

REFERENCES

Abric, J.-C. 2001. A structural approach to social representations. In *Representations of the social: Bridging theoretical traditions*, ed. K. Deaux and G. Philogène, 42–47. Oxford: Blackwell.

Augoustinos, M., I. Walker, and N. Donaghue. 2006. *Social cognition: An integrated introduction*. 2nd ed. London: Sage.

Clémence, A. 2001. Social positioning and social representation. In *Representations of the social: Bridging theoretical traditions*, ed. K. Deaux and G. Philogène, 83–95. Oxford: Blackwell.

Deaux, K. 2001. Meaning and making: Some comments on content and process. *Representations of the social: Bridging theoretical traditions*, ed. K. Deaux and G. Philogène, 312–17. Oxford: Blackwell.

Duveen, G. 1994. Unanalysed residues: Representations and behaviours—A comment on W. Wagner. *Papers on Social Representations* 3:95–232.

———. 2000. Introduction: The power of ideas. In *Social representations: Explorations in social psychology*, by Serge Moscovici and ed. G. Duveen, 1–17. Cambridge: Polity.

———. 2001. Representations, identities, resistance. In *Representations of the social: Bridging theoretical traditions*, ed. K. Deaux and G. Philogène, 257–70. Oxford: Blackwell.

Duveen, G., and B. Lloyd. 1986. The significance of social identities. *British Journal of Social Psychology* 25:219–30.

———. 1990. Introduction to *social representations and the development of knowledge*, ed. G. Duveen and B. Lloyd, 1–10. Cambridge: Cambridge University Press.

Farr, R. M. 1991. Individualism as a collective representation. In *Ideologies et representations sociales*, ed. V. Aebischer, J. P. Deconchy, and E. M. Lipiansky, 129–43. Fribourg, Switzerland: Cousset.

———. 1998. From collective to social representations: "Aller et retour." *Culture & Psychology* 4:275–96.

Hogg, M. 2001. Social categorization, depersonalization, and group behavior. In *Blackwell handbook of social psychology: Group processes,* ed. M. Hogg and R. Tindale, 56–85. Oxford: Blackwell.

Ichheiser, G. 1943. Misinterpretations of personality in everyday life and the psychologist's frame of reference. *Character and Personality* 12:145–60.

Jovchelovitch, S. 1996. In defence of representations. *Journal for the Theory of Social Behaviour* 26:121–35.

Marková, I. 1987. Representations, concepts and social change: The phenomenon of AIDS. *Journal for the Theory of Social Behaviour* 17:389–409.

———. 1996. Towards an epistemology of social representations. *Journal for the Theory of Social Behaviour* 26:177–96.

Moscovici, S. 1982. The coming era of social representations. In *Cognitive approaches to social behaviour*, ed. J. P. Codol and J. P. Leyens, 115–50. La Haye: M. Nijhoff.

Moscovici, S. 1984. The phenomenon of social representations. In *Social representations*, ed. R. M. Farr and S. Moscovici, 3–69. Cambridge: Cambridge University Press; Paris: Maison des Sciences de l'Homme.

———. 2000. The phenomenon of social representations. In *Social representations: Explorations in social psychology*, by Serge Moscovici and ed. G. Duveen, 18–77. Cambridge: Polity.

Tajfel, H. 1981. *Human groups and social categories: Studies in social psychology.* Cambridge: Cambridge University Press.

Tajfel, H., and J. Dawson, eds. 1965. *Disappointed guests.* London: Oxford University Press.

Tajfel, H., and J. C. Turner. 1979. An integrative theory of intergroup conflict. In *The social psychology of intergroup relations,* ed. W. G. Austin and S. Worchef, 33–47. Monterey, CA: Brooks/Cole.

Wagner, W., and N. Hayes. 2005. *Everyday discourse and common sense: The theory of social representations.* New York: Palgrave Macmillan.

Wagner, W., J. Valencia, and F. Elejabarrieta. 1996. Relevance, discourse and the "hot" stable core of social representations—A structural analysis of word associations. *British Journal of Social Psychology* 35:331–51.

CHAPTER 2

MOVING PEOPLE AND SHIFTING REPRESENTATIONS
MAKING IMMIGRANT IDENTITIES

Kay Deaux
Shaun Wiley

THE MOVEMENT OF PEOPLE FROM ONE NATION-STATE TO ANOTHER has become a dominant issue in these early years of the twenty-first century, engaging politicians, social scientists, and the general public throughout the world. The demographic data are striking in terms of both the absolute number of people who are moving and in the steadily increasing trend. In the year 2000, for example, nearly 180 million people were immigrants, moving from one country to another (United Nations 2002). The often-violent ramifications of this human movement can be seen in countries throughout the world—in the vigilante border patrols on the Mexican border of the United States, the unrest of Arab immigrants in Paris suburbs, and the political rhetoric and candidate assassination in the Netherlands.

Our major focus in this chapter, however, is neither the cold data of demography nor the hot rhetoric of the political arena, though both are relevant to our concerns. We look instead at issues of immigration and identification, specifically asking how a social representational analysis can contribute to a greater understanding of this pressing social issue. What are the key images that are framing current immigration debates and how are these images being shaped and reshaped by the political and demographic landscape? And how, within this landscape, do immigrants themselves find meaning and negotiate a sense of ethnic and national identity? These are the questions that we will address in this chapter, assessing whether the concepts of social representation theory can contribute to a deeper analysis of some existent research findings.

IMMIGRATION, IDENTIFICATION, AND SOCIAL REPRESENTATIONS

Immigration offers an important occasion for studying both social representation and identity negotiation. From the perspective of the individual, immigration precipitates a shift of representational fields, a change in the shared understanding about groups and their positions in society and of the boundaries that include or divide one group from another. Reicher (2004) has argued that the key questions of social identities—how we categorize ourselves in terms of group membership, which groups we compare ourselves with, and which domains provide the basis for comparison—are far from set in the real world. He contends that "the issue of how events come to be construed in terms of given categories is a necessary precursor to understanding relations between categories" (2004, 930). We take the position that shared understandings in the new context, to be exemplified by social representations of race and legality, inform and give meaning to immigrants' self-categorizations and social comparisons, shaping both their views of their groups and intergroup behavior. Within these new contexts, people must find some way to position themselves, to anchor the newly encountered representations within their own life experience. Understanding identity as it relates to immigration entails more than knowing the degree to which immigrants categorize themselves in terms of their country of origin or their country of residence. Rather, it also depends on the meaning of each, as well as the meaning of the existing categories they encounter in the new country, often unfamiliar and in need of explication.

At the same time, the existent social representations of a society are also affected by the phenomenon of immigration. As described in more detail by Deaux (2006), government policy, demographic realities, and social representations are interdependent, creating a social context that influences both immigrants and the resident citizens of the country. Policy and demography are clearly interdependent: decisions of governments to open or close the doors to immigration influence the population demographics of a country, and increases or decreases in certain segments of the population can be the impetus for policy changes. Further, both policy and demography contribute to the social representations of immigration generally and of immigrant groups specifically. In the early twentieth century, for example, when immigration to the United States had increased sharply, new metaphorical representations emerged in the public discourse that referred to disease, catastrophe, and subhuman status (O'Brien 2003). Immigrants themselves can also put forward new understandings of old categories, changing the representational landscape. Examples that we will discuss in more detail include redefinitions of race-related categories such as African American, and the development of the concept of undocumented (as contrasted with illegal) by immigrants who have entered the United States without legal papers.

The question of how widely shared these or other representations of immigration are within the society is an important issue for consideration. Moscovici (1988) described three types of social representations: hegemonic, polemic, and emancipated. Hegemonic representations are consensually shared by all members of a society and constitute the collective reality about a given social topic. Representations become polemical to the degree that different groups actively disagree about a representation, putting forward competing positions. Rather than being shared by the society at large, polemical representations are bounded, distinctively associated with particular groups who typically are in conflict with one another. Emancipated representations are also the property of distinctive groups but are characterized as being less polarized, able instead to coexist among subgroups in a society (Breakwell 2001; Liu 2004). Whether a representation is considered emancipated or polemical clearly has critical implications for the relationships between groups and how members of various groups understand themselves.

Also relevant to the shared nature of social representations is the concept of positioning, as introduced by Clémence (2001). For Clémence, social representations are a "network of variations" in which meanings are anchored in the existing knowledge and experience of different groups. Because knowledge and experience vary between groups, representations also vary. Although groups may agree on what a particular object is—for instance, the group of people who make up a given social category—they do not integrate that meaning into their "prior knowledge and beliefs" in the same way. From this perspective, social representations are *shared* in the sense that particular objects organize group thinking, but they are not *consensual*, that is, all groups do not necessarily have the same view of the object despite a common categorization scheme.

This theory of social representations owes much to work by Willem Doise and his colleagues on the representation of human rights (Doise 2001; Doise, Spini, and Clémence 1999). Doise, Spini, and Clémence (1999) argue that, whereas social representations imply a common organization of an object, they do not imply common positions. Different individuals can attach different levels of significance to aspects of a representation. They might anchor the representations in their values, their experiences with conflict, and the nations to which they belong. Predictable patterns of positioning with regard to the representation of human rights are found at the level of the nation. However, demographic categories such as the nation are not the sense in which we make use of Clémence's group positions. We are interested in how positions toward social representations vary as a function of identification with certain groups, not just nominal membership. Although the emphasis in Doise, Spini, and Clémence's (1999) approach has been on individual variations in social representations, it is important to note that each of the anchors they offer implicates group identification. To a large degree, different positions on social representations reflect collective as well as individual values and experiences with conflict.

The views of Clémence (2001) and Doise, Spini, and Clémence (1999) can be contrasted with the structural view of social representations in which meanings are organized around a central core that is consensual and wherein variations are found only in peripheral elements that are not fundamental to shared meaning (Abric 2001). These two views of social representations offer different images of the world and bear more than a passing resemblance, respectively, to the polemic and emancipated versus hegemonic forms described by Moscovici (1988). We will view immigration from each of these lenses, examining which one proves more useful in understanding the phenomena of interest.

In addition to looking at social representations at the level of the group, we also examine the influence of representations on the lives of individual immigrants, moving our analysis from the macrolevel of demographics and laws to the mesolevel of intergroup processes, and further to the microlevel of the individual (Pettigrew 1997). Within the domain of gender, Duveen (2001) has pointed to variability in the social representations of young boys and girls. He attributes this variability to relations of power within the representation of gender, which some children (mostly girls) resist. We adopt a similar perspective in the domain of immigration, considering how social representations vary as a function of the different positions that are associated with different migration experiences and generational statuses.

KEY ELEMENTS OF A REPRESENTATIONAL ANALYSIS OF IMMIGRATION

Fundamental to the reception, treatment, and possible incorporation of an immigrant group by the residents of a country is the issue of status. Almost inevitably, long-time residents believe that they have a higher status, by virtue of settlement and longevity, and they are typically accorded this status by others, as well. The specifics of the status hierarchy will vary across countries, however, shaped by specific policies and cultural norms (for example, see Hagendoorn, Drogendijk, Turnanov, and Hraba 1998). In Germany, for example, until recently, citizenship was defined by bloodline rather than by territorial criteria, so that a person of German descent born in another country was privileged over someone born in Germany but of non-German descent (Joppke 1998). In France, in contrast, citizenship is defined by territoriality, in that residents of Martinique and Guadeloupe, for example, are legally considered equivalent to residents of France, independent of ethnic background (Brubaker 1992).

As we have reviewed the literature that speaks to the representational field of immigrant identity, we find that two key issues predominate: race and legality. Both these concepts are social constructions with histories of changing definitions and boundary lines and, as the examples of France and Germany illustrate, may be conceptualized in different ways at different times and in different places. In our discussion, we will necessarily limit our focus to a few country-specific examples, and we draw most heavily on the U.S. case. We assume, however, that representations of race and legality are critical to the identity construction of immigrants in a majority of circumstances throughout the world.

RACE, ETHNICITY, AND THE SHIFTING COLOR LINES

Dating from the institution of slavery and the social and political structures that surrounded and supported a demarcation defined by color, race has been a powerful representation within the United States. Although the content of the representations of black and white have changed over time (see Philogène 1999; Philogène 2001; and Chapter 3 in this volume), the discourse of race has continued to underlie most discussions and representations of ethnicity within U.S. society. Examples of the power of the race representation within U.S. immigration history are easy to find. The Chinese Exclusion Act of 1882 was the first domestic legislation that explicitly targeted and banned the entry of one ethnic group—a group described by some disgruntled miners as "long tailed, horned and cloven-hoofed" (McLeod, quoted in Daniels 1988, 34).

Yet categories of representation have also shown flexibility over the years. In recounting a history of Chinese-Americans in Mississippi, Loewen (1971) quotes a resident whose classification was simple: "You're either a white man or a nigger here. . . . When I first came to the Delta, the Chinese were classified as nigras." In a representational shift, this respondent goes on to explain that the Chinese are now considered white.

A similar chromatic transformation was described by Ignatiev (1995) in his aptly-titled analysis *How the Irish Became White*. The language used to describe native-born African Americans and Irish immigrants often fused characteristics of the two groups, as when the Irish were called "niggers turned inside out" or blacks were described as "smoked Irish" (Ignatiev 1995, 41). Later, as Ignatiev shows, representations of ethnicity and race shifted. The previously devalued immigrant groups such as the Irish and Italian were upgraded to the status of white ethnics, leaving African Americans as the sole occupants of the category "black."

For an immigrant of African descent who enters a society in which race is a dominant discourse, a major task is to come to an understanding of the societal representations of race and to negotiate the meaning of one's own identity within that context (Tormala and Deaux 2006). This entry entails confronting a discourse that is based not only on color but on status distinctions, as well.[1] Numerous analyses of Caribbean societies, a major source of immigration to the United States and Canada (and, in an earlier period, to England), note that race is conceptualized very differently there (Rogers 2001; Vickerman 1999; Waters 1999). In most countries of the Caribbean, blacks are in the majority, and as a consequence, color can be taken for granted rather than being the distinctive marker that it is in white-majority countries. Focusing specifically on Jamaica, Vickerman (1999) described a society in which "daily interactions . . . are largely independent of race," and where "race has taken on the aspect of a background variable—important, but largely distant" (1999, 36). In these countries, class is the more salient influence, reflecting a relationship between demographics and markers that Bobb (2001) has commented upon, namely the prominence of race discrimination in white-majority societies and of class distinctions in black-majority countries.

Entrance to a white-majority country for the black immigrant involves first a process of categorization in which skin color rather than nationality becomes the defining category. (As one Caribbean immigrant to Canada said to Vickerman, "I had to come all the way to Canada to discover I was Black!" [1999, 24]). With this definition comes the recognition that color categories form the basis of the prevailing status hierarchy within the society, one in which white is at the top and black is at the bottom (Sidanius and Pratto 1999). Immigrants of other ethnic backgrounds also encounter prevailing beliefs about the status hierarchy within the United States, although the lines of demarcation are less sharply etched than they are for black versus white. Nonetheless, Asians tend to be seen as less than white but more than black, and immigrants from Latin America are often placed near the bottom end of the ladder along with Blacks.

These processes are far from perfunctory, however, and are embedded in much more dynamic and culturally influenced systems of meaning. As Reicher and Hopkins observed in their analysis of national identity, it is a "myth that there is always a single valid definition for any given identity" (2001, ix), and the negotiation of ethnic and national identities well illustrates the truth of this premise. Terms such as Asian-American or Hispanic, for example, are from their inception constructed by one set of people (e.g., a government bureaucracy) and then are somehow responded to by those to whom they are thought to apply. Yet to assume a hegemonic basis for these categories, to use Moscovici's (1988) term, would be a mistake. Rather than representing a consensual understanding, ethnic labels are working spaces in which different groups can create quite different meaning systems.

A revealing analysis of the diversity that can exist within a single category is provided by Krystal Perkins (2006), who studied the meaning systems associated with the identity of African Americans by three distinct groups: African-descent persons who were born in the United States (and whose parents were native-born Americans as well), and two groups of immigrants, one group from Africa and the other from the Caribbean. Each of the participants in this study had self-identified as an African American, but as evident from the discussions in her three separate focus groups (each homogeneous in terms of ethnic background), the meanings associated with that categorical label had noticeably different profiles. Participants in each of the groups frequently pointed to experiences with discrimination from the dominant white group as part of their identity as an African American. Yet in a discursive analysis of their comments, Perkins (2006) found differences in the centrality and importance of this theme to identification. For native-born African Americans, their identity was in large part defined by the position of their group in society and their experiences with discriminatory treatment. Although Afro Caribbeans also referred to group-based discrimination, with its implications of victimization and lack of agency, they were more apt also to assign some responsibility to the victim. Both African and Afro Caribbean immigrants showed more inclination to downplay the pervasiveness of discrimination, suggesting some belief in immunity to the oppressive forces of society. Further, African immigrants were the least likely to go beyond the definitional characteristics of being African American, such as skin color and geographical position.

At least two different ideas from social representation theorizing can be brought to bear on the Perkins data. One framework is Abric's (1993, 2001) structural analysis of social representations that distinguishes between core and peripheral elements. The central core of a representation consists of "one or several elements that give the representation its meaning" (Abric 2001, 43). A change in core elements, which are inherently resistant to change, means a fundamental transformation of the representation itself. Peripheral elements, in contrast, "constitute the interface between the central core and the concrete situation in which the representation elaborates or realizes itself" (Abric 2001, 44). These elements allow the representation to be responsive to contextual differences, without necessitating a change in the core representation itself. In the Perkins study, experiences with oppression were central to the definition of African American for all groups, as were defining physical characteristics and African heritage. Thus, these might be considered core elements of the African American representation. In contrast, variations emerged between groups on other elements, including the history of slavery as well as contemporary behaviors and life styles. Using Abric's framework, we might consider these latter features to be peripheral elements whose nature reflects the particular environments of the different immigrant and nonimmigrant groups.

An alternative perspective that can be brought to bear on the Perkins data is Clémence's theory of positionality. As Clémence has described his theory, "Sharing common points of reference does not imply consensual agreement. . . . *Social positioning* derives from the anchoring of the shared knowledge in different groups. These groups are not only different because they do not have access to the same information, but also because their members share specific beliefs and experiences." (Clémence 2001, 87; emphasis original).

Each of the three groups in the Perkins (2006) study was positioned differently with regard to their claims on the identity of African Americans. For those descended directly from the culture of slavery in the United States, the current status hierarchy is easily linked to the earlier, more formalized system of oppression and dominance. The continued existence of one's people within the historical record of the country can neither be minimized nor forgotten. Immigrants from the Caribbean also have a history of slavery, but it is more distant in time and less evident in the present. As residents of countries in which blacks are in the majority, race has lost the force of distinction that it still maintains in the United States. Immigrants from Africa define yet a third position. Although colonialist histories are often part of their heritage, Africans were typically not part of an institutionalized system of slavery. (And indeed, to the degree that slavery was part of their cultural history, they were as likely to be associated with the perpetrators as with the victims.)

Both the Abric and the Clémence models allow for some differences between groups in their social representations of a commonly accepted category. As we will discuss at more length later in this chapter, however, the two models are not totally compatible, having different implications for both the durability and the consensuality of a representation. Although our emphasis in this chapter is primarily on the U.S. context, evidence of race as a pervasive representation can readily be found in other societies. In many countries, the black-white color line observed by W. E. B. Du Bois (1903/1976) in the United States finds close parallels. Such dichotomous categorization systems are far from universal, however. In Brazil, for example, as Edward Telles has so masterfully analyzed, race terms are based almost solely on skin color and physical appearance rather than on history and ancestry. There, although a racial hierarchy exists with its roots similarly based on white supremacy, a different ideology and meaning system defines the hierarchy. The color continuum in Brazil, varying from *blanco* (white), to *preto* (black), exists in a more general social ideology in which miscegenation[2] is foundational (Telles 2004). Further, that continuum is marked by several different categories and tolerates a greater zone of ambiguity than does the white-black color line.

An interesting example of representational shift is seen if we compare data from Marrow (2003) to the findings of Telles (2004). Marrow, using the 1990 U.S. Census data, analyzed the self-categorization of Brazilian immigrants to the United States (defined as all persons in the sample who said they were born in Brazil plus all those who indicated at least one Brazilian ancestor on the long-form census questionnaire) and found that the vast majority of the persons in this sample identified themselves as white. In contrast, Telles (2004) found that only 42 percent of Brazilians self-identified as white (*blanco*) in a 1995 racial survey done in Brazil. Only 8 percent identified as black, consistent with the U.S. data, but almost half described themselves in terms of the alternative midrange categories of *moreno, pardo,* and *moreno claro* (Portuguese terms referring to various shades of brown). Thus, given the availability of socially constructed categories in the society, people in Brazil define themselves in terms that avoid the sharp dichotomies that characterize the U.S. system. Of further interest is the comparison that Marrow (2003) made between first- and second-generation Brazilian immigrants in the United States. Both categories, white and black, were used in self-description more often by second-generation immigrants than by first-generation immigrants.

Although the latter were probably still operating on the basis of racial representations in their country of origin, the second-generation immigrants were now moving toward the acceptance of the dominant U.S. representation, namely the black-white divide.

Thus, our analysis of the use of "color" categories in immigration literature attests to the flexibility and continued reconstruction of the categories, both as they are applied by others and as they are adopted and given meaning by the immigrants themselves. A similar story of positioning and the dynamics of change can be told when we look to the nature of citizenship in the destination country.

LEGALITY, DOCUMENTATION, AND DEFINITIONS OF CITIZENSHIP

As noted earlier, policy and demography often influence the development and change of social representations. Our focus in this section is on how shifting patterns of immigration and legal responses have created a relatively new category of illegal immigrants and how immigrants have contested this categorization. The representations of this category have implications both for individual immigrant identities and group conflict. We will show how individuals and groups position themselves to the new representation, finding diversity among immigrant groups and the native born, as well as between individual immigrants.

Consider the situation in the United States. Hemispheric quotas and long backlogs for legal entry in the United States increased the number of people entering the country illegally in the 1970s (Massey, Durand, and Malone 2002). The adoption of the Immigration Reform and Control Act of 1986 gave a one-year amnesty to immigrants who had come to the United States illegally prior to 1982, but it also increased penalties for hiring illegal workers and militarized the border. Subsequent laws passed in the 1990s continued the militarization of the border and introduced bans for re-entry, such that illegals who were detained faced five- to ten-year bans on applying to return to the United States. The effect of these laws has been to decrease levels of return migration by half, increase the number of illegals living in the United States, and increase the number of immigrant deaths on the border (Massey 2006). Within immigrant communities, the employment focus of the laws has introduced a hierarchy of legal status in which documented people are able to acquire higher-status jobs than the undocumented (Adler 2006). Earlier cohorts of immigrants who were able to normalize their status under the 1986 amnesty find themselves in more favorable positions than those who came later and who now face deportation.

Legal status is also unstable and can take years to resolve, as evidenced by Adler's (2006) examples of Guatemalan migrants to Trenton, New Jersey. In 2004, raids were conducted to identify illegal immigrants in Trenton. Ironically, the raids focused on Guatemalans who had come to the United States during the civil war in their country and had filed for political asylum, rather than those who had not petitioned for legal status. Adler shows that undocumented Guatemalans, as a result of their legal status, occupy the lowest positions in the status hierarchy of the increasingly Latino neighborhood in which she conducted her research. Groups that occupy higher status positions include Italians who immigrated in the first half of the twentieth century and Puerto Ricans who also came earlier and are from a U.S. protectorate. Other examples of relatively privileged groups include immigrants from the Dominican Republic, many of whom were able to normalize their status under the 1986 amnesty (Pessar 1999), and Costa Ricans who, although often undocumented, have nevertheless come to the country without crossing borders illegally because of the relative ease of gaining tourist visas in their country of origin. Adler also suggests that because Guatemalans in Trenton tend to have darker skin and indigenous features, legal status acquires a racial component.

By way of comparison, consider the situation in France as described by Sargent and Larchanché-Kim (2006). Following independence, members of former French colonies were no longer able to travel freely to France as nationals. Open-door immigration policies and a labor shortage after the two world wars, however, made it possible for many economic migrants to travel to France to work and then return to their country of origin. In the mid-1970s, liberal migration policies ended and many migrants were faced with the decision to either stay in France or risk the possibility of being unable to return. These French policies increased the number of migrants who remained in France and gave rise to a new form of "clandestine" migration. Further reforms in the 1980s made receiving and renewing visas increasingly difficult. Migrants were required to show that they had been employed in the previous six months and that they could support themselves financially, and they also had to gain a certification of housing from the local municipality. As a result of these policies, many came to France secretly without proper documentation, and others residing in France failed to renew their papers and did not travel to their countries of origin because they feared they would not be able to return. As Sargent and Larchanché-Kim describe, migrants live under surveillance and instability, threatened by deportation and imprisonment. Within migrant communities, conflicts arise due to the lower status afforded to illegals, creating a new hierarchy within the community.

In both France and the United States, immigration laws and demo-graphic patterns have created a relatively new category of illegal immi-grants[3] who occupy low status positions and face threats of arrest and deportation. Social representation theory raises the question of how these groups come to be represented in host countries and how immigrants position themselves to the representation.

Attitude research suggests that a representation of illegality is central to Americans' views of immigration in general. A 1993 survey found that 68 percent of U.S. respondents believed that the majority of immigrants were illegal (Lapinski, Peltola, Shaw, and Yang 1997). This is in contrast to estimates that around 30 percent of the foreign-born population in the United States is actually illegal (Passel 2005). Beliefs about the attributes of illegal immigrants tend to be more negative compared to legal immi-grants; however, these effects are moderated by ethnic group. Sears, Citrin, Cheleden, and van Laar (1999) found that whites and Asians believe that legal immigrants work harder than illegal immigrants, while blacks and Hispanics make no distinction. Although Sears, Citrin, Cheleden, and van Laar did not examine which variables accounted for these differences, their findings are consistent with Clémence's (2001) assertion that groups' representations about illegal immigrants are anchored in their different experiences and knowledge.

Representations of illegality impact immigrants' identities as well. How do immigrant groups and individual immigrants position them-selves to illegality, which represents them as a low-status, law-breaking, economically and culturally threatening invading force and places them under persistent threats of deportation, nearly constant surveillance, and strips them of the rights afforded to citizens and legal residents?

At the group level, similar positions arise in both France and the United States. Immigrant activists in France have called themselves *les sans-papiers* (those without papers) as an alternative to illegal, both to make their status public and to emphasize that they are not criminals but rather are simply people without documentation (Sargent and Larchanché-Kim 2006). As a parallel, immigrant advocacy groups in the United States have put forward the term "undocumented" in opposition to "illegal," addressing concerns such as difficult border crossings and threats of deportation, and repositioning undocumented people as the recipients of legally sanctioned violence rather than as criminal perpetra-tors of violence (Solis 2003).

The representations of "undocumented" in the United States or *sans-papiers* in France illustrate alternative and conflicting visions of illegal immigrants in both countries, what Moscovici (1988) would term polemical representations. In the spring of 2006, after the U.S. House of Representatives passed a bill that criminalized the provision of services to illegal immigrants, advocated the militarization of the Mexican border, and increased penalties for those living illegally in the United States, hundreds of thousands of demonstrators convened in cities across the United States to call for a reform of the U.S. immigration law. Many of those who marched were themselves illegal. Others were the U.S.-born children of undocumented parents (and thus themselves legal U.S. citizens), and still others were movement sympathizers (Navarro 2006). The issue gained national prominence as the media and all three branches of the U.S. government took up the issue. Movement organizers and immigrant radio stations used the term *no documentado* (undocumented) and adopted the phrase "No human being is illegal." Similarly in 1996, three hundred immigrant families occupied a church in Paris and were later evicted by the Paris police. Immigrant leaders of this movement used the representations of *sans-papiers* to justify their position (Sargent and Larchanché-Kim 2006). These anecdotes show how conflicts over meaning can undergird conflicts between groups.

In addition to intergroup conflict, social representations impact the identities of individual immigrants. The position that an individual immigrant takes to the representation is mediated by his or her personal experience. Solis (2003) shows that undocumented Mexican children struggle with their exclusion from U.S. society in ways that range from anger and violence to a rejection of their Mexican identity. She illustrates the intimate knowledge of representations of illegals that immigrants have and the diverse ways in which they understand these representations. She writes of one child who was representative of many other children in the organization, "David also demonstrated a great amount of cultural knowledge about being 'illegal' in his comments about new immigrants implicitly assumed to be poor and undocumented. He described them as being afraid of the police, easily exploited by employers, and hard working, rather than abusive of government services. David positioned himself repeatedly as an advocate of immigrants, questioning both the ethics and authority of government control along the border" (26). This child demonstrated knowledge of the representation of illegality uncovered in attitude research, but he also contested the representation. In her case study, Solis (2003) finds that although David clearly rejected the representation, he found little space to discover personal meaning and self-efficacy. David did not view illegality as the economic necessity that parents within the organization used to justify the representations. Further, because the representation excludes him from membership in

U.S. society, he could not move his critiques of the representation to action. Faced with such powerlessness, he found efficacy by enacting toughness and violence against others.

In contrast, parents within the organization in which Solis (2003) conducted her research viewed themselves differently in relation to illegality. Although they shared the view of immigrants as occupying a low status and as marginalized, they saw themselves as trying to provide for their families in the United States and in Mexico. Their history of coming to the United States out of economic necessity gave meaning to the discrimination and surveillance they experienced as they worked to overcome economic adversity.

A *New York Times* article based on a small number of informal interviews suggested that many citizen children of undocumented immigrants were involved in the demonstrations (Navarro 2006). That these children would advocate for their parents illustrates one of the legal peculiarities of the illegal representation in the United States. Although undocumented parents are positioned outside of the U.S. nation and thus excluded from political power, their U.S.-born children are positioned within the nation and, on the basis of their place of birth, are given full rights of citizenship. This status offers them a potential not accorded to Solis's David. Because they are positioned as members of the United States, their voices can be heard. Ironically, some undocumented parents with whom the reporter spoke felt ambivalent about their children's position (Navarro 2006), insofar as it created distinctions between family members.

These analyses reveal a pattern of the social representations of race and illegality that are linked to the immigrant generation. As suggested by the earlier example of West Indian immigrants, as second-generation immigrants came to be included in the U.S. system, the relevant social representation of race reduced their status as compared to first-generation immigrants. In contrast, the social representation of illegal excludes the U.S.-born children of undocumented immigrants within the U.S. system, positioning them with a higher status not afforded to their parents. This is not to say that these representations do not work together: Solis (2003) argues that Mexican immigrants must continually negotiate representations of both illegality and race. The representations themselves, however, draw differently the boundaries of membership in the nation.

Solis's (2003) analysis shows both that immigrants and immigrant organizations struggle to position themselves to the representation of illegal and that there is diversity in the positions that they take. They share the view that illegals are outside U.S. society. Some, however, reject the category and position themselves as targets of discrimination. Others view their position as an unfortunate economic necessity, while still others reject it but feel excluded from articulating an alternative representation. These positions link with the experiences, the first adopted by an organization advocating for immigrants, the second by parents trying to provide for their families, and the third by a child who had no choice in migrating and who found himself in a hostile context. Solis's (2003) work thus illustrates the relevance of the social representation of illegal for immigrant identities, as well as the ways in which positions within that category are mediated by personal experience and group memberships. Although polemical representations such as undocumented show the diversity of representational positions between groups in a society, Solis's (2003) work shows that, even among immigrants, legal status and personal history lead individual immigrants to take different positions.

IMMIGRATION AND SOCIAL REPRESENTATION: WHAT IS THE VALUE ADDED?

From the vantage point of these specific examples of race and legality, we are now prepared to look more deeply at the potential contribution of social representation theory to an understanding of immigration and identity. One key issue is the relative utility of central core and positioning theories. We have found both theories useful in capturing the ways in which immigrants establish their social identities with respect to race and legality. Far from debating peripheral elements, proponents of illegal versus undocumented social representations conflict over core meanings. The first position views immigrants as a criminal element and a threat to society, whereas the second group emphasizes immigrant rights and the arbitrary nature of the legal status. In the case of race, first-generation Brazilians operate outside the black-white dichotomy in the United States and resist adopting the one-drop rule that predominates in their new country (in which one drop of African blood makes one black [Du Bois 1903/1976]). For these immigrants, representations of race differ at the most basic level from those encountered in the United States, supporting positioning theory. People who identify as African American, in contrast, share a core of experience with oppression but anchor it differently. Those who are native-born tie oppression to experience with slavery, whereas new immigrants link it to current experiences with discrimination. For these groups, a central core is shared and anchored into group experience with peripheral elements that vary.

In analyzing social representations of immigration, we have also found some utility in Moscovici's (1988) three types, namely hegemonic, polemic, and emancipated, at least as a descriptive vehicle to characterize different types of immigration images. We are less certain, however, whether this triad best represents a categorization system or whether it can be thought to describe stages in the life span of any particular representation, as some authors have suggested. (As Breakwell [2001, 275] notes, "little empirical work has pursued whether the tripartite classification is viable.") Our own feeling at this point is that categorization is more appropriate than a presumed sequence, but with the corollary that a given representation may be characterized differently at different points in time as a function of social-historical events and pressures.

Consider the metaphor of the melting pot in U.S. history as an example. At the inception of this image, as it was offered in a play by Israel Zangwill (1909/1994) and quickly accepted and heralded by President Theodore Roosevelt, the melting pot seemed to qualify as a hegemonic representation, not produced by the group or the nation in a consensual process of development, but rather stamped quickly on the consciousness of the nation by collaborating playwright and politician. And indeed, the longevity of this particular representation in the United States is considerable, still used today despite numerous debates as to its meanings and appropriateness in contemporary society (Gleason 1964; Deaux 2006).[4] Although the meaning of the melting pot was to a large degree shared by the society as a whole, it is also clear that the values associated with those meanings were not consensual. Indeed, as the United States moved toward more restrictive immigration legislation in the early 1920s, heated debates arose as to whether the homogeneity implied by a melting pot was desirable or even possible. The image of the melting pot and metaphors derived from it (e.g., blending, mixing, forming, and the crucible) continue to organize debate (Gleason 1964). Despite different evaluations of the idea, few have questioned the image as a whole. In a recent controversial book, Huntington (2004) offered the image of tomato soup in which white Anglo Saxons predominate and ethnic minorities provide flavor but do not change the whole. It remains to be seen whether this more nativist position can displace the melting pot image. Because of eighty years of dominance of the melting pot and the poor imagery of the tomato soup (tomatoes, unlike white Anglo Saxon Protestants, are native to the Americas), we suspect a change is unlikely.

A better example of polemic representations within the immigration domain is the use of "illegal" versus "undocumented" (*sans papiers*). In this case, the legal definition of citizenship was introduced first, buttressed by specific laws and policies. As the term "illegal" began to be applied to specific individuals, however, essentially giving them an identity, the controversies that define polemical representations became evident. For those who were assigned the label "illegal," an alternative and more satisfying representation emerged, one that challenged not only the value but also the meaning of the representation. Perhaps because this representation is so directly tied to identity (unlike the more amorphous and universal image of a melting pot), it is far more likely to exemplify polemics than hegemony. Polemic representations, because they reflect incompatible positions of different constituencies, press for political resolution (or at least action). Current political debates in the United States and in other countries about citizenship exemplify these currents.

Emancipated representations, defined as compatible but different images held by different subgroups within a society, seem to us most closely tied to questions of ethnic self-definition. Within our coverage, Perkins's (2006) study of representations of African Americans is the best example. In this instance, subgroups of racially similar people with different national backgrounds coexist and share the umbrella label. At the same time, each subgroup has created its own set of meanings associated with that label. In some sense, less is at stake here. We can imagine, however, conditions in which the investment in one or another representation of African Americans could be contentious, in which case they might better be characterized as polemic rather than emancipated representations.

The question remains as to whether these various theories of social representation can be unified. Wary of a teleological process in which representations necessarily move from one stage to another, and questioning the utility of descriptive typologies, we take a different approach to the tripartite distinction between representations. Social representations theory emphasizes the function of meaning and examines the ways in which knowledge is distributed among social groups. Our analysis using the tripartite distinction put forward by Moscovici (1988) suggests that the theory must consider differences in social value as well. As Duveen (2001) has noted, some representations contain more than knowledge about a social object; they prescribe more power to some groups than to others. He argues that girls' resistance to representations of gender is found not in their different views of the world, but instead in the differential status afforded to them by the representations. With regards to immigration, the melting pot is somewhat ambiguous as to status and power—it can be interpreted as immigrants coming to the country and creating something entirely new together with native-born people, or, in contrast, as immigrants being wholly assimilated to the native culture. Other representations are clearer. There is no doubt, for instance, that the documented are afforded more power than those without documents. We argue that responses to a representation and the degree to which that representation is shared within a society will depend largely on how value is distributed among social groups. Polemical representations and intergroup conflict are more likely to develop when value is unequal.

We arrive then at two dimensions by which to understand representations—status and group integration. Hegemonic and emancipated representations differ to the extent that meanings are anchored in similar group histories and experiences. Polemic representations differ from the other two to the extent that group meanings and experiences include sharp differences in status. All these representations involve positioning. In hegemonic representations, the group is positioned together by virtue of its members' shared experience. In emancipated representations, groups are united by a central core—as in Abric's description—but differ in how that central core is anchored as a function of their group history. We used the example of African Americans in the United States. Beyond that specific case, one can also think about ways in which national representations—for example, to be an American or an Australian or a German—could be similarly discrepant. In polemic representations, different experiences with status lead devalued groups to establish new representations aimed at reframing the value of their group. In this view, we unite Moscovici's tripartite distinction with Abric's and Clémence's theories of central core and positioning, arguing that different social processes underlie different kinds of representations.

How can research on social representations and immigration move forward, given this framework? One way of examining the role of value in influencing individual positions to social representations is to examine individuals who move between statuses. Specifically, we think that it would be useful to study identity in individuals, previously undocumented, who are able to normalize their legal status. By examining immigrants who cross the boundaries within a representation, we can understand those boundaries better. A second and continuing aim of research on social representations and immigrant identity is to look within groups. In the cases of race and legal status, we have argued that the immigrant generation is a key component in organizing people's identity positions. Future research should continue in this path, moving beyond generation as a demographic variable to examine how the changes in social networks and status that accompany generational change influence immigrant identities. Native-born African Americans, African immigrants, and West Indian immigrants often find themselves in similar schools and neighborhoods—does group interaction lead to diminished differences over time or do their different identity positions inhibit interaction?

Finally, we have argued that demographic shifts and legal changes can create new social categories and representations. Currently, immigrants in the United States are arriving in places where, historically, there has been little immigration and where racial tensions have sometimes been high. How will these shifting demographic patterns influence conceptions of race? In addition, given high global levels of migration, legislators in many countries are reconsidering their immigration policies. Will representations such as "undocumented" and *sans papiers* influence these debates? And how will new policies impact immigrant identities? These questions provide a challenge for our theories and the opportunity for us to develop and extend these theories to a domain that is so critically important throughout the world today.

AUTHOR NOTE

We thank Susan Meiklejohn, Krystal Perkins, Jana Sladkova, and other members of the City University of New York Graduate Center Immigration Research group for their comments on earlier versions of this chapter.

NOTES

1. Within the social science discourse, immigrants of African descent from the Caribbean are often referred to as West Indians. The social construction of this category reflects the colonial history of the Caribbean, in that the term originally referred to residents of those societies that were colonized by the British, the western reach of the British empire. The boundaries of the category have become more permeable in recent years, and scholars often include residents of non-English speaking countries, such as Haiti, in their categorization (Vickerman 1999).

2. *Mestizaje* has similar connotations in Latin America, referring to a mixture of races.

3. Technically the category of illegal immigrant was created in the United States with the National Origins Act of 1924, but a focus on enforcement was not prominent until the Immigration Reform and Control Act of 1986.

4. Canadian society offers another example of hegemonic representation in the image of a cultural mosaic, which emerged early in the twentieth century in literature (Foster 1926) and then was formally established in governmental policy in the 1960s. (See Deaux 2006, chapter 2 for a more detailed discussion of the Canadian representation.)

REFERENCES

Abric, J.-C. 1993. Central system, peripheral system: Their functions and role in the dynamics of social representation. *Papers on Social Representations* 2 (2): 75–79.

———. 2001. A structural approach to social representations. In *Representations of the social: Bridging theoretical traditions*, ed. K. Deaux and G. Philogène, 42–47. Oxford: Blackwell.

Adler, R. H. 2006. "But they claimed to be police, not la migra!": The interaction of residency status, class, and ethnicity in a (post-PATRIOT Act) New Jersey neighborhood. *American Behavioral Scientist* 50 (1): 48–69.

Bobb, V. F. B. 2001. Neither ignorance nor bliss: Race, racism, and the West Indian immigrant experience. In *Migration, transnationalism, and race in a changing New York,* ed. H. R. Cordero-Guzmán, R. C. Smith, and R. Grosfuguel. Philadelphia: Temple University Press.

Breakwell, G. M. 2001. Social representational constraints upon identity processes. In *Representations of the social: Bridging theoretical traditions,* ed. K. Deaux and G. Philogène, 271–84. Oxford: Blackwell.

Brubaker, R. 1992. *Citizenship and nationhood in France and Germany.* Cambridge, MA: Harvard University Press.

Clémence, A. 2001. Social positioning and social representation. In *Representations of the social: Bridging theoretical traditions,* ed. K. Deaux and G. Philogène, 83–95. Oxford: Blackwell.

Daniels, R. 1989. *Asian America.* Seattle: University of Washington Press.

Deaux, K. 2004. Immigration and the color line. In *Racial identity in context: The legacy of Kenneth B. Clark,* ed. G. Philogène. Washington, DC: American Psychological Association.

———. 2006. *To be an immigrant.* New York: Russell Sage Foundation.

Doise, W. 2001. Human rights studied as normative social representations. In *Representations of the social: Bridging theoretical traditions,* ed. K. Deaux and G. Philogène, 96–112. Oxford: Blackwell.

Doise, W., D. Spini, and A. Clémence. 1999. Human rights studied as social representations in a cross-national context. *European Journal of Social Psychology* 29 (1): 1–29.

Du Bois, W. E. B. 1903/1976. *The souls of black folk.* New York: Alfred A. Knopf.

Duveen, G. 2001. Representations, identities, resistance. In *Representations of the social: Bridging theoretical traditions,* ed. K. Deaux and G. Philogène, 257–70. Oxford: Blackwell.

Foner, N. 2001. Introduction. West Indian migration to New York: An overview. In *Islands in the city: West Indian migration to New York,* ed. N. Foner. Berkeley: University of California Press.

Foster, K. 1926. *Our Canadian mosaic.* Toronto: Dominion Council of the YWCA.

Gleason, P. 1964. The melting pot: Symbol of fusion or confusion? *American Quarterly* 16 (1): 20–46.

Hagendoorn, L., R. Drogendijk, S. Turnanov, and J. Hraba. 1998. Inter-ethnic preferences and ethnic hierarchies in the former Soviet Union. *International Journal of Intercultural Relations* 22 (4): 483–503.

Huntington, S. P. 2004. *Who are we? The challenge to America's national identity.* New York: Simon and Schuster.

Ignatiev, N. 1995. *How the Irish became white.* New York: Routledge.

Joppke, C. 1998. Multiculturalism and immigration: A comparison of the United States, Germany, and Great Britain. In *The immigration reader: America in a multidisciplinary perspective*, ed. D. Jacobson, 285–319. Malden, MA: Blackwell.

Lapinski, J. S., P. Peltola, G. Shaw, and A. Yang. 1997. Trends: Immigrants and immigration. *Public Opinion Quarterly* 61 (2): 356–83.

Liu, L. 2004. Sensitising concept, themata, and shareness: A dialogical perspective of social representations. *Journal for the Theory of Social Behavior* 34 (3): 249–64.

Loewen, J. W. 1971. *The Mississippi Chinese: Between black and white.* Cambridge, MA: Harvard University Press.

Marrow, H. 2003. To be or not to be (Hispanic or Latino): Brazilian racial and ethnic identity in the United States. *Ethnicities* 3 (4): 427–64.

Massey, D. 2006. The wall that keeps illegal workers in. *New York Times,* April 4, p. A1.

Massey, D. S., J. Durand, and N. J. Malone. 2002. *Beyond smoke and mirrors: Mexican immigration in an era of economic integration.* New York: Russell Sage Foundation.

Moscovici, S. 1988. Notes toward a description of social representations. *European Journal of Social Psychology* 18 (3): 211–50.

Navarro, M. 2006. Taking to the streets, for parents' sake. *New York Times,* June 11, p. 1.

O'Brien, G. V. 2003. Indigestible food, conquering hordes, and waste materials: Metaphors of immigrants and the early immigration restriction debate in the United States. *Metaphor and Symbol* 18 (1): 33–47.

Passel, J. S. 2005. *Estimates of the size and characteristics of the undocumented population.* Washington, DC: Pew Hispanic Research Center.

Perkins, K. M. 2006. *Diasporic representations of African American: Exploring the contours of identity.* Unpublished manuscript, Graduate Center of the City University of New York.

Pessar, P. R. 1999. The role of gender, households, and social networks in the migration process: A review and appraisal. In *The handbook of international migration: The American experience*, ed. C. Hirschman, P. Kasinitz, and J. DeWind, 53–70. New York: Russell Sage Foundation

Philogène, G. 1999. *From black to African American: A new social representation.* Westport, CT: Greenwood-Praeger.

———. 2001. From race to culture: The emergence of African American. In *Representations of the social: Bridging theoretical traditions, ed.* K. Deaux and G. Philogène, 113–28. Oxford: Blackwell.

Pettigrew, T. F. 1997. Personality and social structure: Social psychological contributions. In *Handbook of personality psychology*, ed. R. Hogan, J. Johnson, and S. Briggs, 417–38. New York: Academic Press.

Reicher, S. 2004. The context of social identity: Conflict, resistance, and change. *Political Psychology* 25 (6): 921–45.

Reicher, S., and N. Hopkins. 2001. *Self and nation: Categorization, contestation and mobilization*. London: Sage Publications.

Rogers, R. 2001. "Black like who?" Afro-Caribbean immigrants, African Americans, and the politics of group identity. In *Islands in the city: West Indian migration to New York*, ed. N. Foner. Berkeley: University of California Press.

Sargent, C. F., and S. Larchanché-Kim. 2006. Liminal lives: Immigration status, gender, and the construction of identities among Malian migrants in Paris. *American Behavioral Scientist* 50 (1): 9–26.

Sears, D. O., J. Citrin, S. V. Cheleden, and C. van Laar. 1999. Cultural diversity and multicultural politics: Is ethnic balkanization psychologically inevitable? In *Cultural divides: Understanding and overcoming group conflict*, ed. D. A. Prentice and D T. Miller, 35–79. New York: Russell Sage Foundation.

Sidanius, J., and F. Pratto. 1999. *Social dominance: An intergroup theory of social hierarchy and oppression*. Cambridge: Cambridge University Press.

Solis, J. 2003. Re-thinking illegality as violence *against*, not *by* Mexican immigrants, children, and youth. *Journal of Social Issues* 59 (1): 15–31.

Telles, E. E. 2004. *Race in another America: The significance of skin in Brazil*. Princeton, NJ: Princeton University Press.

Tormala, T. T., and K. Deaux. 2006. Black immigrants to the United States: Confronting and constructing ethnicity and race. In *Cultural psychology of immigrants*, ed. R. Mahalingam, 131–50. Mahwah, NJ: Lawrence Erlbaum.

United Nations, 2002. *International migration report 2002*. Population Division. Department of Economic and Social Affairs.

Verkuyten, M. 2005. *The social psychology of ethnic identity*. Hove, England: Psychology Press.

Vickerman, M. 1999. *Crosscurrents: West Indian immigrants and race*. New York: Oxford University Press.

Waters, M. 1999. *Black identities: West Indian immigrant dreams and American realities*. Cambridge, MA: Harvard University Press; New York: Russell Sage Foundation.

Zangwill, I. 1909/1994. *The melting pot: Drama in four acts*. New York: Ayer.

SOCIAL REPRESENTATIONS OF ALTERITY IN THE UNITED STATES

Gina Philogène

IN THIS CHAPTER, I WANT TO EXPLORE FURTHER THE NOTION of black Americans as the "Serviceable Other," a categorization introduced by Toni Morrison (1992). This term encapsulates the alterity of Americans of African descent as an excluded group, that is, a racial group that by virtue of this representation assumes an immutable position. This group's representation as the "Other" serves as a necessary counterpoint to the experience of an ideal white identity (Miles 1989; Philogène 2000; Sampson 1993).

We will focus our discussion on a dynamic model of identity production. It is a perspective in which social identity is a dynamic social structure anchored in the in-group while getting objectified through contradistinction to a constructed Other. In the United States, there are two categories of social groups that have come to be defined as the Other. On the one hand, various waves of immigrants have served as a background against which to refine more accurately what it is to be an American, so the immigrants have been perceived as the Other. On the other hand, the racial history embedded in the collective mind has systematically ostracized black Americans as the Other.

In the context of American culture, we thus face a dual meaning of alterity. The first one refers to the relative status of immigrant groups as they gradually become American. The other state of alterity centers on the persistent exclusion of black Americans from full participation in American society. Both groups have been represented as the Other. However, the "immigrant experience" does not seem to carry the same weight of negativity as the one associated with the "black experience." In reviewing the patterns of immigration in Newark followed by white flight, Toni Morrison remarks that the overwhelming majority of African-Americans serves the function of defining whites as the "true" Americans. She states, "So addictive is this ploy that the fact of blackness has been abandoned for the theory of blackness. It doesn't matter anymore what shade the newcomer's skin is. A hostile posture toward resident blacks must be struck at the Americanizing door before it will open" (Morrison 1993).

In the following discussion, immigrant groups are characterized as the *Cultural Other* while black Americans are perceived as the *Social Other*. Following an elaboration of these two representations of otherness, the immigrant experience will be contrasted to that of black Americans to demonstrate the immutable nature of race as an intergroup barrier.

IDENTITY AND ALTERITY

In today's fast moving, technologically driven, densely interconnected, and globalizing society, we no longer belong to fixed groups. We live in a society that is perpetually in transition, forcing its individuals to play multiple roles and adopt several identity fragments in order to cope with high levels of specialization and displacement. Such a complex and mobile society shifts the focus from what an identity is to how an identity is produced (Boyd 2006; Luhmann 1995). Identities are no longer essentialized, but instead exist in contradistinction to others. What defines individuals is their processing of difference with others on the basis of which they integrate their identity fragments and multiple roles through participation in groups and differentiation with others. Thus, today, identity can no longer be separated from the processes of constructing otherness.

Conversely, groups generally define themselves by instilling in their subjects a sense of belonging. While such solidarity may contain positive attributes as foundations for a shared identity, groups also have a tendency to define themselves in juxtaposition to others who manifestly do not belong because they are different. Cultures thus often end up with a bipolar vision of "us" versus "them," with the former being a representation of what it means to be human, and the latter implying something less than human. Groups define their collective Self by presuming superiority over the Other whom they do not allow to belong.

Groups need to build an internal consensus from which the group members derive a sense of belonging as a source of self-esteem and pride. This consensus is more easily constructed by imposing norms and drawing boundaries, both of which produce a positive group identity by comparing one's group with other, negatively valued groups. We can trace such contradistinction between in-groups and out-groups to postcolonial theories (Said 1978), postmodernism (Foucault 1988), and critical theory (Habermas 1998; Iragaray and Guynn 1995). In social psychology, that kind of argument about social hierarchization is central to social identity theory (Tajfel 1981). The construction of otherness thus plays a crucial role in societies to the extent that any group defines itself in comparison to a presumed Other who is construed as inferior.

It is precisely this differentiation of one's identity with the Other which the concept of *alterity* embodies so well. Its meaning, according to Cartledge (1993), refers to "a condition of difference and exclusion suffered by an 'out' group against which a dominant group and its individual members define themselves negatively in ideally polarized opposition" (2). When applied conceptually to human objects, alterity does not denote a basic description of individual difference, but rather a systematic and comprehensive crystallization of difference between classes of people. The emphasis goes beyond the basic categorization process, which aims at structuring and ordering the world. Instead, alterity involves the construction of entire categories of individuals as other than normal people, as less than human. A classic example of this construction of otherness embodied in the meaning of alterity is the early intelligence tests in America around World War I that included a catchall group category of "feeble-minded," comprising the poor, the insane, most immigrants, and later on, also blacks (Goddard 1914; Goddard 1917).

THE DUAL MEANING OF ALTERITY

When looking at the concept of alterity more closely, its application implies a dual meaning of unfamiliarity and exclusion. In its first definition, when implying a sense of unfamiliarity, alterity is a characteristic of cultural otherness that can be overcome by learning about the unfamiliar and anchoring it. This process of getting to know the stranger is precisely how various immigrant groups entering the United States are eventually included in mainstream society, once they have become familiar with the host country's culture and those belonging to the majority in-group of that country have in turn become familiar with them.

But alterity can also mean social otherness. This version conjures a sense of nonbelonging. It is of a more permanent nature, impervious to the moderating effects of growing familiarity over time. It rests on an act of exclusion that separates everyone else from the assigned Other.

But why do people need to marginalize others as more or less permanently excluded from their in-group? Most likely, the essential characteristics of the Other resonate with something that is fundamentally within the person and that he or she is afraid of. In trying to objectify difference, one can make it appear as if it is not inside oneself. The first step in this process is to select a demographically distinct group as the Other. We then endow it with characteristics that make its members appear less than fully human. In the process, one projects onto the group representing the Other various qualities that one fears and rejects in oneself. Eventually, any member of that group ends up being viewed not as a variable and unique individual, but rather solely in terms of these perceived group qualities that one abhors. Alterity so becomes a carrier for prejudice and stereotyping.

In setting such a boundary with this constructed Other, one is defining oneself by defining who one is not. Thus, individuals project what they would not accept about themselves onto an objectified and externalized Other, a constructed otherness to which they can ascribe an objectively unalterable difference (e.g., skin color). With such markers ruling out any synthesis between the Self and the Other, exclusion becomes a more or less permanent condition. In the United States, we find persistent beliefs in race as a decisively determinant category of marginalization, while in other countries, such long-term exclusion may be justified on the basis of differences in religion (e.g., Jews and now also Muslims in Europe). As a matter of fact, the Other can be justified on many different grounds. Irrespective of the specific justification, the production of images about the Other aims always at demeaning and assuming control over the group to be dominated. These images and descriptions of the Other are never ideologically or cognitively neutral (Ahmad 1992).

CULTURAL VERSUS SOCIAL OTHERNESS IN THE UNITED STATES

In the United States, a multicultural society composed of a constantly changing mix of immigrant groups trying to become Americans, the distinction between cultural otherness and social otherness is uniquely important. These two conceptions of alterity enter into a dialectical relationship with each other whose resolution plays a crucial role in shaping American society.

On the one hand, the United States has been shaped by its immigrant population ever since its inception. The irresistible draw of opportunity and freedom in the New World has attracted generations of immigrants from all corners of the world to the shores of America. The United States is thus truly a nation of immigrants whom this society has been able to integrate in a remarkably effective fashion. Of course, when the immigrants first arrive, they are seen as strangers and thus regarded with suspicion by the native population. In this context, we can see many attempts to characterize unfamiliar groups of immigrants as a threat to the existing social order. There is a rich history of Americans targeting newly arrived groups as the (Cultural) Other, including the Anglo Saxon majority of Americans initially considering Italian or Irish immigrants to be of a different race or imposing ethnically discriminatory restrictions on immigration in recurrent fashion (Jacobson 1998).

Cultural otherness refers to the Other in the sense of unfamiliarity. The Other is seen as strange, as the stranger who appears different. In this construction, alterity reflects the cognitively unfamiliar. We need to distinguish two types of cognitive unfamiliarity, an epistemic one that occurs when we do not know or understand something, and a practical one that occurs when we do not know how to handle a challenge. The Cultural Other marks the boundaries of our comprehensive capability and our dependency on expectations. Cultural otherness may be resolved through learning about the unfamiliar group and thereby reducing social distance to it.

Newly arrived immigrants protect themselves against being targeted as the Cultural Other by grouping together in the urban centers of America, drawing support from other members of their own group and acquainting themselves with American culture. This recipe has enabled generations of immigrants to assimilate by becoming comfortable in their new home country while demonstrating to the rest of society their will to pursue the American Dream. As both sides become more familiar with each other, they overcome initial stereotypes. Most immigrant groups face enormous intergenerational and intracultural tensions when their children are torn between cultural allegiance to their parents' country of origin and integration in their country of birth and citizenship. But this struggle also helps facilitate the transformation of immigrants into mainstream Americans—a process that for most immigrant groups occurs within a generation or two.

That process of integration dissolves the cultural otherness of the targeted group. The immigrant community becomes a hyphenated group of Americans with a dualistic group identity (e.g., German-Americans and Korean-Americans), a condition best characterized as "dual consciousness" (Du Bois, 1903/1965), in pursuit of the American Dream like everybody else. In that transformation, cultural specificities associated with that group's country of origin (e.g., Germany and South Korea) are incorporated into the fabric of American society through such channels as food, language, customs, holidays, parades, fashion, and so on. There exists a reciprocal and mutually enriching relation between mainstream American society and its constituent populations of once-immigrant, now-hyphenated Americans. Anyone can partake in that relation as long as she learns how to speak English and agrees to the system of values, beliefs, and goals anchored in the American Dream crystallizing around the combination of hard work, home ownership, individual enrichment, religious tolerance, and allegiance to the U.S. Constitution.

While most immigrant groups have been allowed fairly rapid integration, there is one group to whom this privilege has been systematically denied. For over two centuries, millions of Africans were brought to the United States involuntarily to work and die as slaves. This subhuman status prevented Americans of African descent from enjoying the rights and protections granted to all other citizens of the United States. Such systematic exclusion, marking Americans of African descent as the Social Other by using the device of a "race apart" on the basis of a different skin color continued after the end of slavery. The emancipation of slaves in the wake of the Civil War (1861–65) was followed by a century of segregation under the "separate, but equal" doctrine that the U.S. Supreme Court had ratified in *Plessy v. Ferguson* (1896). Even today, four decades after the Civil Rights movement ended segregation, racist practices continue against Americans of African descent who still face widespread discrimination in employment, housing, health care, and education.

The kind of persistent discrimination practiced against Americans of African descent points to the Social Other. This type of otherness results from drawing the boundaries that place targeted individuals outside the in-group. Such exclusion may even extend to originally included group members. Alterity in the sense of social otherness may only be resolved by the inclusion of the out-group. But that is very difficult to do, because the initial representation of the Other is fixed in concrete categories (e.g., race, ethnicity, class, and gender) and, once created, takes on a persistent life on its own. The history of the United States, from slavery during its first century and the civil war of the early 1860s to the Civil Rights movement a century later, has largely been shaped by the contradiction between America's self-definition as a democracy and its systematic exclusion of one group of Americans on the basis of race (Philogène 1999).

THE INTERPLAY OF THE TWO TYPES OF ALTERITY

The maintenance of the Social Other requires a categorization that unalterably sets apart the object to be excluded. An effective way to mark the Social Other for exclusion is by racializing the category. This process, whereby race is invoked to denote a subhuman status, allows the setting of clear boundaries and facilitates ostracism by characterizing the targeted group as deviant. Such racialization is not just occurring in the heads of individuals sharing that representation, but also gets institutionalized into our laws, customs, and social organizations.

The two types of alterity, comprising both the Social Other and the Cultural Other, play themselves out in unique fashion here, because both Americans of African descent and newly arriving immigrant groups have settled in America's major urban centers. They thus have come to share the same densely populated space where they together constitute the majority of the population. The two groups are in a way connected by their respective otherness vis-à-vis the dominant Anglo Saxon culture of the mainstream. Urban blacks provide immigrants with much material in their learning about their new home country.

While both groups share much in common, their intergroup dynamic cannot escape the instrumentalization of race at the center of American society. As immigrants try to transform themselves into Americans, they typically recreate the "us" versus "them" framework imposed by the prevailing social order. Race, used primarily to exclude the group representing the Social Other, now becomes an instrument of group differentiation to facilitate the integration of groups representing the Cultural Other. When immigrant groups start to internalize the same race-based exclusion of "blacks," they do so for the most part in order to reduce their social distance to the mainstream. Blacks thus constitute the "Serviceable Other" through which immigrant groups relativize their status as Cultural Other and integrate more easily (Philogène 2000).

Americans of African descent may in turn oppose immigration, since they are likely to be the group hurt most by a large influx of immigrants competing with them for scarce jobs and affordable housing (Lim 2001). And it is surely difficult for members of this marginalized group to be constantly reminded that newly arrived immigrants, still strangers a short while ago, are now pulling ahead of them in socioeconomic terms. Government data (see Table 3.1) do indeed confirm that immigrant groups tend to do better than Americans of African descent (Fears 2003). This is especially true for Asian-Americans, whose median household income and average years of schooling exceed even the respective levels of whites. African-Americans earn less than Latinos, even though the latter group has comparatively less education. African immigrants as well as Afro Caribbean immigrants, both of whom tend to be highly educated, have managed to reach median household income levels that exceed significantly those of African-Americans. Their unemployment rates also compare favorably with those of Americans of African descent.

Table 3.1   Socioeconomic indicators in the United States (by ethnic background)

Group	Median household income	Average schooling[1]	Unemployment rates (March 2003)
White Americans	$52,000	13.5 years	5.1%
Asian-Americans	$64,000	13.9 years	6.3%
Africans	$40,000	14.5 years	5.1%
Afro Caribbeans	$40,300	14.5 years	7.3%
African Americans	$33,500	12.5 years	9.9%
Hispanics	$37,000	10.7 years	7.5%

Source: U.S. Census (2000), U.S. Bureau of Labor Statistics
[1]Average schooling is inclusive of the first Kindergarten year

Obviously, neither African nor Afro Caribbean immigrants have been held back by the stigma of race to the same degree as Americans of African descent, most likely because they were higher wage earners and part of a better-educated elite in their country of origin. Bringing their upper-class consciousness with them, both immigrant groups tend to use race in much the same polarizing fashion as nonblack immigrants. They set themselves deliberately apart from black Americans, with whom they typically share the same neighborhoods in America's largest cities. Their group positioning within America's multiethnic spectrum is more like that of recently arrived Asian-Americans and Latinos, and they seem to have succeeded in that assimilation effort.

The relative success of black immigrant groups (e.g., Jamaicans, Haitians, Nigerians, Senegalese) is especially conducive to making one wonder why black Americans have not been able to make similar progress. Americans of African descent hear this question often, implying that it must be their own shortcomings at fault here. As James Baldwin put it so succinctly more than three decades ago in his dialogue on race with Margaret Mead (1971),

> Alas, most white people until this hour, for a complex of reasons which there may be no purpose in going into, partly willfully and partly out of genuine ignorance and a lack of imagination, really do not know why black people are in the streets. And God knows, the mass media do not help to clarify this at all.
>
> Every time you see a riot, you see all these people stealing TV sets and looking like savages, according to the silent majority's optic. If you do not know why they are in the streets—especially with various ivy league colleges and Arrow-collar-ad-men, and all the symbols and tokens of progress—there is a danger of another polarization, at least on the surface. Because then the world, the white American and the world, looks at, let us say Harry Belafonte, to use arbitrarily a famous public figure, and those

people rioting on the South Side, and they conclude, as they are meant to conclude, really, that if those people on the South Side washed themselves and straightened up they could all be Harry Belafonte. There is nothing wrong with the system, so the American thinks; there is something wrong with the people. This is the greatest illusion, and the most dangerous delusion of all, because it exacerbates the rage of the people trapped in the ghettos. They know why they are there, even if America doesn't. (154–55)

Many nonblack Americans continue to believe that black Americans have mostly themselves to blame for not being able to enter the mainstream.

This widespread belief ignores, of course, that black Americans represent *social otherness* marked by race for exclusion, while all other groups, even black immigrants from Africa and the Caribbean, embody *cultural otherness* that diminishes over time with familiarization to the strange. That distinction between two different types of alterity gains additional meaning when immigrants are allowed to join the multicultural dynamism of a rapidly diversifying society in juxtaposition to the black-white dichotomy evoked by race as a marker of permanent exclusion and the legacy of racism. Race is a social construct that applies to a particular group subject to ostracism. As long as the targeted group gets defined by that categorization, it remains tied to its representation as *Social Other* to whom the benefits of belonging to that society are denied. The fundamental difference in the nature of their group-specific alterity renders any comparison of progress between black Americans and immigrants meaningless, except to highlight the lasting and detrimental effects of race-based discrimination.

FROM RACE TO CULTURE AND BACK

The validity of this argument about the importance of race as a marker of permanent exclusion has ironically been proven by Americans of African descent themselves. To the extent that the civil rights legislation of the 1960s did open the door to a modicum of political empowerment and economic opportunity, a black middle class has arisen whose numbers are steadily growing. This subgroup, demographically characterized as young, urbane, college educated, professional, and politically engaged, has succeeded to create a more positive and inclusive representation by referring to themselves as African-Americans (Philogène 1994; Philogène 1999). Launched in 1989 at a conference of civil-rights leaders, this new group denomination is the first name applied to Americans of African descent that breaks the association with race. By choosing for themselves an alternative name whose semantic structure is the same applied to all other groups (e.g., Italian-Americans or Irish-Americans), and anchoring in this way a new representation of themselves fully in line with the values and aspirations prevailing in mainstream American society, African-Americans have succeeded to dismantle the primacy of race in favor of a cultural designation, thus avoiding the stigma of the Social Other. Even more hopeful is the fact that the new denomination has now become the most widely used name for the whole group in public discourse, portending a future in which the racial categorization of Americans of African descent will have given way to their re-presentation as a culturally defined group placed centrally within the multicultural spectrum of contemporary America.

This future may have already arrived. The shocking events of September 11, 2001, have created within the United States a heightened sense of national unity against an array of presumed foreign adversaries. There is now a superordinate goal shared by the vast majority of Americans, focused on homeland security and the worldwide defense of liberty. In that new context, old domestic divisions on the basis of race have lost much of their meaning, especially since Americans have now become much more vested in conceiving their multiethnic diversity, religious tolerance, and various (economic, political, and legal) freedoms as societal strengths worth defending and propagating. Race-based exclusion applies to Americans of African descent today much less than it did just five years ago.

This change, however, does not mean that race as a marker of exclusion has disappeared. This social construct has just shifted the object to which it applies. With the United States under attack by Islamic fundamentalists, Americans have grown extremely wary of the Arab world in particular. While they profess—from President Bush on down—continued tolerance toward Islam, there clearly exists in the United States strong suspicion and prejudice toward Arab-Americans in particular and Muslims in general. One could even say, on the basis of officially sanctioned racial profiling in the name of homeland security (by police, customs officers, and so on) and commonly heard stereotypes sanctioned in the mass media, that we are seeing the first steps toward a racialization of Arabs (and, by extension, Arab-Americans). The official U.S. policy of mass arrests, indefinite detention, forced deportation, and tighter identity checks—all in the name of preventing the target group from violating immigration rules or posing security threats—feeds that attempt at the systematic exclusion of a group now seen as representing the enemy. Targeting Muslims as the Social Other and doing so on the basis of race-based differentiation (where religious fundamentalism and anger against

Western values appear as innate character flaws) demonstrates once again the durability of social otherness and the power of race.

REFERENCES

Ahmad, A. 1992. *In theory: Classes, nations, literatures.* New York: Verso.

Baldwin, J., and M. Mead. 1971. *A rap on race.* Philadelphia: J. B. Lippincott.

Boyd, D. 2006. Identity production in a networked culture: Why youth heart MySpace. Paper presented at the meeting of the American Association for the Advancement of Science, St. Louis, MO, February 19.

Du Bois, W. E. B. 1903/1965. *The souls of black folk.* New York: Mentor Books.

Cartledge, P. 1993. *The Greeks. A portrait of self and other.* Oxford: Oxford University Press.

Farr, R. 1996. *The roots of modern social psychology.* Blackwell: Oxford.

Fears, D. 2003. Disparity marks black ethnic groups, report says. *Washington Post*, March 9, p. A7.

Foucault, M. 1988. *Madness and civilization: A history of insanity in the age of reason.* Trans. Richard Howard. New York: Vintage.

Goddard, Herbert, H. 1914. *Feeblemindedness: Its causes and consequences.* New York: Macmillan.

———. 1917. Mental tests and the immigrant. *Journal of Delinquency* 2:243–77.

Habermas, J. 1998. *The inclusion of the other: Studies in political theory.* Cambridge: Massachusetts Institute of Technology Press.

Iragaray, L., and N. Guynn. 1995. The question of the other. *Yale French Studies* 87:7–19.

Jacobson, D., ed. 1998. *The immigration reader: America in the multidisciplinary perspective.* Malden, MA: Blackwell.

Lim, N. 2001. On the back of blacks? Immigrants and the fortunes of African Americans. In *Strangers at the gates: New immigrants in urban America*, ed. R. Waldinger, 186–227. Berkeley: University of California Press.

Luhmann, N. 1995. *Social systems.* Stanford, CA: Stanford University Press.

Miles, R. 1989. *Racism.* London: Routledge.

Morrison, T. 1992. *Playing in the dark: Whiteness and the literary imagination.* Cambridge, MA: Harvard University Press.

———. 1993. On the backs of blacks. In The new face of America. Special issue, *Time*, December 2.

Philogène, G. 1994. African American as a new social representation. *Journal for the Theory of Social Behavior* 24:89–109.

———. 1999. From black to African American: A new social representation. Westport, CT: Praeger/Greenwood.

———. 2000. Blacks as "serviceable other." *Journal of Community & Applied Social Psychology* 10:391–401.

Said, E. 1978. *Orientalism: Western conceptions of the Orient.* London: Routledge.

Sampson, E. E. 1993. *Celebrating the other: A dialogic account of human nature.* Boulder, CO: Westview.

Tajfel, H. 1981. *Human groups and social categories.* Cambridge: Cambridge University Press.

CHAPTER 4

IDENTITY REPRESENTATIONS WITHIN ISRAELI SOCIETY

A KALEIDOSCOPE OF MINORITY PHENOMENA

Emda Orr

IN THIS CHAPTER, I DESCRIBE THREE STUDIES in which aspects of social representations theory (SRT) are demonstrated in the specific characteristics of minority societies in Israel: immigrant high schoolers from the former Soviet Union and Ethiopia, parents from the religious Zionist settler society and their high school children, and "slow learners" in an elementary school. Whereas membership in an immigrant society is clearly not a matter of choice, membership is a personal choice for individuals in the religious-settler society. However, both cases share an inherent conflict between preservation of their social identity and identification with the majority. Each of these studies describes a distinct societal identity construction in representing this problem: the coexistence of logically incompatible identity representations of cooperation and rivalry in the case of immigrants, and representing the conflict as an inherent part of one's identity system in the case of the religious Zionist society. The third study also demonstrates a representational incompatibility, but within a hegemonic institution: the school. In this case, the school ideology consists of democratic egalitarian representations, but representations of stratification define some children as incompetent outsiders, thus creating a stratified society and a minority within an egalitarian school culture. The situation is not represented as contradicting democratic representations, but rather as a self-evident compromise between one's representations and a sad reality of incompetent children. I begin with a short description of SRT and the present version of the concept of identity representation. I then pinpoint the contribution of each study to the theory of social representations.

SOCIAL AND IDENTITY REPRESENTATIONS

Social representations are the verbal and behavioral forms by which members of a society co-construct the world they live in (Marková 2000; Moscovici 1984). According to social representations theory (SRT), human beings construct that world by their individual cognitive capacity, but they do so as members of a particular society by communicating with each other within specific social contexts. Hence, these representations are shared to a certain extent by members of a given society within a specific historical time. The progression in which representations are constructed is evolutionary, such that new representations are anchored in former ones and rooted into the societal historical representational system. When a society faces a new chaotic reality, such as phenomena without form or name, and the existing social representations (SR) system does not provide a ready-made appropriate clue, members of a society *objectify* (construct) this situation as a new object they are able to act upon, speak about, and feel. This kind of construction does not necessarily obey the rules of formal logic, yet it is not chaotic; rather, it has its own special logic that makes perfect sense to those who have constructed it, such that it facilitates their adaptation to the surrounding social reality.

As a scholar who desires to make sense out of the seemingly chaotic social life of my own country (Israel), SRT seems a promising tool. With the collaboration of my university students over a number of years in this endeavor, we have not only expanded our understanding of our society, but have also been able to clarify and demonstrate some aspects of SRT. The aim of this chapter is to share some of these insights with you.

One of the main concepts we used was identity representations. Following Gerard Duveen (2001), our definition of the concept is of representations that locate a group and its members *vis-à-vis* other societal sectors. Distinctively, however, identity representations as we define them are not features of individuals; rather, like other representations, they are negotiable among individuals and between them and the societal media and other institutions (Ben Asher, Wagner, and Orr 2006). More specifically, identity representations are not only those by which individuals and societies represent themselves verbally; they are also constructed by observers and include representations that society members are not necessarily aware of. These representations are derived by the social scientist from what members of a certain society say and do, which distinguish one society from others. Hence, Duveen's (2001) question of whether identity or representations come first becomes irrelevant, as identities *are* representations, and their specificity is derived from their function as societal markers. That is, they are the social reality as constructed by a specific society, and the social reality of a society as constructed by other relevant spectators. Thus, for instance, group-related self-definitions (e.g., a person identifying as Israeli), a societal shared language, and forms of speech and action distinguishing a society from others all fall into the category of identity representations.

At first glance, this definition may seem to somewhat overlap the concept constructed by self-categorization theory (Haslam, Turner, Oakes, McGarty, and Reynolds 1998) in which identity is conceived as the tendency to extend the self-concept to include others in one's society, as if one becomes a depersonalized exchangeable unit of others in the society and an expert of its cultural representations. However, there are two critical differences between the concept of identity representations presented here and the self-categorization concept. The latter is defined as an *individual universal process* motivated by the desire to *mark one's social borders* as a means for self-enhancement. In contrast, identity representations are steps made by a *collective* of *interacting individuals* while *making sense of their social reality*. This distinction is clearly highlighted by a comparison with two additional social identity research sectors. According to Henry Tajfel's (1981) original version of social identity theory, the motive behind social identity is self-empowerment through identification with one's collective, thus gaining its social status. Marilyn Brewer (2001), in an elaboration of that theory, assumes a balance between the motive to be connected and close to a group of others and the opposing motive for differentiation and distinctiveness, which account for the individual's multiple identifications.

From the SRT approach, as will be demonstrated later, each of these supposedly universal individual motivations are possible goals that societies in specific contexts may or may not harbor. For instance, in the studies that are reported in the following sections, representations of empowerment and inclusion were simultaneously employed by adolescent immigrants to Israel, whereas the issue that the religious Zionist settlers' society represented was that of marking borders (i.e., categorization) between themselves and the Jewish, nonreligious, hegemonic Israeli society. The school teachers in the third study demarcated a category of slow learners as distinct from other students. In each of these studies, however, a context-specific rather than a universal factor was revealed as operating, and collective rather than individual factors were tapped and investigated.

In the following sections, then, I examine identity representations from a number of complementary perspectives. In the first study, adolescent immigrant identity was defined by the shared verbal expressions of high school students regarding their adaptation as immigrants to life in Israel, complemented by the construction of these immigrant identity representations by the relevant society of "others," native Israeli peers (Mana 2005; Orr, Mana, and Mana 2003). The second study defined the identities of religious settlers from their membership in their specific society, their unique lifestyle compared to other Israeli societies, their shared verbal expressions and attitudes about other societal sectors, and their value priorities (Paryente 2002; Paryente and Orr 2003). Finally, the last study (Tuval 2004) gleaned the identity of "slow learning" children from how relevant others, such as teachers, treated them (clearly, to get the full picture, the perspectives of the children, including their speech and activity, need to be documented as well). The descriptions of the identity of each minority group opened a window through which we were able to see how SRT enhances our understanding of societies and how each group's specific findings expand our understanding of that theory.

IMMIGRANT MINORITIES: REPRESENTATIONS OF POWER AND ACCULTURATION

The first research I describe is based on two studies carried out by Adi Mana as part of her PhD thesis (Mana 2005; Orr, Mana, and Mana 2003). Mana was interested in the identity construction of Jewish immigrants from Ethiopia and the former USSR to Israel. Immigration to Israel is unique in certain ways: the number of newcomers over the past two decades has been about a sixth of the entire population in Israel and immigration is officially represented as repatriation—coming home from exile.

I wish to highlight several questions from this research. The first question I would like to address is whether and to what extent immigrants and their old-timer hosts share a representational system regarding immigrant representations. This question was posed within a changing historical context: To what extent do immigrants represent their identity in keeping with Israeli historical hegemonic representations, according to which immigrants should turn their backs on their original identity and assimilate as soon as possible into the identity of their local hosts? Or, rather, do they construct their identity by the more recent worldwide representations of multiculturalism, according to which distinct identities within a shared societal frame of reference are legitimately represented?

The second question I wish to discuss is how power issues are represented in the Israeli immigration context. Though largely ignored by SRT, power issues seem to be intrinsically involved in identity issues. In the present study, the social situation was that immigration to Israel was officially represented as repatriation, but simultaneously unequal power was delegated to each of the involved parties. The ideological and official representations indicated that newcomers should gain a status equal and similar to that of their hosts (e.g., according to law, every Jewish immigrant, from the moment he or she sets foot on the land, is entitled to the full rights and obligations inherent in Israeli citizenship). Socially, however, this rule, though designed as a means of empowerment, was ironically twisted, and the newcomers were expected to surrender their social power, abandon their original identity, and talk, behave, and look as similar as possible to native Israelis, replacing their native language with Hebrew (spoken with the local accent). The majority of immigrants, who were unwilling or unable to represent themselves this way, were labeled *olim chadashim* (newcomers), and their economic, cultural, and social power were much lower than that of their hosts (Ben-Rafael 1982). Mana's second theoretical aim, then, was to discover whether, how, and to what extent power issues appeared in the identity representations of the research populations.

In an attempt to uncover answers to these two research questions, Mana first conducted a pilot study, in which participants from two samples of immigrant adolescents (from the former USSR and Ethiopia) were asked to describe what they thought was involved in their adaptation to life in Israel. The immigrants' responses were categorized and constructed into a forty-four–item Likert-style questionnaire, which was then administered in two waves (1997 and 2002) to two large-scale samples of fifteen- to sixteen-year-old high school students. The schools in which participants studied were located throughout Israel, and they were attended by native Israelis and immigrants from the former USSR and Ethiopia. The immigrant students were asked to refer to their actual adaptation as immigrants, while the native Israelis were asked to describe their attributions regarding one of the immigrant groups. The data obtained from each wave was analyzed by Guttman's Small Space Analysis (SSA; Guttman 1968), a method originally devised with the aim of theory construction.

In answer to the first research question, results showed similar two-dimensional maps[1] for male and female immigrants from Ethiopia and the former USSR, as well as for native Israelis. The findings indicate that, despite their distinct social positioning and distinct cultural background, host and immigrant students who shared a school constructed the immigrant identity by similar *shared representations*. That is, the two immigrant groups of Russian intelligentsia and Ethiopian nomads, despite their distinct origins and nature, constructed their adaptation to Israel by similar representations, and their Israeli hosts shared this construction.

The question of whether immigrant adaptation was represented as "multiculturalism" or "assimilation" was addressed through the identification of five immigrant identities. The assimilation category appeared in a small number of items, with a very low mean value, indicating that historical representations of the melting pot ideology—according to which immigrants are required to represent themselves as native Israelis and indeed attempt to do so—were quite marginal. In contrast, multiculturalism was represented in the multi-item, high mean category of extended identity. Opposite the latter on the SSA map were the items for secluded Identity—such as representations of immigrants' wishes to maintain their original culture and to avoid that of their hosts. Power issues appeared in the items of the fourth category, rivalry identity, in which immigrant students represented their former identity and their original culture as equal and even superior to that of their hosts, and demanded to be heard more loudly, especially in the state-owned media.

The findings indicate, then, that although SRT does not include power issues as an intrinsic part of the theory, such issues were manifest in the *content* of the societal representations that were gleaned. There seem to be two conditions for the appearance of such power issues. First, they need to be a relevant, conspicuous part of the societal social context. Second, the research methodology must be such that societal representations are not presumed in advance.

SRT explicitly assumes (Moscovici 2000) that social logic, unlike scientific logic, tolerates incompatibilities between social rules, and that logical contradictions may simultaneously coexist between historical sources, present interests, and aspirations and hopes. Social incongruities are ignored, and social consensus replaces rules of logic. Indeed, in the case of the recent Jewish immigration to Israel, the results confirmed this SRT postulate by the discovery that adolescent immigrants constructed their adaptation by means of their context-related social rationality, in which seemingly antagonistic themes appear to coexist. Simultaneous to the representations of the extended bicultural identity, they identified themselves as rejecting the symbols of the new culture and revering the former original culture exclusively. This kind of representational system does not abide by rules of formal logic; rather, societal logic prevails where power and conflict representations of the world and basically harmonious representations coexist.

Whereas Mana's study illustrates the SRT-related aspects of shared social construction, power issues and the nature of social thinking, other distinct aspects of the theory, are illustrated by the next study. This research demonstrates the status of values within SRT and the distinct intergenerational transmission of *hegemonic* and *emancipated* values and identity representations.

THE RELIGIOUS ZIONIST SETTLER IDENTITY: INTERGENERATIONAL TRANSMISSION OF HEGEMONIC AND EMANCIPATED REPRESENTATIONS

The studies performed by Bilha Paryente (Paryente 2002; Paryente and Orr 2003) confirm Moscovici's speculation that *values* should be considered core representations around which other representations (such as those of identity) are organized. Paryente was able to clarify the concepts of *hegemonic* and *emancipated* representations, to define their distinct nature, and to offer a system of operational definitions by which these phenomena could be investigated with quantitative measures. Once hegemonic and emancipated identities were clarified, she applied the concept with the aim of enriching our understanding of the specific minority society in which she was interested. Her results surprisingly indicated that parents transmitted societal *hegemonic* values and identity representations to their children to a lesser extent than they transmitted *emancipated* values and identity representations.

The specific Israeli minority group Paryente investigated was that of religious Zionist settlers. In the beginning of the twentieth century, members of this ideological political faction identified themselves as strictly religious (as distinct from the Israeli Jewish secular majority) and as Zionists (as distinct from ultra orthodox Jewry from a European background). In contrast to the traditional religious leadership, which ideologically opposed the Zionist political agenda and believed in a messianic Jewish redemption, the religious Zionists joined the secular Zionist political movement as a minority faction. However, following the 1967 war between Israel and the surrounding Arab countries, members of this group began to settle in the newly occupied territories, beyond the former Israeli borders, with the conviction that the Israeli occupation of the Palestinian territories was a heavenly directed event by which God returned the "Promised Land" to the Jews (Sobel and Beit Halachmi, 1991).

With this historic background in mind, I would like to refer to a number of important minority characteristics specific to this society. Contrary to other minority groups, such as immigrants whose identity is *imperative*, the identity of the religious Zionist settlers is *contractual* (Duveen 2001). The borders of this society are permeable, membership is a personal choice rather than imposed, the social status of its members within Israeli society is relatively high, and their interaction with other sectors in hegemonic Israeli society is quite extensive. Contrary to ultra orthodox society, members of this society enlist in the Israeli army—where the younger generation encounters nonreligious Jews—and take an active role as consumers and creators of the country's cultural life. As such, the borders around this group are quite open, and its members, especially the younger ones, are at risk of attrition. Hence, members of this society need to protect the younger generation from the "negative" effects of the surrounding hegemonic society.

Paryente's research was grounded within this societal background, and her investigation dealt with the issue of how this society transmits its societal minority identity to the younger generation. Specifically, she examined the transmission of parental- and societal-specific values and identities to children.

In the first stage, the identity representations of this society were defined through intensive interviews with parents and their adolescent children. Based on the taped interviews, a questionnaire was devised and administered, together with a standardized value questionnaire (Schwartz 1992) to a large sample of 1470 participants (490 families—two parents and their adolescent child) across a wide variety of communities within Israel and the occupied Palestinian territories. Values were conceptually defined as core representations (Moscovici 2000), and the results of Multi Dimensional Scaling (MDS) and SSA in each of the research groups (mothers, fathers, sons, and daughters) pointed to three identity regions posited around the core of values.

The first region (labeled religious settler identity) was a structure with a *large number of items, a high mean, and relatively small variance*, reflecting a wide range of religious-settler interests combined with a sense that the younger generation was in danger of being negatively affected by their communication with out-group secular Israelis. The other two identity regions—Israeli identity and conflict identity—were similarly apparent in each subgroup, negatively related to the first region, and consisted of a *smaller number of items, a lower mean, and larger variance*. The contents of these identities reflected a sense of being part of the surrounding Israeli society, and a sense of discontent regarding the incompatibility between their religious-settler and Israeli identities. The religious-settler identity was correlated with the values of tradition and benevolence, whereas the Israeli and conflict identities were correlated with the values of self-enhancement and universalism. These findings provided instrumental definitions for the concepts of *hegemonic* and *emancipated* representations.

Moscovici (1988, 221) draws attention to the different ways in which societies acquire their representations. Hegemonic representations are constructed by communication within a society; they are widely shared, uniform, and somewhat coercive. In contrast, subgroups within a society share the emancipated representations to a varied extent, and we assume, also, that they are acquired by communication with surrounding societies within a shared overall social context. The critical point is that they are not those that define the societal borders. These representations enjoy certain autonomy with respect to the interacting segments of a society. David Canter and Circe Monteiro (1993) assert that "the challenge of social representations theory is to see if the range of people who share any particular representations can be identified. If they can, the subsidiary methodological problem is to establish ways of distinguishing between the all-pervasive, hegemonic representations, and the emancipated ones" (226).

In her study, Paryente rises to this challenge. The religious-settler identity was defined as hegemonic to this society and as distinct from the identity representations of the surrounding Israeli hegemonic society. Its hegemonic position was empirically evident from its dominance in the identity structure of most people in each of her research groups, parents and children alike. It also included intolerance and a sense of threat regarding the surrounding nonreligious society. The finding of high means and small variance across each subgroup of the religious-settler society indicated its *hegemonic* position. The Israeli and conflict identities, in contrast, were shared by members of this society to a lesser extent; individual families varied in the degree they sensed it as their identity, and it was unrelated or modestly negatively related to their hegemonic identity. The findings indicated, then, that the Israeli identity was not the hallmark of the religious-settler society, nor was it unanimously represented in a negative light. The relatively large variance of both Israeli and conflict identities indicates that individuals and families were free in the extent that they could identify themselves as part of the surrounding Israeli society, or with the sense of conflict between these two societies. As such, the Israeli identity and the sense of conflict were defined as *emancipated* representations.

The next question, then, was of the extent to which parental hegemonic and emancipated identities were transmitted to their children. The hypothesis was that the hegemonic identity, being highly important, is transmitted to children to a greater extent than the emancipated identity and sense of conflict. Findings from a path analysis, however, did not confirm this hypothesis. In fact, the correlation between parental hegemonic values and identities and the values of their children was *smaller* than the correlation between parental emancipated values and identities and the values of their children. Furthermore, instead of being correlated with parental variables, as predicted, the children's hegemonic values of tradition were predicted mostly by their own political position (right wing) and the extent of their religiousness.

Our post-hoc interpretation of these findings is that hegemonic representations (values and identities) are transmitted to children mainly by the institutions of the community, such as the society-oriented schools (*yeshiva*, higher Jewish education for males, and literally meaning sitting together, and the *ulpana*, or school for females), the youth movement, the community-specific media, and informal communication in the societal neighborhoods. The emancipated representations, in contrast, are not transmitted by the societal institutions, and the extent of their endorsement depends on the extent of parental transmission.

To conclude, in describing a highly local Israeli minority group, Paryente has discovered highly general social phenomena. In accordance with Moscovici's (2000) postulation, values were found to be constructed as the core of the representational system, and identity representations were constructed in more peripheral positions. Moreover, operational definitions were discovered for his concepts of hegemonic and emancipated representations.[2] This definition led to the discovery of a distinction between two kinds of intergenerational transmission of identity representations and values. It was the adolescent children's emancipated representations that were related to those of their individual parents. The children's hegemonic representations, in contrast, were related less to those of their own parents and more to the extent of their self-definition as religious and their political agenda. It appears that hegemonic representations are constructed by children within community institutions, and less so by communication with individual parents. This speculation merits further theoretical and empirical inquiry.

The last study to be described here is Smadar Tuval's ethnographic research. Like Paryente, she was interested in how a society transmits its hegemonic representations to the next generation. The context of her study, though, was the school rather than the family. She wished to trace how the hegemonic representations of a society as stratified, and the elementary school humanistic values of egalitarianism, are represented such that some children and not others become members of the invisible "slow learners" society.

SELF-EVIDENT DISCRIMINATORY ACTIVITY
IN THE ELEMENTARY SCHOOL

Socrates suggests that an efficient regime of the Hellenic Republic needs its citizens to be positioned in one of three echelons: rulers, soldiers and craftsmen. The stability of a society, he claimed, depends on the respect that members of society attribute to these echelons, as well as their acceptance of their own position within the system. "But is it possible?" his disciple asks, and Socrates answers that one needs to tell the people a story that attributes this social division to the gods. The gods created all men, but added gold to the creation of rulers, iron and copper to soldiers, and left the rest as they were originally created. "But would people believe the story?" the disciple asks. Socrates replies, "They will believe if they accept this division as self-evident truth" (Plato 1975, vol. 6, 414–15).

In reality, it is rarely possible to uncover how some individuals are represented socially as a low-status minority and how this kind of status is accepted as a self-evident reality. Usually, society members are born into their status identification, and it is unusual to locate an instance in which identification can be tracked. Smadar Tuval, in an unusual ethnographic study (2004), was able to follow this kind of event. She offers an interpretative social analysis of how six-year-old children enter first grade, where all are supposed to equally acquire reading skills, but some, through a set of school representations, are identified as "slow learners" (in Hebrew, literally "weak learners") and put into exclusionary social frameworks. Tuval did not investigate these children's self-identification; instead, she looked for the ideology, common sense, and activity by which school teachers and the administration, despite their egalitarian ideology regarding the elementary school, represented these children as having a distinctively lower status.

The study makes an important contribution to our understanding of two SRT-derived concepts. Each of these concepts—self-evident representations, on the one hand, and the interplay of ideological, verbal, and activity representations, on the other—facilitates the obliviousness of society members to the incompatibilities between what they think is the right thing to do and what they really do. Each of the incompatible representations reflects one facet of the conflicting ideologies and values of a society. In the present case, it was the capitalistic values of social

stratification versus the egalitarian values of human equality as they feature in the life of the elementary school.

Self-evident representations are those social representations that societal members do not recognize as such; instead, they represent them as
undeniable reality. The nature of these representations facilitates their
ability to perpetuate themselves and relieves societal members of their
responsibility to account for them. Thus, they become oblivious to the
conflicts and incompatibilities within their representational world.
Tuval's study illustrates and develops this concept within the elementary
school setting.

The second contribution of her study to SRT is the illustration of how
ideological and verbal representations and those of action are combined
within a social system (the elementary school) such that the incompatibilities between representations are ignored. By acting in accordance with
a self-evident reality, society members become oblivious to—and live by
routines that mask—the incompatibilities of their representational world.

Tuval's study demonstrates (similar to Jodelete 1989/1991 regarding
psychiatric patients within a French village) the coexistence of two
incompatible sets of representations within a specific societal institution,
the Israeli elementary school. One set of representations reflects the ideological aspect of the society as democratic, relating to human rights, and
fighting discrimination; the other reflects the nature of this society as
stratified, where society members are treated discriminatively. The
incompatibility is either ignored or explained as an admittedly sad but
undeniable reality.

The novel contribution of this study is the demonstration of the chain
of institutionalized events through which minorities of children from a
supposedly homogeneous group were marked as different and socially
represented as "slow learners." By a sequence of institutional representations, teachers, following school procedures, systematically treated these
children distinctively from other students, so that they were ultimately
permanently identified as in need of integration. The paradox is that they
were first secluded, and then this seclusion was represented as a need for
integration.

An additional characteristic of this representational activity of seclusion is that specific cultural criteria marked certain children as targets of
discrimination. Only those who were slow in acquiring reading competence were treated this way; those who exhibited slow acquisition of cal-
culation skills, for instance, or those who did not conform to school
regulations regarding obedience and conformity were not. Furthermore,
the number of children who were targeted was more or less fixed (six to

eight children from each class of about thirty-five students), and a disproportionate quantity were from families that had immigrated to Israel from Ethiopia during the 1980s (but not those who had come from the former USSR). Thus, the school's stratifying activities in terms of academic criteria converged with societal institutional stratification.

The study demonstrates and reflects how schools in Israel mirror the society's incompatible formal ideologies. On the one hand, Israeli institutions and ideology are part of the Western democratic, humanistic approach, resting on egalitarian values; on the other hand, the social structure is stratified in accordance with the capitalistic agenda. Tuval's data reveals a similarly complex scenario with regard to elementary schools. This reflects the incompatible representations of the state of Israel as an all-embracing democracy and as a stratified, status-based country. The findings demonstrate, also, how the Israeli elementary school system copes with the incompatibility between egalitarian and stratified representations. Specifically, the conflict within the educational system was between its central ideological representations of humanistic, democratic, egalitarian principles and the academic, achievement-based activity of stratification. Ironically, this combination was labeled as the principle of *inclusion*. This label combines a tacit assumption of an innate value-laden difference between bright and slow students and an explicit declaration that this inequality should be amended. Alternative humanistic representations of accepting *variance* as the school's core representations are ignored. For instance, when Tuval interviewed the elementary school principals and teachers in her sample, all told her spontaneously that they are committed to accept and teach all children without exception, independent of their level of academic achievements. What she actually observed, however, was quite different and much more complex.

Stratification, it turned out, was not a one-step event. Initially, every six-year-old child who completes his or her kindergarten education enters a first-grade class. That is, elementary school is supposed to and does accept and *include* all. However, even before first grade begins, the teachers, following information they receive from kindergarten teachers, sort their future students into two groups so that each prospective teacher has a small number of those reported as academically slow in his or her classroom.

The first step taken in any given institution highlights its fundamental representations. As the teachers reported and Tuval observed, children with varied academic interests and abilities sit together in small working teams, such that they are able to learn not only from their teacher's instructions, but also from each others' varied kinds of competence.

However, on her visits to classrooms a number of weeks after the start of the academic year, she observed, to her amazement, that a number of students in each class were not sitting like the rest. Instead, they sat near the teacher, and their desks were positioned along one of the classroom walls. In response to Tuval's inquiry, the teachers said that these children were slow in acquiring reading skills, and they required more time and assistance. It seems, however, that such extra help was unfruitful; the same children, with minimal changes, remained excluded throughout their first-grade year, as well as throughout the two subsequent years that Tuval visited the same group for her research.

The above stratification representations were evident not only in the classification of the children and in their physical location in the classroom, but also in the efforts made to help them "catch up." While teachers spent more time with them, they did not adapt their teaching methods to the needs of these specific children. Rather, probably on the assumption that they were "slow," teachers worked with them longer than the others, using the same methods as for the rest of the class. Unsurprisingly, this had no positive effect on their academic and social status, as what these children really needed was an individually adapted method of teaching. Interestingly, teachers evaluated the academic achievements of these children by means of the psychiatric representation of *diagnosis*. Indeed, at some later point, usually during their second or third year at the school, a psychologist was asked to "diagnose" them.

These differential representations were also obvious during formal meetings in which teachers, the principal, and a counselor took part. A list of students' names was given to each, and the lists were arranged such that the student at the top was the one evaluated as the best in the class based on academic achievement (labeled "abilities"). The last students to appear on the list were those who were evaluated as academically problematic. The possibility of listing students in alphabetical order was ignored. Most of this meeting time was devoted to discussing the last children on the list, but instead of devising new methods for teaching them, the discussion involved descriptions of their academic incapacities.

Interestingly, but not surprisingly, the school teaching personnel was not aware of their actions as stratifying representations. The stratification activity was represented as a sad reality, quite close to a special kind of illness, which the team members tried to ameliorate. When they failed, they attributed the failure to circumstances in the family, and called upon external agencies, such as psychologists, for help. It was a very rare occasion that the children's level of academic performance was attributed to the school's pedagogical skills and activity.

How did the school system represent the entire situation? Tuval described the overall scene as a kind of *compromise*. When the school professionals discussed the situation, they represented their activities as attempts at inclusion. Over time, what the school actually did with the "slow learners" was to refer them to a special teacher for individual "treatment," and ultimately, some were referred to some kind of remedial school. In the meantime, the "problematic" children were taken out of their classrooms for a specified period of time to receive individual tutoring sessions. These tutors were paradoxically called "integrators," although, from a social perspective, their actual function was to segregate these children. The "compromise" was achieved by *camouflage*; verbal representations such as the "integrator" disguised the meaning of this activity as exclusionary.

This study reflects social scenes in which two incompatible representations of the social world coexisted: it was simultaneously represented as varied, egalitarian, and classless, on the one hand, and stratified by certain criteria—in this case, academic performance and ethnicity (Ethiopian)—on the other. The school professionals exercised a kind of compromise by which the stratification was represented as a given, and the school's role in reinforcing it was ignored. In other words, part of the stratification was represented as legitimate pedagogic *activity* in a *given* self-evident stratified world. What the school system was doing, or trying to do, was represented on the surface as curative activity. That was the point at which therapeutic representations fitted into the representational scheme.

CONCLUSIONS

Each of the three studies presented here demonstrates the "logical incompatibility" of representations. Mana illustrates the coexistence of identity representations of social harmony (integration) and power struggle (rivalry and seclusion) regarding immigrants. Paryente demonstrates the coexistence of a hegemonic religious-settler identity and its inconsistent emancipated Israeli-democratic identity among members of the religious Zionist society. Both try to show that the logical incompatibility is socially reasonable.

Tuval takes this a step further by demonstrating an incompatibility between two incongruent hegemonic representations, showing their interplay and its function in a stratified democratic society. She shows how school professionals preached an all-inclusive ideology according to which education is for all, yet, by means of a distinct set of representations, the administrators divided elementary school students into two echelons: a high-status bright majority and a low-status "slow-learning" minority. The incompatibility was tolerated because the children were tacitly represented as coming to school with varied innate capabilities for learning. The underlying assumption was that methodological teaching skills should be suited to "normal" children; as "slow learners" are beyond these skills, they should be taken care of by parents, counselors, psychologists, special schools, and so forth. The representation of intellectual incapacity did not appear to the school professionals as contradicting their representations regarding respect for variance, because the "incapacity" was represented as *self-evident*.

The last point I wish to make has to do with methodology. Unlike the case with other social psychological theories, researchers of SRT are not expected to use a specific methodology to test its speculations (see also Wagner and Hayes 2005). Instead, SRT supports the legitimacy of applying an array of methodologies. The specific methods any given researcher chooses to use depend on the specific aim of the investigation. In two of the present studies—that of Mana dealing with the identities of immigrants, and that of Paryente dealing with parental transmission of values and social identities to their adolescent children—the choice was a combination of qualitative and quantitative methods. First, the culture-specific identity representations were recorded via intensive interviews with representative groups from the societies of interest. These were expected to reflect the specific content and structure of the groups' identity representations. Then quantitative methods were used to: construct group-specific questionnaires, investigate the magnitude of the identity representations, analyze interrelationships between representations, and reveal within- and between-group differences. Paryente also used the statistical procedure of Path Analysis with the aim of documenting parental transmission of values and identities to children. Tuval, in contrast, applied an ethnographic methodology, whereby she documented the incompatible ideological and practical representations of speech and action in the elementary school.

It is my deep conviction that the SRT nonconservative research strategy is not only prolific, but it is also the flesh and bones of the social representations body of theoretical thinking. Social representations are not universal, but are rather context-specific; it is appropriate, then, that the methods for their discovery should be specific as well.

NOTES

1. In the SSA method, data is usually displayed on a map in accordance with the multiple nonparametric correlations between each of the items and the rest of them.

2. How does the distinction between hegemonic versus emancipated identities relate to that of imperative versus contractual obligations (Duveen 2001, 269)? Identity representations as defined here are not a distinctive individual identity category interacting with those of the social metasystem; instead, they are defined as a specific facet of the representational system along with the facets of knowledge and communication (Moscovici 1984). In each of these facets, two perspectives, the individual and the social, are simultaneously in action. The term "identity" as defined by Duveen, then, refers to the individual perspective within the general representational system, and as such, his categories of imperative versus contractual obligations refer to the relationships between the individual and the social metasystem. In the first case, society imposes an imperative obligation on the individual to adopt a particular identity, whereas in the case of contractual obligation, the individual voluntarily joins a social group and voluntarily takes a particular identity. Hence, an imperative obligation such as gender is the individual facet of societal hegemonic identity representations, whereas contractual obligation, such as an occupation, is the individual facet of societal emancipated identity representations.

REFERENCES

Ben Asher, S., W. Wagner, and E. Orr. 2006. Thinking groups: Rhetorical enactment of collective identity in three Israeli kibbutzim. *Asian Journal of Social Psychology* 9:112–22.

Ben-Rafael, E. 1982. *The emergence of ethnicity: Cultural group and social conflict in Israel.* Westport, CT: Greenwood.

Brewer, M. B. 2001. Social identities and social representations: A question of priority? In *Representations of the social: Bridging theoretical traditions*, ed. K. Deaux and G. Philogène, 305–11. Oxford: Blackwell.

Canter, D. V., and C. Monteiro. 1993. The lattice of polemic social representations: A comparison of the social representations of occupation in favelas, public housing, and middle-class neighborhoods of Brazil. In *Empirical approaches to social representations*, ed. G. M. Breakewell and D. V. Canter, 223–47. Oxford: Clarendon.

Duveen, G. 2001. Representations, identities, resistance. In *Representations of the social: Bridging theoretical traditions*, ed. K. Deaux and G. Philogène, 257–70. Oxford: Blackwell.

Guttman, L. 1968. A general non-metric technique for finding the smallest coordinate space for a configuration of points. *Psychometrica* 33:465–506.

Haslam, S. A., J. C. Turner, P. J. Oakes, C. McGarty, and K. Reynolds. 1998. The group as a basis of emergent stereotyped consensus. In *European review of social psychology*, vol. 8, ed. W. Stroebe and M. Hewstone, 203–39. Chichester, UK: Wiley.

Jodelete, D. 1989/1991. *Madness and social representations*. Trans. T. Pownall. Ed. G. Duveen. Hemel Hempstead, UK: Harvester Wheatsheaf.

Mana, A. 2005. *Social representations regarding the adaptation of "Ethiopian" and "Russian" adolescents in Israel: Actual and successful identity*. PhD diss., Ben Gurion University (translated from Hebrew).

Marková, I. 2000. Amédée or how to get rid of it: Social representations from a dialogical perspective. *Culture and Psychology* 6:419–60.

Moscovici, S. 1984. The phenomenon of social representations. In *Social representations*, ed. R. M. Farr and S. Moscovici, 3–69. Cambridge: Cambridge University Press.

———. 1988. Notes towards a description of social representations. *European Journal of Social Psychology* 18:211–50.

———. 2000. *Social representations: Explorations in social psychology*, ed. G. Duveen, 18–77. Cambridge: Polity.

Orr, E., A. Mana, and Y. Mana. 2003. Immigrant identity of Israeli adolescents from Ethiopia and the former USSR: Culture-specific principles of organization. *European Journal of Social Psychology* 33:71–92.

Paryente, B. 2002. *Identity conflict and intergenerational transmission of values among religiously observant Zionists from "settlements" and outside of them*. PhD diss., Ben Gurion University (translated from Hebrew).

Paryente, B., and E. Orr. 2003. Social identity structure: The case of religious Zionist communities in Israel. *Journal of Cultural and Evolutionary Psychology* 1 (3–4): 205–26.

Plato. 1975. *Plato in twelve volumes*. Vols. 5–6. Trans. Shorey Paul. Cambridge, MA: Loeb Classical Library, Harvard University Press; London: Heinemann.

Schwartz, S. 1992. Universals in the content and structure of values: Theoretical advances and empirical tests in 20 countries. In *Advances in experimental social psychology*. Vol. 25. Ed. M. P. Zanna, 1–65. New York: Academic Press.

Sobel, Z., and B. Beit Halachmi. 1991. *Tradition, innovation, conflict: Jewishness and Judaism in contemporary Israel*. Albany: State University of New York Press.

Tajfel, H. 1981. *Human groups and social categories: Studies in social psychology*. Cambridge: Cambridge University Press.

Tuval, S. 2004. *Social representations of inclusion, exclusion and stratification in the school, and as a factor in channeling children to a career in special education*. PhD diss., Ben-Gurion University (translated from Hebrew).

Wagner, W., and N. Hayes. 2005. *Everyday discourse and common sense: The theory of social representation*. New York: Palgrave Macmillan.

CHAPTER 5

SOCIAL REPRESENTATIONS AND THE POLITICALLY SATIRICAL CARTOON

THE CONSTRUCTION AND REPRODUCTION OF THE REFUGEE AND ASYLUM-SEEKER IDENTITY

Gail Moloney

IN *DISAPPOINTED GUESTS*, TAJFEL ASKS WHAT IT MEANS to be socially defined as a particular group—specifically for people of color in Britain in the 1960s (Tajfel and Dawson, 1965). Irrespective of how the African, Asian, and West Indian students in Tajfel's accounts felt about themselves, how they were seen by others in this particular social context became a powerful force in establishing who they were (Tajfel 1981). The content of identification, or how we are seen by others, is also beholden to other influences exercised through social representations, such as the imperative obligation imposed on individuals to adopt particular identities (Duveen and Lloyd 1990). In the specific instance in which an ethnic group is forced to migrate to a new country, the content of that imposed identity positions the migrant into the social matrix even before he or she arrives (see Philogène 2000; Tajfel 1965).

The focus of this chapter is on how the identity, and thus the social position, of refugees and asylum-seekers is not only predetermined before their arrival in a host country, but also on how it is reproduced *after* they arrive. I elucidate this by drawing from research that has investigated how refugees and asylum-seekers are depicted in the editorial cartoon; this analysis transmutes into a visual slice of how identity is located within social knowledge (see Duveen 2001).

INTRODUCTION

The editorial cartoon is a regular feature of all the major newspapers in Australia. Taking up one-third of the space on the editorial page, the cartoon could be accused of being nonchalant as it satirically passes comment on the news events of the day. But how should we understand this indifference, these sideline heckles, these caricatured scribbles, and their engaging irreverence? Is it mere titillation to brighten up the dry, grim retelling of world events, or is there a potency to these cartoons that is obscured by frivolity?

In addressing this, it is first necessary to frame the question within the relationship that has been argued to exist between mass media communications and social representations. From the inception of social representations theory, social representations have been argued to exist in the conversations, narratives (Moscovici 1984; Rouquette 1996), texts, ritualized practices (Jodelet 1989), cultural artifacts, and images of a society (de Rosa 1987; Jodelet 1989), all of which are communicable through the mass media.

As social knowledge, social representations are distinctive through their construction, which is concerted across individuals, groups, and institutions as a symbolic and dynamic system that melds both cognition and behavior (Duveen 1994; Moscovici 1973; Wagner, Valencia, and Elejabarrieta 1996). Through its conceptualization of social knowledge, social representations theory challenges traditional approaches in social psychology by arguing that perception should not be delineated from the social issue, nor the individual from their society. As "a system of values, ideas, and practices" (Moscovici 1973, xiii), a social representation *is* the social issue, not a representation of it (Wagner 1998). Similarly, to investigate what the individual understands about a social issue is to investigate also how that issue is socially derived, as it is individual activity that constitutes the social, and socially derived, understandings that inform individual thinking about social issues. While recognizing that the individual alone does not constitute the social, and that the social cannot be reduced to the individual (Jovchelovitch 1997), it is their interdependence and inseparability in the construction of social knowledge that defines social representations theory (Marková 1996).

MEDIA COMMUNICATIONS AND REPRESENTATION

As a disseminated product, the transmission of media communications is often perceived to be unidirectional: the producers of the media disseminate the news to the receivers of the media, being the viewers and readers. Conceptualized within social representations theory, however, mass media communications are underpinned by representational systems, and because the producers and the receivers reside within the same historicity, both are seen as constructors of media communications (Rouquette 1996).

Repeated, reflected, distorted, and innovated upon in accord with the structures of society, representations are always situated between stasis and transition, creating a dynamism that is also their malleability and thus susceptibility to influence by those who have the agency and the resources (Wagner 1998). Such inequities in media access allow for the proliferation of one version of events over others (Jovchelovitch 1997), which not only reproduces the identities of voiceless groups in society but also reconstructs them. Indicative of many "othered" groups, often known vicariously through the media, refugees and asylum-seekers do not have the means or the opportunity to reply to their depiction. Thus, the juncture between *what is* and *the reporting of what is* becomes asymmetrical, and the gap between *what is* and *what is reported as is* widens.

As representational discourse, the editorial cartoon is not excepted from this circularity. As a visual exemplar of the media's relationship with representations, the uniqueness of the cartoon's silent voice makes explicit the interdependence between identity and social representations.

The research presented in this chapter analyzes how the editorial cartoon is constructed and how this construction is perceived, providing a glimpse into the meshed relationship between the processes and content of identity to exemplify how an understanding of social identity needs first to be situated within concomitant representational systems. In doing this, I argue that the power of the satirical cartoon is twofold. First, in order to communicate political satire, the caricature in the cartoon needs to be irrefutably recognized as such. That is, the caricature must resonate with how the viewers perceive that group to be. Second, when the caricaturized group is known vicariously through the media, the exaggeration, ridicule, and humor of caricature distorts these boundaries. And, when little redress to this content exists, the potential is created for the content to be appropriated as the identity of that group.

REFUGEES AND ASYLUM-SEEKERS IN AUSTRALIA

Refugees and asylum-seekers do not arrive into an empty social space. Despite the host country's lack of experiential knowledge about their origins, refugees and asylum-seekers arrive into a social network of pre-existing ideas, beliefs, and values that position them in the social matrix of their new country (see Philogène 2000).

The morphogenesis of what constitutes an asylum-seeker, or, possibly more accurately, *who* constitutes an asylum-seeker, was crystallized for many Australians on August 27, 2001, when Captain Arne Rinnan asked Australian authorities for permission to land the 433 Afghani people he had rescued from their sinking boat in the Indian Ocean close to Australia.[1]

Australia takes approximately thirteen thousand people each year under its humanitarian program (Department of Immigration and Multicultural and Indigenous Affairs [DIMIA] 2007a), which is a small number by international standards (Pickering 2001). In addition to these figures, and prior to 2001, three "groups" of unauthorized "boat people"[2] had arrived at Australia's borders: the Vietnamese arrived post-1975, after the Vietnam war; the Cambodian and Chinese arrived after 1989; and the Vietnamese and Chinese arrived between 1994 and 1998 (Brennan 2003).[3]

What epitomized the 433 Afghani people rescued by the MV *Tampa* as "asylum-seekers" was the government's reaction to Captain Rinnan's request to land these people: firstly by ordering the *Tampa* to leave Australian waters, ignoring reports that the *Tampa* was dangerously unsea-worthy, and secondly by having the Special Air Service board the *Tampa* to ensure that none of its passengers disembarked (Pugh 2004). The period from 1997 until the end of 1999 was definitive in Australia's response to asylum-seekers (Pickering 2001). In Australia, immigration is a federal issue that typically receives bipartisan support from the two major political parties.[4] The government's approach to immigration was grounded in the prime minister's own anti-Asian (white Australia) position on immigration, as well as an increase in public support for minor right-wing anti-immigration parities (Pickering 2001). When Captain Rinnan made his request, a federal election campaign was well underway and both major political parties were keen to demonstrate that they could take a firm stand against the "other": those whose entry into Australia was not through legitimate channels (Brennan 2003). The government's response to the *Tampa* incident was seen as a symbolic attempt to address a growing unease over Australia's cultural identity as a young country, located near Asia but historically identified with Europe and North America (Pickering 2001). This fear was capitalized on by Australian authorities after the September 11, 2001, terrorist attack, when links were made between terrorism and asylum-seekers (Colic-Peisker 2005; Pugh 2004). *"The Twin Towers in New York were attacked as the Tampa affair continued to reverberate, and the*

Australian Defence Minister Peter Reith, and Howard himself, crudely linked the two events, claiming that terrorists might hide among asylum-seekers" (Pugh 2004, 55–56).

Two months after the *Tampa* incident, and at the height of the election campaign, a vessel identified as the *SIEV-4*[5] was intercepted on suspicion of people smuggling, and found to be carrying asylum-seekers. On October 7, 2001, one month before the federal election, the minister of immigration produced photographic "evidence" that a number of children had been thrown overboard the *SIEV-4* in an attempt to force the Royal Australian Navy to rescue them and thus grant them asylum. Although the Australian Defence Force and the defense minister knew that this photographic evidence was of a different event, the public was still unaware of the falsity of these claims at the time of the federal election a month later. These events developed into a political scandal (Herd 2006), countless analyses of the motives behind this deception have been produced. In short, the incident served to intensify the public's reaction to the *Tampa* by demonizing and dehumanizing more unwanted asylum-seekers as child-abusers and cheats (Herd 2006).

SEEKING REFUGE OR ASYLUM?

Forced migration to Australia is either couched in terms of those seeking refuge or asylum. The term refugee is used to describe those whose entry is via the *Refugee or Special Humanitarian Program*,[6] which requires that the person be living outside their home country and that the person make application through a formal, and frequently lengthy, process. Thus the entry is authorized and considered lawful (Healey 2002). The term asylum-seeker is used to describe either those whose entry is unauthorized and considered unlawful or those who have entered on an authorized and lawful visa but seek asylum during (or after) the term of this visa. Interestingly, contrary to what is commonly thought, most asylum-seekers in Australia enter via the latter means, that is, they arrive lawfully by plane and seek asylum during the term of their visa (Brennan 2003; Department of Immigration and Multicultural and Indigenous Affairs [DIMIA] 2007b; 2007c).

In 2001, Australia was resettling refugees fleeing civil war and famine in Africa concurrently as people were arriving unauthorized at Australia's borders from countries such as Afghanistan, Iran, and Iraq. The government's response to the former group was to resettle them in regional towns in Australia, while their response to the latter group was to "house" them in detention centers in the Australian desert, or divert their arrival to countries such as Nauru and Papua New Guinea[7] until formal, and lengthy, processing could determine the legitimacy of their applications. Although the government's treatment of asylum-seekers became very contentious internationally (Australia was found to have breached the 1951 Refugee Convention; Pugh 2004), the government's handling of this issue mustered a great deal of national public support, becoming "one of the most socially divisive and politically salient issues in Australia" (Augoustinos and Quinn 2003).

REFUGEES, ASYLUM-SEEKERS, AND THE EDITORIAL CARTOON

While this political and socially divisive debate occurred at the national level, refugees from Africa were being resettled at the local level into regional Australian towns. The interplay between this national debate and one local regional community's understandings held about this resettlement program became the impetus for a research program into the social understandings of refugees (Moloney 2004). In order to find out what the local people were being told about this program, a search of the regional newspaper was conducted. Much to our surprise, a disproportionate number of editorial cartoons in comparison to text reports about refugees and asylum-seekers was unearthed. This brought attention to the editorial cartoon and the role that it might play in the construction and reproduction of the identities of these groups, and constitutes the research presented in this chapter.

There were four stages to the research program that ensued. The first stage investigated the extent to which refugees and asylum-seekers were the subject of editorial cartoons. The second stage focused on what was understood by the terms "refugee" and "asylum-seeker" that is, the social representations of these terms in the Australian context. The third stage drew from the work of van Leeuwen (2000; 2001) to analyze how three typical cartoons about refugees and asylum-seekers were visually constructed, while the fourth stage investigated how the caricatures in these three cartoons were perceived by viewers. The remainder of this chapter presents the findings of this research, and discusses their implications for elucidating how identity is forged through social knowledge.

CARTOON COVERAGE OF ASYLUM-SEEKER AND REFUGEE ISSUES

Three Australian newspapers—one national, one state, and one regional newspaper[10]—were searched between January 2001 and January 2004, yielding 237 cartoons pertaining to refugees and asylum-seekers. One noticeable feature of these cartoons was the lack of distinction between asylum-seekers and refugees. In some instances, both terms were used in the one cartoon, while at other times, the term "refugee" was used while the issue clearly concerned people arriving unlawfully at Australian borders. However, what was clear was that the cartoon caricatures were recognizable as depicting asylum-seekers and refugees (Moloney 2006).

Having established that the editorial cartoon was a medium frequently used for communicating information about refugees and asylum-seekers, the next stage of the research sought to find out what was understood by the terms "refugee" and "asylum-seeker" in the Australian context. Despite the generic usage of these terms worldwide, it is the communicative action between individuals, groups, and the institutionalized structures of the society that the refugees and asylum-seeker are entering into that defines the localized meanings of these terms.

SEMANTIC NETWORK ASSOCIATED WITH REFUGEES AND ASYLUM-SEEKERS

A technique commonly employed in the investigation of social representations is the word-association task, in which respondents are asked to list the first responses that come to mind when they think of a stimulus word (see Wagner 1997; Wagner and Hayes 2005). Such tasks are argued to elicit habituated, unconscious, and often automatized responses that may not necessarily be revealed within the constraints of formal discourse (Deese 1965; Marková 1996; Szalay and Deese 1978). Because respondents are not called to reflect on or justify their answers, word-association tasks often elicit more spontaneous and less politically correct responses than those obtained through interviews, focus groups, or Likert scales, and thus indicative of socially derived historical meanings about the issue and constituents of social representations (Marková 1996; Moloney, Hall, and Walker 2005).

Social representations are conceptualized here as a tacit framework of meaning that directs and informs, but does not constrain, discourse about the issue. This conceptualization allows for the possibility of contradiction, agreement, and negotiation about the issue because the participation occurs within a consensual framework of meaning, as well as a dynamism to the representation that facilitates representational change (Moloney, Hall, and Walker 2005; see also Rose, Gervais, Jovchelovitch, and Morant 1995; Wagner and Hayes 2005).

The word-association task asked 115 participants[11] to write down the first 5 words that came to mind when they thought of either the term "refugee" or the term "asylum-seeker."[12] In total, 570 associations were elicited, revealing a common group of word categories[13] for both the terms "refugee" and "asylum-seeker": these included *boat, poor, escape, war, scared, politics, country of origin, immigrant,* and *unwanted.*

In order to examine the relationships between word categories, the associations for both stimulus words were pooled and new word categories were formed that were then subjected to Individual Differences Scaling (INDSCAL), also known as three-way multidimensional scaling.[14]

The INDSCAL solution can be interpreted by investigating the associations that cluster around the centroid,[15] and by a dimensional interpretation of the differential subject weights (Kruskal and Wish 1978).

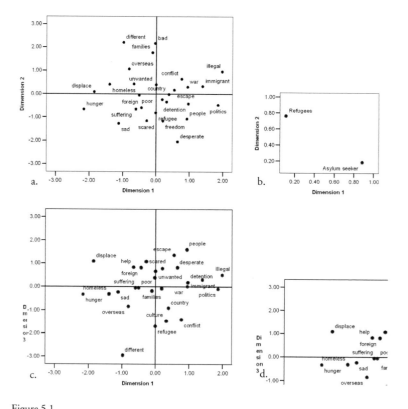

Figure 5.1
a. Scatter-plot of the INDSCAL solution for both the stimulus terms "refugee" and "asylum-seeker." Dimension 1 by Dimension 2 of the 3-dimensional solution (Stress = 0.14, RSQ = 0.88).
b. Subject weights for Dimension 1 by Dimension 2.
c. Scatter-plot of Dimension 1 by Dimension 3.
d. Subject weights for Dimension 1 by Dimension 3.

Associations that cluster around the centroid are argued to be central to the representation due to their high frequency and high co-occurrence (Moloney, Hall, and Walker 2005; Wagner, Valencia, and Elejabarrieta 1996), which suggests a shared-ness and a semantic network, in this instance, for both "refugee" and "asylum-seeker." The implication is not that participants themselves agreed with this semantic network, but rather that these were the words that sprang to mind most frequently within and across participants. Cleary, it is possible to be aware of how an issue is socially understood yet not subscribe to this understanding.

The most interesting finding from this analysis was the elicitation of the category *boat*. Refugees do not generally arrive by boat, nor do the majority of asylum-seekers, who, in the main, come by plane and overstay their visas (Mares 2002). Yet central to the semantic network for both the terms "refugee" and "asylum-seeker" was the idea of a boat, attesting to the socially constructive nature of representational discourse. Further analyses revealed that the categories *escape*, *help*, and *unwanted* also clustered around the centroid.[16] The category *escape* is self-explanatory in that refugees and asylum-seekers are escaping from something or somewhere, yet *help* appears antithetical to *unwanted*, indicating a contradictory representational field. One explanation for this contradiction is that there are normative and functional dimensions within the representational structure (Guimelli 1998; see also Moloney, Hall, and Walker 2005).

Guimelli (1998) posits that the normative dimension of a representation is marked by ideological and historical factors that allow evaluative judgments to be made about the social object, while the functional dimension conveys the instrumental relations that individuals have with the social object as exemplified through their social practices. Conceptualized therein, the categories *boat* and *help* appear as normative elements, while *unwanted* is functional. At an ideological or intellectual level, these people were recognized as being in need of help, yet at a functional level—when the issue directly concerned Australia—they were unwanted: they were *intruders*, *queue jumpers*, *a threat to Australians*, and simply *not our problem*. These latter associations concur with Grove and Zwi (2006), who argue that such metaphors emphasize the difference between "us" and "them"—"we are law-abiding, they are law-breaking" (1934)—and facilitate public acceptance of controversial immigration policies such as the detention of asylum-seekers, by shifting the focus from the protection of the refugee to protection from the refugee.

In contrast to two-way multidimensional scaling (MDS), INDSCAL provides subject weights that allow the differential salience of the associations to each stimulus word to be compared against the referent structure that the aggregated data represents, yielding a dynamic interpretation of the representational field. In Figures 5.1a and 5.2b, associations central to the dimension most salient to asylum-seekers (Dimension 1) are shown as polarizing the dimension central to refugees (Dimension 2). For example, the categories of *bad* and *family* can be seen to differentiate understandings of asylum-seekers from those of refugees (*bad* is a category indicative of derogatory associations such as *dirty, scum, opportunist,* and *liar,* while the category *family* suggests that asylum-seekers are seen either to arrive in family groups or to bring their family to Australia once they have obtained asylum). *Bad* and *family* also cluster antithetically with *scared* and *freedom,* indicating an understanding of the plight of asylum-seekers concomitant with a negative evaluation. In sum, the responses from the word-association task reveal a contradictory representational field pertaining to both refugees and asylum-seekers, central to which is the image of a boat and a pitiful group of people who, although clearly in need of help, are not wanted in Australia.

Similar results were found in a 2004 study investigating Australian adolescents' understanding of refugees and asylum-seekers, suggesting that this contradictory image has persisted over time (Worboys and Moloney, 2004).[17] This also concurs with Augoustinos and Quinn (2003), who found that significantly more negative than positive attributes were ascribed to the labels of "asylum-seekers" and "refugees" in Victoria, Australia, and with Grove and Zwi (2006), who describe the public perception of refugees in Australia as "needy, helpless and a drain on resources" (1935). Grove, Zwi and Allotey (2007) suggest that similar to metaphors of unlawful entry, notions of being uninvited are used to justify controversial government policies toward these people:

> One of the most powerful ways in which asylum-seekers and forced migrants are portrayed is as uninvited. . . . Notions of the "uninvited guest" have been employed by politicians to justify sensational attempts at deterring boat people. The Australian government has intercepted refugees at sea and refused entry of vessels thought to be carrying refugees into Australian waters. These actions were accompanied by the Prime Minister John Howard's defiant declaration: "We will choose who comes to these shores and the circumstances under which they come." (216)

WHOSE IDENTITY?

Rajaram (2002) describes the refugee identity as an identity lost and replaced by a vacuous administrative label (Colic-Peisker and Walker 2003). Grove and Zwi (2006) argue that the identity of refugees is constructed by their host country, and cite how metaphors of threat, natural disaster, war, and contagion have been used to construct who these people are. Joffe (Chapter 11, this volume) argues that the dominant group's identity drives the construction of the "other," for, by serving as a contra, the "other" defines who the members of the dominant group are by who they are not. Weiss (1995) elaborates (from the writings of Edward Said [1985]), stating that as all identities are constructions, they must, by course, be constructed in relation to others. Thus, the identity we give to the refugee and to the asylum-seeker legitimizes our responses to these people. The image of the *Tampa* (and the 433 people that the Australian government vigorously prevented from landing on Australian shores), eclipses who these people are and their individuality and incogitable survival against appalling hardships and oppressive regimes. Thus, what it is to be Australian is defined by those who want to be Australian.

THE EDITORIAL CARTOON

What is the relationship between socially derived patterns of association with an issue, and the portrayal of that issue through media such as the editorial cartoon? Both are arguably representational discourses not created by the media but are, rather, socially derived through the interactions among those who read, produce, and inform the media. A constituent of representational discourse is the state of being somewhere between stasis and transition; thus, representational discourse disseminated by the media is not immutable from the comportment of the media in its retelling of the news.

But what is the editorial cartoon? Is it news or not news? The nexus of the cartoon with other news forms is argued by Buell and Maus (1988) to be shadowy. Editorial cartoonists are neither reporters nor news editors, yet their material flows from the news. While a single cartoon has the potential to crystallize an issue protracted in text, this depends on satirical commentary being understood. Gamson and Stuart (1992) argue that often, this is simply not the case, citing the research of Carl (1968) that revealed that only 30 percent of those surveyed fully grasped (15 percent) or partially grasped (15 percent) the satirical comment of the cartoons they were shown. While clearly a valid point, this does not mean that the characters in the cartoon are not recognized as intended.

THE CARTOON IDENTITY

How does the cartoonist create a caricature? An obvious requirement is that the caricature of a group be recognizable as that group, otherwise the satirical commentary could not be conveyed. Caricature predominately works at the group level: the caricature of a person is representative of a group or institution. For example, a caricature of Australian Prime Minister John Howard is parodying the institution of the government (Barrow 2003). Similarly, a caricature of a refugee is representative of *refugees*. It is this enigmatic leap from individual to group that affords the cartoon, and particularly the caricature, its power (Barrow 2003). These clear concise visually repeated images reinforce the image portrayed by the caricature as that group, especially when only one form of caricature is used to depict a group time after time.

In his *Handbook of Visual Analysis*, van Leeuwen (2001) argues that the visual interpretation of images must be inclusive of the image in its entirety. That is, it must look beyond the physical objects or subjects to include such things as social distance, the positioning of people relative to each other and to the viewer, the culturally denotative meaning associated with the presence and placement of cultural artifacts, and the depiction of individuals versus types through the use of physiognomic stereotypes, generality, or attention to detail, posture, and stance.

Clearly, the cartoon is a medium of representational discourse, a visual slice of the socially derived pattern of meanings held about an issue. And it is this socially derived knowledge that Duveen and Lloyd (1990) argue is drawn upon in the construction and reproduction of social identity.

SOCIAL IDENTITY WITHIN SOCIALLY DERIVED KNOWLEDGE

In arguing for a position where identity is resourced from social knowledge (Duveen and Lloyd 1986, 1990), it is first necessary to elucidate the relationship that is seen to exist between the individual and society. The interdependence between the social and the individual, and thus their inseparability in the construction of social knowledge, is pivotal in the theory of social representations (Marková 1996). Duveen and Lloyd (1986) argue that the dichotomy between the individual and the social is untenable, as the categorical separation between the individual and the social is itself a social representation. In effect, as social beings, social relations are inextricably part of the individual, rendering the understanding of individuality devoid of a social network that is itself a misrepresentation (see Farr 1989). Individuals constitute society through their social grouping, and, as many of these social groupings are prescriptive and imposed (for example, gender and ethnicity), any delineation between the individual and society is forced (Duveen and Lloyd 1986).

Nonetheless, the relationship that the individual has with society is socially constructed by the individuals, groups, and institutional structures of that society, and is thus intertwined with resource availability, not only to those to whom it pertains but also to others in relation to those individuals. This asymmetry allows for the imposition, entrenchment, and acceptance of these representations as ontological reality (see Augoustinos and Riggs, Chapter 7, this volume; Jovchelovitch 1996). The editorial cartoon is one arena that reflects the outcome of differential media access (Gamson and Stuart 1992) that has the means to convey particular representations about groups and their relationships to the mainstream.

THE CONSTRUCTION OF THE EDITORIAL CARTOON

This editorial cartoon appeared in *The Australian* newspaper on Wednesday, September 5, 2001, when Prime Minister John Howard was "relocating" the Afghani people rescued by the *Tampa*. A satirical commentary on the insensitivity of governments to the plight of asylum-seekers, the cartoon has, as Manning and Phiddian (2004) describe, indignation cartooning as its intent: the legitimacy and office are not the urgent issues; rather, the action and the manner in which the office is dealing with the issue are. This form of cartooning draws the reader

Figure 5.2

"emotionally and intelligently" into the issue (Manning and Phiddian 2004, 35). However, regardless of the cartoon's intent, it is the construction of the character that is the asylum-seeker that is important here.

The first point in such an analysis is social distance. Van Leeuwen (2000) argues that the distance in visual representation is symbolic of the relationship that "society" has with the people in the image. Depicted as "not one of us," distance in the lens shot can convey notions of othering. For example, a long shot in which a person is positioned further back in the image connotes a social distance between the viewer and that person, particularly when that distance is differential to other distance shots in the image. In the cartoon reproduced above, the Afghani people are positioned farther back than both John Howard and New Zealand Prime Minister Helen Clark, indicative perhaps of the difference in our familiarity with these people (see van Leeuwen 2000). The synchronized pose of the asylum-seekers augments this social distance through typification, which itself is accentuated by the individuality conferred by the fine detail given in the portrayal of John Howard and Helen Clark. Helen Clark carries a handbag; John Howard wears a tie.

Physiognomic stereotypes—exaggerated noses and accentuated moustaches—are used to depict the asylum-seekers, denoting the ethnicity or country of origin of the group, despite the word "Afghanis" being included in the cartoon text. With their uncanny resemblance to Saddam Hussein, these people may be from regimes associated with evil and terror, or they may quite simply be camel drivers from central Asia. Whoever these people are, the use of physiognomic stereotypes implies that they are not like us. The averted gaze of the asylum-seekers (from the viewer) signifies quite subtly that these people are not the viewer's problem (see van Leeuwen 2000, 2001). There is no need to engage with these people or, more importantly, to engage with their plight.

Similar constructions can be seen in the two cartoons reproduced in Figure 5.3 a & b, which appeared respectively in the national *Australian* newspaper and the regional *Coffs Coast Advocate*. The cartoon in Figure 5.3a appeared on November 1, 2001, as comment on the Australian government's continued treatment of asylum-seekers. The one in Figure 5.3b appeared on August 13, 2004, as a comment on the treatment of refugees fleeing famine in Sudan. Both are examples of how caricature inadvertently begets a distant other, despite a cartooning style designed to engage the viewer with the issue (Manning and Phiddian 2004). The headscarf and physiognomic stereotype of an exaggerated nose in the cartoon on the left suggest that the asylum-seekers are central-Asian Muslims, while the infantile stereotype (large head and bulbous eyes) in the cartoon on

Figure 5.3a   Nicholson 2001-11-08

The Australian, November 8, 2001

Figure 5.3b   Broelman 2004-08-13

Coffs Coast Advocate, August 13, 2004

the right intimates helplessness and naïvety. In both instances, the stereotyping and typification construct a social distance between the viewer and the people, augmented by a vertical distance that denotes asymmetrical power relations between asylum-seekers and the government in the cartoon in Figure 5.3a, and between refugees and world institutions in the cartoon in Figure 5.3b. This symbolism conveys their dependency not only on these institutions but, by course, on the viewer, as well.

In all three of the cartoons reproduced in this chapter, the image is one of helplessness and dependency, but also, through typification, one that negates individuality, thus casting these groups as "others" from the point of view of Australians (Grove and Zwi 2006; see also Joffe, Chapter 11, this volume). This cartooning style was a consistent feature of the 237 cartoons found across the three newspapers over the three-year period surveyed. Table 5.1 presents the frequency of the styles as found across the cartoons.

Table 5.1   Frequency of cartooning characteristics in 237 cartoons

Cartooning Characteristic	Frequency
Physiognomic Stereotype	
Large nose	63
Large mustache	46
Long beard	31
Bulbous eyes/infantile	30
Synchronized Pose	
Group with same features	41
Group in same position or direction	57
Single individual	13
Presence of Symbol or Cultural Artifact	
Boat	38
Detention center	42
Burqa (full)	6
Burqa (open face)	29
Headscarf	8
Turban	29
Robe	27
Symbolic Distance and Passivity	
Vertical distance from non-refugee	14
Horizontal distance from non-refugee	16
Bowed head or shoulders	19
Non-refugee is larger	27

HOW IS THE CARICATURE VIEWED BY OTHERS?

The next stage of the research investigated how the caricatures in the cartoons were perceived by viewers. To this end, 115 participants were asked to rate how they thought the caricatures in the three reproduced cartoons portrayed refugees and asylum-seekers. The respondents each rated one

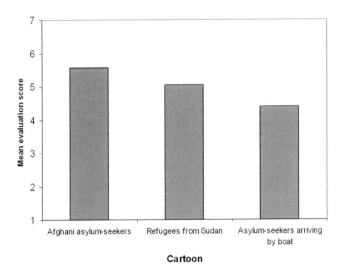

Figure 5.4   Mean scores for the positive-negative evaluation scale for the three cartoons. (Total M = 4.97; SD = 0.99. Cartoon 1: M = 5.56, SD = 0.60; Cartoon 2: M = 5.04, SD = 0.91; Cartoon 3: M = 4.40, SD = 0.99)

of the three cartoons on nine seven-point semantic differential scales (adapted from Voci and Hewstone 2001; Wright Aron, McLaughlin-Volpe, and Ropp 1997),[18] that measured one underlying negative–positive construct. Across all three cartoons, the caricatures of refugees and asylum-seekers were perceived negatively by participants, with ratings well above the midpoint of the scales (see Figure 5.4).[19]

IDENTITY WITHIN THE CARTOON

Where does fact stop and suggestion begin? Van Leeuwen (2000) argues that the ability of images, particularly photographic images, to mechanically reproduce what is in front of the lens leads us to conclude that the viewer reads the meaning into the image. This, however, juxtaposes the cartoon with society in the same way that a two-dimensional view communicates stasis of what is in reality three-dimensional.

Connotative meaning is premised upon an interdependence between the viewer and the image, as reiterated by the analyses presented in this chapter. When the visual construction of the cartoon was examined, differential lens shots, physiognomic stereotypes, and cultural artifacts effected a negative image of a helpless, pitiful group of people paradoxical to the satirical comment. The satirical comment urges the viewer to engage with how the institutions involved are dealing with these people (Manning and Phiddian 2004), while the caricature itself visually devalues them.

One explanation for this apparent paradox is the dichotomy between reflexive and nonreflexive[20] thought and its relationship to social representations. Nonreflexive and habituated responses have been associated with culturally shared beliefs (Marková 1996), that is, the social knowledge that is derived through communication and interaction across institutions, groups, and individuals. However, this social knowledge does not always equate with reflexive knowledge or considered thought. Consider, for example, the responses an individual may give when asked about asylum-seekers or refugees.

In urging the viewer to engage with this issue, the satirical commentary is supportive of the plight of asylum-seekers and refugees, while the negative image implicit in the caricature is the nonreflexive, habituated social representation of asylum-seekers and refugees—the iconic image of how these people are socially identified by Australian society.

IN CONCLUSION: POWER, COMMUNICATION, AND THE CONSTRUCTION OF IDENTITY

Joffe (see Chapter 11, this volume, p. 323) states that "a distinctive aspect of being the 'other' is that one is the object of someone else's fantasies, but not [one] with agency and voice." The imposed refugee and asylum-seeker identity is one informed by Australia's concern over border protection, nationalism, and sovereignty. This identity does not represent these people, their histories, or their cultures. It is instead a vacuous, administrative identity that is a construction of how they are seen in relation to us. As an imposed social identity, the refugee and asylum-seeker represent a location in our social knowledge about these issues and an identity predetermined before these people set foot on Australian soil. It is from this position that they must negotiate their new life (see Philogène 2000). "Outside of the detention centres, refugees is an undesirable identity which the mainstream views with suspicion; it is a pariah status that gives welfare and social entitlements but little else. Rather than viewing themselves as heroes, who have stood up to and escaped oppressive regimes, many refugees are reluctant to admit their status" (Colic-Peisker and Walker 2003, 343).

But to say that this is how those who are refugees respond to this imposed identity is to ignore Duveen (2001) who talks of resistance—a point at which "an identity refuses to accept what is proposed by a communicative act" (269). For example, Colic-Peisker and Walker (2003) cite cases of refugees arguing against this identity by stating that they arrived in Australia with a valid passport from their home country, and instances of Red Cross workers who recognize this need to resist the imposition of a negative image and do so by greeting refugees at the airport and stating immediately "that they are no longer refugees but permanent residents of Australia" (342).

But what of the innocent cartoon, satirically poking fun at the institutions that denigrate these people, yet unable to reflect on their contribution in constructing these identities? It is argued here that the editorial cartoon reproduces the content of the refugee and asylum-seeker identity in much the same way as well-intentioned charity institutions adorn Christmas cards with pitiful images of helpless refugees and asylum-seekers. The cartoon simply goes further, adding to this reproduction through its tools of hyperbole, exaggeration, and humor. Through this enticing humorous veneer, the viewer is encouraged to engage with the issue—but not with the socially constructed identity.

Most Australians' knowledge of asylum-seekers and refugees is predominately vicarious, and obtained primarily through the media. While politicians and everyday Australians may also be subjected to caricatured constructions of identity, the difference lies in the fact that politicians can redress these images. In constructing caricatures of voiceless groups in society, there are huge inequities in communication. Groups such as refugees or asylum-seekers do not have the means or the opportunity to reply to their depiction. Thus, the gap between *what is* and *the reporting of what is* widens, contributing further to the inequity of discourse about these groups (Duveen 2001). Without the means to redress that reproduction, and left unchallenged, the reproduction is gradually distorted through caricature, and through the prescriptive nature of representation is incorporated into the identity of that group.

The humor and engaging irreverence of the editorial cartoon masquerades its potency as communicative action and draws the viewer into its reproduction of this single shot of identity. When viewed within the framework of social representations, the cartoon is analogous to a lock and key. The viewer needs to be apprised with the layered meaning implicit in the cartoon in order to interpret the cartoon. Thus, the power to create identity lies not in the caricature itself, but rather in the prescriptive power of representation when inequitable communicative processes exist and the identity of groups is imposed.

It has been argued in this chapter that the construction of social iden-tity is resourced from social representations (Duveen and Lloyd 1990; Duveen and Lloyd 1986). While this chapter has focused on the medium of the cartoon to exemplify the relationship of the identity of asylum-seekers and refugees to social knowledge, it does so in order to highlight the asymmetrical construction of identity that exists in society for many other voiceless groups.

NOTES

1. As a direct result of their response to this incident, Captain Arne Rinnan, his crew, and the ship owner of the MV *Tampa* received the Nansen Refugee Award (UNHCR: United Nations High Commissioner for Refugees) in June 2002 for distinguished work on behalf of refugees (Pugh 2004).
2. The word "group" is used here to avoid the commonly used phrase "waves of boat people" (see Mares 2002 and Pugh 2004 for a comprehensive dis-cussion of this issue).
3. The most recent group arrived between 2000 and 2003 from central Asia and include the 433 Afghani persons discussed here.
4. The two major political parties in Australia are the Liberal and Labour parties.
5. SIEV is the acronym used by the Australian Defence Force or Coast Guard for suspected illegal entry vessels, that is vessels suspected to be attempting to reach Australia without authorization. These vessels are given numerical designations, hence the maritime vessel referred to here had been identified by the Australian Defence force as SIEV-4 (SIEVreader, 2007).
6. Persons entering Australia via the *Refugee Program* have been identified by UNHCR as being subject to persecution in their home country. Entry via the *Special Humanitarian Program* occurs when discrimination in the refugee's home country amounts to a gross violation of human rights and his/her entry into Australia is sponsored by groups within Australia (Healey 2002).
7. This is often referred to as "the Pacific solution."
8. Although refugees from other parts of Africa were also resettled into this regional coastal town in New South Wales from 2003 onward, between 2001 and 2003, the refugees were predominately from Sudan.
9. One plausible explanation for this disparity is that the editorial cartoons were produced for a syndicate of papers of which the *Coffs Coast Advocate* was one. The cartoons were part of a national debate on refugees and asy-lum-seekers, and were not directly commenting on the local resettlement occurring in this community.
10. These three papers constitute a cross-section of the papers available in this regional town.
11. These participants were undergraduate university students enrolled in busi-ness and tourism studies.

12. The stimulus words for the word-associations tasks were randomly assigned to the participants.

13. The raw associations were homogenized into word categories. Plural forms were reduced to the singular, and synonyms were grouped together into one category.

14. New word categories were formed across stimulus words. Similarity matrices were computed for the twenty-one highest-frequency categories, followed by INDSCAL (Individual Differences Scaling) or a three-way multidimensional scaling (see Moloney, Hall, and Walker 2005 for a similar procedure).

15. This draws from Kruskal and Wish's (1978) neighborhood interpretation that focuses on the similarities in distances between items in the configuration.

16. A Hierarchical Cluster Analysis (HCA) solution was extracted from the three dimensions.

17. A very similar semantic pattern of associations was found in Worboys and Moloney (2004), which investigated the social understandings held by Australian high school students about refugees and asylum-seekers at a local high school where Sudanese refugee students had recently been enrolled. *Boat, unwanted,* and *help* were again central associations made to both stimulus terms.

18. The scale items were "negative–positive, warm–cold, suspicious–trusting, disgust–admiration, hostile-friendly, dangerous–safe, type–individual, you–me, same-other " The last three items were an extension to the original scale. The items were randomly ordered, reversed scored, and subjected to Principal Components Analysis (PCA), which revealed a robust underlying dimensional construct for the first six items listed (Evaluation scale: Cronbach's alpha .82).

19. Ratings on the six-item evaluation scale were well above the midpoint (Total Mean (M) = 4.97, Standard deviation (SD) = .99; Cartoon 1: M = 5.56, SD .69; Cartoon 2: M = 5.04, SD = .91; Cartoon 3: M = 4.40, SD =.99), while item means for individuals–types (Total M = 5.53, SD = 2.02), me–you (M = 4.8, SD = 1.57), same–other (M = 4.56, SD = 1.76) revealed a similar negative bias.

20. See Marková 1996; conscious and unconscious thought are also terms that could be used here.

References

Augoustinos, M., and C. Quinn. 2003. Social categorization and attitudinal evaluations: Illegal immigrants, refugees or asylum seekers? *New Review of Social Psychology* 2 (1): 29–37.

Barrow, H. 2003. *Hired assassins: Political cartooning in Australia.* Evershine; Lindfield NSW: Film Australia, 2003.

Bauer, M. W., and G. Gaskell. 1999. Towards a paradigm for research on social representations. *Journal for the Theory of Social Behaviour* 29 (2): 163–86.

Brennan, F. 2003. *Tampering with asylum: A universal humanitarian problem.* St. Lucia, Queensland: University of Queensland Press.

Buell, E., and M. Maus. 1988. Is the pen mightier than the sword? Editorial cartoons and 1988 presidential nominating politics. *Political Science and Politics* 21 (4): 847–58.

Colic-Peisker, V. 2005. At least you're the right colour. Identity and social inclusion of Bosnian refugees in Australia. *Journal of Ethnic and Migration Studies* 31:615–638.

Colic-Peisker, V., and I. Walker. 2003. Human capital. Acculturation and social identity: Bosnian refugees in Australia. *Journal of Community and Applied Social Psychology* 13:337–60.

de Rosa, A. S. 1987. The social representations of mental illness in children and adults. In *Current issues in European social psychology*, vol. 2, ed. W. Doise and S. Moscovici, 47–138. Cambridge: Cambridge University Press.

Deese, J. 1965. *The structure of associations in language and thought.* Baltimore: John Hopkins University Press.

Department of Immigration and Multicultural and Indigenous Affairs (DIMIA). 2007a. *Fact sheet 60: Australia's refugee and humanitarian program.* http://www.immi.gov.au/media/fact-sheets/60refugee.htm (accessed January 10, 2007).

———. 2007b. *Fact sheet 61: Seeking asylum within Australia.* http://www.immi.gov.au/media/fact-sheets/61asylum.htm (accessed January 17, 2007).

———. 2007c. *Fact sheet 71: Processing unlawful boar arrivals.* http://www.immi.gov.au/media/fact-sheets/75processing.htm (accessed March 3, 2007).

Duveen, G. 1994. Unanalysed residues: Representations and behaviours—A comment on W. Wagner. *Papers on Social Representations* 3:95–232.

Duveen, G. 2001. Representations, identities, resistance. In *Representations of the social: Bridging theoretical traditions*, ed. K. Deaux and G. Philogène, 257–70. Oxford: Blackwell.

Duveen, G., and B. Lloyd. 1986. The significance of social identities. *British Journal of Social Psychology* 25:219–30.

———. 1990. Introd. to *Social representations and the development of knowledge,* ed. G. Duveen and B. Lloyd, 1–10. Cambridge: Cambridge University Press.

Farr, R. 1987. Social representations: A French tradition of research. *Journal for the Theory of Social Behaviour* 17:343–69.

Gamson, W. A., and D. Stuart. 1992. Media discourse as a symbolic contest: The bomb in political cartoons. *Socialogical Forum* 7 (1):55–86.

Grove, N. J., and A. B. Zwi. 2006. Our health and theirs: Forced migration, othering, and public health. *Social Science & Medicine* 62:1931–42.

Grove, N. J., A. B. Zwi, and P. Allotey. 2007. Othering of refugees: Social exclusion and public health. In *A reader in promoting public health. Challenge and controversy*, ed. J. Douglas, S. Earle, S. Handsley, C. E. Lloyd, and S. Spurr, 213–24. London: Sage.

Guimelli, C. 1998. Differentiation between the central core elements of social representations: Normative vs. functional elements. *Swiss Journal of Psychology* 57:209–24.

Healey, J. 2002. *Australia's immigration debate*. Rozelle, Australia: Spinney.

Herd, A. 2006. Amplifying outrage over children overboard. *Social Alternatives* 25 (2): 59–63.

Huguenot Society of Great Britain & Ireland. 2007. http://www.huguenotsociety .org.uk (accessed May 21, 2007).

Jodelet, D. 1989. Representations sociales, un domaine en expansion. In *Les Represetantions Sociales*, ed. D. Jodelet, 31–61. Paris: Presses Universitaires de France.

Jovchelovitch, S. 1996. In defence of representations. *Journal for the Theory of Social Behaviour* 26 (2): 121–35.

———. 1997. Peripheral communities and the transformation of social representations: Queries on power and recognition. *Social Psychology Review* 1 (1): 16–26.

Kruskal, J., and M. Wish. 1978. *Multidimensional scaling*. Beverly Hills, CA: Sage.

Manning, H., and R. Phiddian. 2004. In defence of the political cartoonists' licence to mock. *Australian Review of Public Affairs* 5 (1).

Mares, P. 2002. *Borderline: Australia's response to refugees and asylum-seekers in the wake of the Tampa*. Sydney: University of New South Wales Press.

Marková, I. 1996. Towards an epistemology of social representations. *Journal for the Theory of Social behaviour* 26:177–96.

Moloney, G. 2004. *The tourist, the refugee and Coffs Harbour: Social representations and social identity*. Paper presented at the Society of Australian Social Psychologists Conference (SASP), Melbourne, July 1–2.

———. 2006. *Political satire and the construction of identity within social knowledge: refugees, asylum-seekers and the editorial cartoon*. Paper presented at the VIII International Conference on Social Representations: Media and Society, Rome, August 28–September 1, 2006.

Moloney, G., R. Hall, and I. Walker. 2005. Social representations and themata: The construction and functioning of social knowledge about donation and transplantation. *British Journal of Social Psychology* 44 (3): 415–41.

Moscovici, S. 1973. Foreword to *Health and Illness*, ed. C. Herzlich, ix–xiv. London: Academic Press.

———. 1984. The phenomenon of social representations. In *Social representations*, ed. R. M. Farr and S. Moscovici, 3–69. Cambridge: Cambridge University Press; Paris: Maison des Sciences de l'Homme.

Philogène, G. 2000. Blacks as "servicable other." *Journal of Community and Applied Social Psychology* 10:391–401.

Pickering, S. 2001. Common sense and original deviancy: News discourses and asylum seekers in Australia. *Journal of Refugee Studies* 14 (2): 169–86.

Pugh, M. 2004. Drowning not waving: Boat people and humanitarianism at sea. *Journal for Refugee Studies* 17 (1): 50–69.

Rajaram, P. K. 2002. Humanitarianism and representations of the refugee. *Journal of Refugee Studies* 15 (3): 247–64.

Rose, D., D. Efraim, M. C. Gervais, H. Joffe, S. Jovchelovitch, and N. Morant.1995. Questioning consensus in social representations theory. *Papers on Social Representations* 4:150–55.

Rouquette, M. 1996. Social representations and mass communications research. *Journal for the Theory of Social Behaviour* 26 (2):221–31.

Said, E. 1985. *Orientalism*. Harmondsworth: Penguin.

SIEVreader .2007. http://sievxreader.com (accessed May 21, 2007).

Szalay, L., and J. Deese. 1978. *Subjective meaning and culture: An assessment through word associations*. Hillsdale, NJ: Lawrence Erlbaum Associates.

Tajfel, H. 1981. *Human groups and social categories: Studies in social psychology*. Cambridge: Cambridge University Press.

Tajfel, H., and J. Dawson, eds. 1965. *Disappointed guests*. London: Oxford University Press.

van Leeuwen, T. 2000. Visual racism. In *The semiotics of racism: Approaches in critical discourse analysis*, ed. M. Reisigl and R. Wodak, 333–50. Vienna: Passager Verlag.

van Leeuwen, T., and C. Jewitt. 2001. Semiotics and iconography. In *Handbook of visual analysis*, ed. T. van Leeuwen and C. Jewitt, 92–117. London: Sage.

Voci, A., and Hewstone, M. 2003. Intergroup contact and prejudice toward immigrants in Italy: The mediational role of anxiety and the moderational role of group salience. *Group Processes and Intergroup Relations* 6(1): 37–54.

Wagner, W. 1997. Word associations in questionnaires: A practical guide to design and analysis. *Papers in Social Research Methods: Qualitative Series*. London: School of Economics.

Wagner, W. 1998. Social representations and beyond: Brute facts, symbolic coping and domesticated words. *Culture and Psychology* 4 (3): 297–329.

Wagner, W., and N. Hayes. 2005. *Everyday discourse and common sense: The theory of social representations*. New York: Palgrave Macmillan.

Wagner, W., J. Valencia, and F. Elejabarrieta. 1996. Relevance, discourse and the "hot" stable core of social representations—A structural analysis of word associations. *British Journal of Social Psychology* 35 (3): 331–51.

Weiss, L. 1995. Identity formation and the process of "Othering": Unravelling sexual threads. *Educational Foundations* 9:17–33.

Worboys, J. and G. Moloney. 2004. Adolescent understandings of refugees: The role of social identity and intergroup contact. Unpublished thesis. Coffs Harbour, NSW: Southern Cross University.

Wright, S. C., A. Aron, T. McLaughlin-Volpe, and S. A. Ropp. 1997. The extended contact effect: Knowledge of cross-group friendships and prejudice. *Journal of Personality and Social Psychology* 73:73–90.

Chapter 6

A Narrative Theory of History and Identity

Social Identity, Social Representations, Society, and the Individual

James H. Liu
János László

THE CONCEPT OF SOCIAL IDENTITY, as described by social identity theory (Tajfel and Turner 1979) and its subsequent elaboration, self-categorization theory (Turner et al. 1987), provides a nucleus from which psychologists can understand the relationship between individuals and the social worlds they inhabit. Identity from this perspective is not something *belonging* to the individual, as a set of fixed traits, but rather something that *emerges* out of an interaction between the person and the situation. The interplay between a person's self-concept and the situation, containing the social forces emanating from other people and institutions that direct him how to think, feel, and behave is at the heart of the process of identification (Reicher and Hopkins 2001; Oakes, Haslam, and Turner 1994; Turner et al. 1987). A person has a fluid repertoire of self-categorizations that enable self-positioning as "one" with different in-groups and responses to being positioned as "other" by other people (Dresler-Hawke and Liu 2006). Self-categorization activates socially shared cultural knowledge that allows the individual to conform to situation-appropriate group norms for behavior. The same person may sometimes act as a mother, as a social worker, or a nationalist. A person's subjective sense of social identification provides a navigation system for dealing with the different demands of these different in-groups and enables differentiation from various out-groups. This fluidity in social identification allows a person to sometimes activate maternal norms for caring, to other times conform to nationalistic beliefs about defending the motherland, and still to other times react against prejudice, and so on.

Most of the literature on social identity and self-categorization theory has focused on individual-level processes, examining how a person's sense of self-identification is primed or made salient by different situational factors, along with subsequent implications for thinking, feeling, and acting. Through social comparison, a person strives for positive distinctiveness, coming to understand herself as part of a group or category that is positively distinct from out-groups. Self-categorization appears to be both a cause and consequence of socially shared beliefs among group members (Bar-Tal 2000), and is associated with a move toward the homogenization of beliefs within the group and an enhanced polarization of differences between groups (Turner et al. 1987).

By contrast, less effort has been devoted to theorizing about the societal factors at play shaping the *content* of social norms or societal beliefs for appropriate group behavior. Because the situation consists of a multilevel and complex aggregate of social forces, in experimental social psychology, the situation is treated as an impenetrable "black box" with functions corresponding to experimental analogues (for example, majority or minority status, high or low power, and so on) whose distribution, content, and structure in society is either unknown or assumed to consist of an abstract universal.

Recent work in the area of social representations (Moscovici 1988, 1984; for a comprehensive review, see Wagner and Hayes, 2005), the "other" great European theory of social psychology, has demonstrated that behavior in culture-specific intergroup situations may be more precisely delineated by an analysis of the content and sources of relevant collectively shared systems of knowledge and belief. In particular, James Liu and Denis Hilton (2005) have outlined the ways that socially shared representations of history condition nations and peoples with objectively similar interests to take qualitatively different actions and attitudes with respect to international relations and issues of internal diversity. Borrowing from dynamical systems theory, we argue for a "sensitive dependence on initial conditions" for collective actions. That is, the same political situation could engender quite a different probability space of responses from different peoples, depending on their representations of the historical experiences that have shaped them as a people.

History endows certain peoples (and nations) with "charters" (Malinowski 1926) that use the accumulated wisdom of the past to justify societal arrangements for the distribution of resources and the allocation of social roles both internally and internationally. History provides legitimizing myths or ideologies (Sidanius and Pratto 1999) that explain how things are and ought to be based on different forms of collective remembering (Halbwachs 1950/1980; Pennebaker, Paez, and Rimé 1997) and their application to current situations (Spellman and Holyoak 1993; Southgate 2005). Moreover, cumulative historical experience can result in the formation of cognitive narrative templates (Wertsch 2002) or a societal ethos (Bar-Tal 2000) that structure and interpret new experiences based on recurring historical patterns. In this way, social representations of history structure the "objective" situation through a process of selective interpretation, biased attribution, restricted assessment of legitimacy and agency, and by privileging certain historically warranted social categories and category systems above other alternatives. They provide an important avenue of integration between universal theories of identity and intergroup relations and culture-specific formulations based on the specific *content* of knowledge and beliefs.

Following Jerome Bruner (1986; 1990), authors such as Sandra Jovchelovitch (2002), János László (1997), and Uwe Flick (1997) suggest that social representations are organized not simply as cognitive categories, but contain narrative forms as well. Historical narratives are stories that communicate symbolic and practical meaning over and above the "bare facts" of history. The validity of narrative hinges on its credibility, authenticity, relevance, and coherence, which in turn are dependent on the proper use of narrative features—time, plot, characters, perspective, narrative intentions, and evaluation. The paradox of narrative is that it is a universally human mechanism of communication and cognition, but at the same time, the form of knowledge created by this mechanism is validated and maintained in time and space as a part of a particular society's beliefs. This dual nature of narrative has created productive points of contact between history and social psychology, beginning with Wilhelm Dilthey's work on the history of ideas (Blanco and Rosa 1997). This interface allows the introduction of cognitive structures with psychological content into the analysis of historical narrative as an explanation or interpretation.

Bruner (1986, 43) views narrative as a medium for constructing psychological and cultural reality so that history may be "brought to life." Through such devices as perspective and story structure, narrative connects individuals to a collective through symbols, knowledge, and meaning. Studying how people tell and understand stories, including performances of their own history or mythology, enlightens us about the process of how a group creates a social reality (Shore 1996, chaps. 9, 10). The process of how these stories collide or collude with stories told by others, especially other groups, enables a person to construct a personal sense of self amid this confluence of story elements, collective and private, accepted and rejected (McAdams 1993). One of the major lessons of social psychology is that behavior is not consistent across situations; what a narrative approach asserts is that our systems of meaning are well adapted to make sense of such incongruities by telling stories of how these different realities we encounter cohere from a subjective point of view.

Jan Assmann (1992) offers a synthetic theoretical framework for collective memories and identity that explicitly relates past and present representational processes to group identity. He distinguishes between *cultural* versus *communicative* memory. Communicative memory embraces memories from the proximate past, shared with contemporaries. A characteristic example is generational memory that emerges in time and decays with the death of its carriers. The span of communicative memory is thus about sixty to eighty years, or three to four generations. Studies of autobiographical memory that concern the communicative memory of a society from the perspective of the individual have found that events experienced in late adolescence or early adulthood—between the ages of eleven and twenty (see the reminiscence phenomenon in Fitzgerald 1988; Schuman and Rodgers 2004)—prove to be the most memorable for each generation. Forty years, or, half the communicative memory period, is again a critical threshold. After elapsing forty years, those who experienced a significant event early in their adulthood, fearing that their memories will disappear when they have departed, feel motivated to record and transmit their experiences. A salient example is the proliferation of the Holocaust literature during the mid-1980s.

Cultural memory, on the other hand, goes back to the supposed origins of the group. Culture objectifies memories that have proven to be important to the group, encodes these memories into stories, preserves them as public narratives, and makes it possible for new members to share group history. In modern societies, the task of generating cultural memory is often assigned to professionals (Liu and Hilton 2005; Southgate 2005, chaps. 3, 4). Some, like historians and museum curators, adhere to disciplinary standards of objectivity and fact-finding. Others, like politicians, use the past for different purposes, such as for motivating and justifying political actions. Hence it behooves us to understand the content of lay representations of history and their potential for maintaining group identity and mobilizing political action.

The Content of Socially Shared Beliefs about History

The central characteristic of lay conceptions of history is that they privilege recent events (for example, the last one hundred years) in politics and war. The survey research of Liu et al. (2005) found that over two-thirds of both the people and events nominated as the most important in world history across twelve cultures concerned politics and war, with war taking up the lion's share (see Pennebaker et al. 2006 for similar findings). This pattern is repeated with variation for national histories; for New Zealand (Liu, Wilson, McClure, and Higgins 1999), Malaysia and Singapore (Liu, Lawrence, Ward, and Abraham 2002), and Taiwan (Huang, Liu, and Chang 2004), political events are again dominant, but as relatively peaceful young nations, the percentages devoted to war are lower. Hungary, on the other hand (László, Ehmann, and Imre 2002), shows a popular history that is dominated by warfare and violent revolution, and draws more deeply from the distant past when the Magyar nation was formed. The topics of technological and economic advance, which are often central to expert histories (Hart 1992; Kennedy 1987), are almost invisible in lay histories (where ordinary people nominate events or figures and importance is determined by consensus). The implication of these data is that according to the popular imagination, history and the peoples inhabiting it are created by the politics of warfare. The idea put forward by sociologists of history (Anderson 1983) that the modern nation-state is a product of the collective imagination made possible by advances in literacy and mass communication has no currency among lay peoples. Rather, they believe the alternative theory that "the growth of the modern state, as measured by its finances, is explained primarily not in domestic terms but in terms of geopolitical relations of violence" (Mann 1986, 490; though Mann's own view is more complicated).

Politicians, media, and lay people alike appear to act under the premise that war is what makes the nation-state. It is no wonder that war is glorified in the collective memory of victorious nations (see Olick 2003) and that the availability of such memories correlates with the willingness to fight in future conflict (Paez et al. forthcoming). The phenomenon of "rallying around the flag" during conflict with another nation must also be considered normative. Selective recall of historical events appears to be essential for legitimizing myths or ideologies that portray objection to war as illegitimate, disloyal, or incorrect; such arguments were employed repeatedly by British Prime Minister Blair in justifying the invasion of Iraq (Southgate 2005, 60).

Collective memories of war are refreshed by new conflicts (Schuman and Rodgers 2004), and behavior in war weighs heavily on attitudes toward nationalities, as illustrated by internationally negative perceptions of America in the wake of the Iraq War (Pew Global Attitudes Project 2006). In extreme cases of protracted conflict, as in Israel, the collective emotional orientation may become contaminated by fear, producing a societal ethos characterized by deep mistrust of the out-group and perpetual readiness for conflict (Bar-Tal 2001; see also Staub 1988). More generally, the extent to which the social identities of peoples are forged in the crucible of conflict and defined by their behavior in war may be a product of long-term trends in the evolution of social power, particularly the development of the state (Mann 1986). Charles Tilly (1975) may be read from a psychological perspective to suggest that the preparation, prosecution, and consequences of war drove the development of European societies to become the first capable of producing mass identification with the state. At present, it is primarily nationalities, ethnicities, and religions that can mobilize collectivities to kill *en masse*, and it cannot be coincidental that these are the groups for which history and its promise of immortality (see Solomon, Greenberg, and Pyszczynski 1991) matter most.

On the other hand, there is great variation in the type of event that is nominated as the most important in a single nation's history. This has definite implications for a whole range of group-specific attitudes and behaviors, particularly in managing internal diversity. First, certain events predispose the use of certain category systems. The Treaty of Waitangi, signed between Maori (Polynesian) chieftains and the British Crown (representing European settlers who arrived six to eight hundred years after Maori) in 1840 is widely regarded as the most important historical event in New Zealand (NZ). This privileges the signatories of the treaty, Maori and the Crown (representing NZ Europeans), above other social categories. Numerous historical accounts (King 2004) portray the nation as a "partnership" established between members of these groups dating back to the colonial era (Liu 2005). The partnership is depicted in most national iconography, including passports, the national museum, the singing of the national anthem (in both Maori and English), and in public education. Perhaps as a consequence, even in the domain of implicit associations, these two groups are closer to national symbols than other demographically numerous ethnicities in NZ, such as Asians (Sibley and Liu, forthcoming).

Similarly, the status of Mingnan Chinese as the prototype for Taiwanese national identity is bolstered by their standing as the aggrieved party in the February 28 incident, the most important event in Taiwanese history (in which mainland Chinese soldiers in the Kuomintang (KMT) killed and imprisoned large numbers of Mingnan people to establish political control). Outside-province Chinese, who arrived in Taiwan from the mainland following World War II, may see their demographic heritage as a "problem." Hence, some young outside-province people prefer to call themselves "New Taiwanese" to avoid the taint of the February 28, 1947, legacy (see Huang, Liu, and Chang 2004).

Second, history privileges certain political issues as perennially central to national identity. For NZ, Maori-Pakeha issues are often center stage, whereas in Taiwan, the cross-straits relationship with the mainland is never far from public consciousness. These two factors predispose an ethnocultural frame of reference in Taiwan and NZ that contrasts sharply with the category system privileged under a communist reading of history, where the dialectics of class (such as workers versus owners) rather than ethnicity predominate (Reicher and Hopkins 2001). James Liu and Tomohide Atsumi (forthcoming) found in their review of contemporary Chinese history that Maoist readings of history officially endorsed by the communist state focused on the international solidarity of workers, collaboration between the military industrial complexes of Japan and the United States, and collusion between ethnic Chinese (such as those in the KMT) and Japanese imperialists. Under such a narrative, class struggle rather than nationality is privileged. The collapse of global communism has been associated with increased national tensions between China and Japan regarding the historical remembrances of war, as China reasserts a more nationalistic narrative of history where Japanese war crimes are more central (Liu and Atsumi forthcoming). Similarly, religious readings of history of the variety advocated by extreme fundamentalists like Al-Qaeda (Al-Zawahiri 2001) prioritize religious categories and Islamic unity in direct contradiction to competing secular, ethnocultural, and national categories.

James Wertsch (2002) proposes that certain peoples derive cognitive narrative templates that summarize in a general way the major historical dilemmas that have faced them throughout history. According to Wertsch, schematic narrative templates emerge out of the repeated use of standard narrative forms produced by history instruction in schools, the popular media, and so forth. The narrative templates that emerge from this process are effective in shaping what we can say and think because they are largely unnoticed, or "transparent" to those employing them, and they are a fundamental part of the identity claims of a group. They can be said to impose a plot structure on a range of specific characters, events, and circumstances.

His work, focused on the former Soviet Union, has identified the following sequence of moves resulting in a cognitive narrative template for

Russian history: An initial situation in which the Russian people are living in a peaceful setting where they are no threat to others is disrupted by the initiation of trouble or aggression by alien forces. This leads to a time of crisis and great suffering for the Russian people that is overcome by the triumph over the alien force by the Russian people, acting heroically and alone. This template has been used to provide explanatory insight into the actions of Russia in signing the Molotov-Ribbentrop Pact that partitioned the states between the Soviet Union and Germany at the beginning of World War II. Stalin was not being malevolent or aggressive, but was instead just acting defensively to bide time before the inevitable battle with Hitler for the survival of the Russian people. This template can be applied to make sense of any number of conflicts involving Russia—from WWII to the Napoleonic Wars to wars with the Mongols, Poles, and Swedes—and it is a model for the sturdiness of Russian identity when faced by an external threat.

János László, Bea Ehmann, and Imre (2002) show how narrative schemes predict events that are "elevated" in collective memory. In their study, participants had to name and briefly narrate positive and negative events in Hungarian history. There were three typical patterns of events: "long term victory" (up until the sixteenth century), when Hungarians were victorious; "first victory then defeat," when Hungarians won battles for freedom and independence but eventually failed (in wars of independence against the Turks and then the Habsburgs); and "long term defeats," when Hungarians lost (for example, World Wars I and II). It turned out that the "first defeat, then victory" schema was missing from the Hungarian collective memory. This missing schema at least partly explains why Hungarians mentioned the regime change marking the end of Russian occupation in 1989 at a very low frequency among positive events. A more discursive approach has been used to establish bicultural versus liberal democratic accounts of NZ nationhood (Liu 2005).

THE PROCESS OF CONSTRUCTING
SOCIALLY SHARED BELIEFS ABOUT HISTORY

There are at least two fundamental reasons for the pre-eminence of warfare in lay histories. The first is its narratability. Socially shared beliefs are above all communicated, and the basic template for human storytelling, as shown in Vladimir Propp's (1968) classic work on folktales, is conflict. Propp shows that he could decompose the basic structure of collected Russian folktales into approximately thirty "moves." While these contain a rich tapestry of events, including support from helpers, gifts from donors, missions from rulers, and obstacles to test worthiness, the basic story arc of every folktale involves conflict between a protagonist (hero) and antagonist (villain) from an initial state of affairs to a resolution. Stories of conflict channel our hopes and fears into a system of meaning in which they can be managed and sometimes resolved. A similar narrative structure of conflict for mythological and religious stories has been theorized by Joseph Campbell (1949).

Given how basic folktales and mythology are to human narrative, there is reason to believe that this is the type of story that people tell one another when they gather around the campfire. Anthony Lyons and Yoshihisa Kashima's (2001, 2003) findings using Frederic Bartlett's serial reproduction paradigm suggest that the prototypical form of folktales may be a product of social features of story transmission. They found that when a short written narrative is passed along a dyadic communication chain, stereotype inconsistent information is filtered out, leaving predominantly stereotype consistent information after about three to four transmissions of the story. This effect is due to communication goals (for example, high stereotype endorsement and stereotype sharedness) rather than memory biases. Peripheral information is very quickly lost in a communication chain. The essential organizing features of a plot—involving the major story arc of conflict between the protagonist and antagonist—are likely, however, to be retained. Marques, Paez, Valencia, and Vincze (2006) used a similar paradigm to show that negative historical information (in this case, a massacre of Native Americans committed either by Portuguese or Spanish colonists) dropped out more over the course of a communication chain if the event was reported as having been committed by the in-group instead of by the out-group.

Second, conflict generates emotion, and collective remembrances are keyed around extreme emotion, both positive and negative (Bar-Tal 2001; Cabecinhas 2006; Rimé 1997). Bernard Rimé (2007) reports that people share an emotional event by talking about it to someone else after the episode 80 to 90 percent of the time, and that this is repeated more often for intense emotions. When an emotional event happens in a person's life, it ripples through that person's community. Once an emotional event is shared once, it is quite likely to be shared again by the listener to a new hearer; Rimé estimates that 50 to 60 people in a social network may learn about an emotional event affecting one of its members within hours. Collectively shared events, like the September 11, 2001, terror bombing, are like a thousand stones hitting the community lake all at once, with ripples of emotional sharing carrying seeds of information to create a shared new representation at great speed (Rimé 1997). The paradox of

socially shared emotions, according to Rimé (2007), is that people will-
ingly share a negative emotion even when it reactivates an aversive experience. Because the evidence suggests that socially sharing negative
emotions does *not* aid a person's recovery from a traumatic event, it
appears that the function of the social sharing of emotions is purely social:
it is about community building and showing empathy rather than instrumental action. Negative events function no less effectively in this regard
than positive. Emotions live in the present. Hence, the relative prepon-
derance of recent and negative events in representations of world history
(Liu et al. 2005) may be a function of the social sharing of emotions.

However, there are also strong instrumental motives at work in the
production of lay perceptions of history. Some theorists have argued that
war makes the nation-state, and the nation-state thrives on war (Tilly
1975; Winter and Sivan 1999). Perhaps the most concentrated nexus of
social science research on collective memory concerns the influence of the
state on institutional forms of remembering, such as those exhibited in
museums and enacted at commemorations (for example, LeGoff 1992;
Olick 2003; Linsroth 2002; Schwartz 1997). Theorists in this area tend
to see memory as mediated by institutions that are subject to manipula-
tion and control by the state. The past is mobilized in the service of political agendas such as promoting national unity, and it is not so much
recalled as performed through rituals, like parades or docent tours. Paez,
Liu, Techio, Slawuta, Zlobina, and Cabecinhas (forthcoming) characterize the collective remembering of war as institutionally mediated in-
group favoritism grounded in dominant values and mobilized by
present-day political issues; they view biases in this recollection as con-
strained by interstate and intergroup power relations, as well as personal
experiences and word of mouth. Research on commemoration reminds
us of the dynamic influence of the present in re-creating an idealized past,
and the central role of artifacts and social practices in communicating
these reconstructions in societal processes.

THE RELATIONSHIP BETWEEN THE INDIVIDUAL AND SOCIETY

In comparison to social identity theory, social representations theory
(SRT) has struggled to define the relationship between the individual and
society (see Wagner and Hayes, 2005, chap. 10). The problem is that
social representations reside at the level of the collective, whereas what is
to be explained in psychology is generally at the individual level. No one
person could be said to have a "social representation of history," but social
representations of history are argued to influence behavior and cognition

at the individual level. A simple semantic solution is to refer to attitudes or arguments *derived from* social representations when talking about history used to causally influence opinions at the individual level (Sibley, Liu, and Kirkwood 2006). Liu and Sibley (2006) argue that an individual's attitudes are anchored to not only an intrapersonal set of beliefs, but also to an interpersonal network of communications and contacts. An even more theoretically sophisticated solution is provided by Willem Doise (1986), who divides social research into four levels ranging from intraindividual to ideological and is cautious about using data or theory from one level to explain phenomena at another level. However, such an analysis led Wagner and Hayes to eschew causal explanation for SRT altogether, and to consider it as a circular theory "in which theoretical terms mutually presuppose each other" (2005, 312; a reflexive group maintains a discursive representation and thereby determines its identity and belongingness). Such a stand is entirely incompatible with a mainstream psychology that privileges experimentally derived causal inferences as the most valuable form of knowledge.

Perhaps a more satisfactory solution can be generated from the fact that social representations of history are by definition temporal structures that relate occurrences linked together thematically through time. This means that they can be approached as *narratives*, or stories of events with a temporal structure that can be related thematically from a particular point of view (see Wyer, Adaval, and Colcombe 2002 for a more sharply limited definition). Bruner (1986, 1990) argues that narrative is a fundamental mode of human thinking that is predicated on the pragmatic considerations of communication rather than the dictates of formal logic.

If social representations of history are considered as narratives, then two key properties of narratives, perspective and the ability to generate empathy, can be enlisted to bridge the gulf between the individual as the recipient of the narrative, and the society that is the repository of narratives. Moreover, composition and discursive features of narratives such as coherence, evaluation, agency, and spatial-temporal organization are indicative of the psychological orientation and identity of the narrator. In the case of historical narratives, these stories reflect group (national or ethnic) identity on the one hand, and connect individuals to the group on the other. In this sense, not only can historical texts be analyzed as carriers or vehicles of national identity, but other forms of narratives, such as romance or heroic fiction, can be, as well. For example, László and his colleagues studied the five most popular Hungarian historical novels (László, Vincze, Kőváriné Somogyvári 2003, László and Vincze 2004) and pinpointed the role these novels play in the transmission of basic features of Hungarian national identity, like prototypical heroic traits and coping strategies.

NARRATIVE PERSPECTIVE

The content of a narrative, including elements such as events, characters, and circumstances, must be presented from a point of view (Prince 1987). The only truly omniscient third-person voice belongs to God and to authors of fiction. Historians as august as Jacob Burckhardt (1979) in the nineteenth century wrestled with the problem of narrative perspective being part of the craft, and those following Hayden White (1981, 1987) acknowledge that despite the best of academic intentions to honor truth, history inevitably involves the selection and interpretation of events. It includes a storytelling element that can at best be minimized through careful adherence to explicit disciplinary practices, and at worst can include willful distortions in the service of a national unity projected by the state (Hein and Selden 2000; Hobsbawm 1990; Kohl and Fawcett 1996). While the invention of tradition (Hobsbawm and Ranger 1983) and the projection of nationalism into history are problem areas for historians (Burke 1989), they are grist for the mill of social psychologists, who see in these distortions manifestations of the interaction between processes of social identity and social representation.

Narrative perspective can be thought of as a relational concept (Bal 1985) between the producer and the recipient of narrative. This is communicated by the distance in time and space the author takes vis-à-vis the content, and by the possibility that the narrator may express a character's beliefs, emotions, or evaluations (Wiebe, 1991). The latter component is sometimes called a psychological perspective (for example, Uspensky 1974). Through these components, narrative perspective establishes a *surface structure empathy hierarchy* (Kuno 1976) that influences how the reader or listener constructs the meaning of the narrated event and opens the way for *participatory affective responses* (Gerrig 1993).

For instance, Tóth, Vincze, and László (2005) compare the depictions of the Austro-Hungarian monarchy in contemporary Austrian and Hungarian textbooks. One of the major differences they found was that the Hungarian texts included more personal agents as opposed to institutional agents, and mental inferences (for example, words such as "knew," "thought," "felt," and so on) as opposed to direct actions or statements. These narrative devices lead the reader to form the landscape of action according to the landscape of consciousness (Bruner 1986, 16), thereby facilitating interpretation and empathy from a Hungarian point of view, effectively personalizing the events. These results could be interpreted in terms of the historical tradition of the Habsburg imperial versus the Hungarian small-state identity, with the latter requiring a comparatively stronger and more personalized adherence to the nation. Also, the longer established and stronger democratic traditions and more institutionalized view of Austrian society may be reflected in the way historical events are selected and reported, as the impersonal actions of institutions rather than the agency of individuals.

How the narrator relates past events to the current situation has significant influence on impression formation and identity judgments about the narrator, even when the same events are described. Tibor Polya, László, and Joe Forgas (2005) found that narrators using a retrospective perspective to describe autobiographical events were generally judged to be better adjusted, more desirable socially, and less anxious than narrators describing the same events in the present tense, as though they were re-experiencing the events. Similar results were obtained by Ehmann, Garami, Naszodi, Kis, and László (forthcoming) when a linear retrospective time perspective was judged to better reflect trauma elaboration after the event. For historical narratives, particularly when relatively recent traumas are narrated, time perspective can be a sensitive indicator of elaboration and coping.

What efforts such as these do is allow us to ascribe influence to non-human agents widely distributed throughout society. Artifacts such as textbooks communicate narratives in sometimes subtle ways that suggest a relationship between the subjects of the text and the readers, and the authors of the text and its readers. So by examining textbooks designated by the state to teach history in schools, and also by investigating institutions of public commemoration such as museums and national holidays (LeGoff 1992), we can probe into the influence of institutional agents of collective remembering and social representation without requiring a "group mind" (Wilson 2004). By tracing the production and effects of institutionalized forms of collective remembering, we can examine specific components of how societies communicate their traditions, the psychological reactions to these narratives, and the rise and fall in popularity of different representations over time.

It has been established that from time to time, collective memory and the social representation of history are revised. These representations appear as narratives and work as folk histories in accordance with the identity needs of groups. Narrative is not merely a natural, economical, or cognitive tool for preserving information; rather, it is a form that is suitable for establishing a personal relationship with an audience and for identifying oneself with something. As Ricoeur (1991) writes, identifying the self proceeds through identification with others—through history grounded in reality and through fictional narratives taking off from the imagination.

By means of empirical studies, we can reveal the characteristic features of group identity in the language of social psychology from professional and folk historical stories. Thus, the question is not in what way and to what extent these stories correspond to a scientifically reconstructed reality (although this may also be an interesting question); instead, what we want to know is what psychological state of being—balanced or imbalanced—what sense of security or threat, what sort of continuity or discontinuity, and what temporal orientation, intergroup relationship, motivation, and evaluation are reflected by the stories (László 2006). In other words, what types of collective symbolic coping (Wagner, Kronberger, and Seifert 2002) are taking place?

NARRATIVE EMPATHY

The fact that narratives are produced from a particular perspective or point of view suggests that there will be individual differences in how they will be received. One way to characterize the reception of a narrative by audiences is to consider how much empathy they have for the characters, events, and point of view expressed. This conceptualization capitalizes on the property of narrative that its comprehension is enhanced by momentarily yielding to its premises, and suspending disbelief about its reality (Gilbert 1991). If Bruner (1986, 1990) is correct in asserting that narrative thinking is driven by a search for plausible, lifelike connections between events—establishing verisimilitude rather than truth—then empathy would appear to be the key mediator of narrative impact.

Stephanie Preston and Frans de Waal (2002) provide a broad definition, claiming that empathy is any process of attending to another's state in a way that induces a state in oneself more appropriate to the situation of the object attended to than to one's own situation (see Eisenberg and Strayer 1987 for additional perspectives). Such experiences as laughter, tears, joy, anger, fear, hope, and frustration are not uncommon to readers of books or watchers of movies. The reader, viewer, or listener momentarily suspends disbelief and participates vicariously in the narrative to the extent that he shows empathy for the point of view expressed and the characters and situations depicted. Alternatively, the audience may find the narrative lacking in coherence and verisimilitude, and fail to relate to it for any number of reasons ranging from aesthetic to political. Many officially sanctioned histories must surely have provoked apathy rather than empathy among their adolescent readers; indeed, Liu and Atsumi (forthcoming) found that many best-selling authors providing influential accounts about the Sino-Japanese War in Japan were nonhistorians happy to employ narrative devices and factual distortions eschewed by professional historians. For narrative representations to have influence on the individual, there must be some degree of sympathy for the situation or empathy for some of the characters. The degree of empathy provides a measure of the extent to which the individual relates to representational aspects of the narrative, bridging the gap between the individual and society.

Not only does this link the subjectivity of the individual to societal narratives rich in social axioms (Leung and Bond 2004) and normative beliefs (Bar-Tal 2000), but it also does so in a way that expands our vocabulary beyond that of social identity theory. The key point is that empathy does not require identity between the individual and the characters or situation with which she empathizes, though it is certainly facilitated by similarity and familiarity. It does not require a homogenization of attitudes and conformity of opinion, though there may be empirical tendencies in that direction. The capacity to respond empathetically is a fundamental biological heritage shared among higher social animals that enables the coordination of behavior with those clearly different than oneself (and sometimes even belonging to different species; see Preston and de Waal 2002). Empathy according to the perception-action model of Preston and de Waal (2002) contains a predisposition for action common to a complex of states, including sympathy, emotional contagion, and prosocial behavior. What the concept of narrative empathy does is extend the perception-action model to situations of vicarious learning and cognitive sympathy mediated by narration rather than personal experience. Such learning is the hallmark of culture and central to what makes human society a "thinking society" (Billig 1993)—its reliance on the accumulated wisdom of the past transferred through such processes as modeling and narrative agency (Bandura 2004) rather than personal trial and error.

Some narratives will achieve great empathy with audiences, over time becoming canonical for a particular genre. By furnishing an alternative operationalization of social representations as narratives widely known and accepted in society, SRT can avoid the problem of hermeneutic circularity (see Ricoeur 1974; Wagner and Hayes 2005). Survey data involving aggregate analyses of individual data can continue to be used to identify how social representations are collectively shared, but this can be corroborated at the individual level by measuring the empathy for particular societal narratives embodying core features of these representations. For instance, the degree of empathy for characters or actions in canonical historical narratives (see László and Vincze 2004), or the degree of sympathy for events described using different writing styles and inferring alternative relationships with the past, could reveal how prototypical individuals are in their orientation toward canonical narratives for the group. We might be able to see an individual drawing on representational resources from different groups, producing a "laminated self" that draws together in personal layers canonical elements from diverse cultural traditions. Investigations of the interaction between canonical histories produced by professionals and personal memories or oral accounts transmitted by families would appear to be an ideal site to elucidate the relationship between individual and collective memory (see Halbwachs 1950/1980; Wilson 2005).

Such an approach avoids the problem of circularity in which theoretical terms such as "social identity" and "representation" mutually presuppose one another. An individual may have empathy for historical narratives that stand well outside the boundaries of his social identity and the representations dominant in society, and he may have a self-repertoire that is more complex than the homogenized accounts that can be produced when a dominant identity is made salient. A narrative approach employing indicators of empathy opens up a new frontier for group and intergroup psychology by enabling theorists to establish linkages at the individual level *between* the content of manifestly different identities and social representations.

For instance, audiences around the world participated vicariously in the narrative of the young star-crossed lovers of different social classes in the blockbuster movie *Titanic*. Some of these viewers would have been members of groups with social representations of sex and marriage at odds with the individualistic and sexually permissive point of view presented in the movie. Yet, the popularity of the film, a canonical representative of the Hollywood genre of disaster romance, was unprecedented in countries in Asia and the Middle East where having premarital sex and going against parents in marital choice would have been counternormative. Investigating the extent of empathy for the old mother trying to save her family fortunes by marrying her daughter into a wealthy but cold family versus that for the young lovers would go a long way toward establishing the personal orientation of individuals toward societally normative representations of sex and marriage. Research along these lines would bring SRT into dialogue with the burgeoning area of acculturation (Ward, Bochner, and Furnham 2001) and bring a further element of dynamism into the study of social representations.

Further down the line, research should examine whether the action propensities of empathy are reduced for reactions to narratives compared to firsthand experiences. It may also be appropriate to investigate other states, particularly intergroup emotions such as guilt or hatred (Branscombe and Doosje 2004; Smith and Mackie 2005), but these may not be as generally relevant to narrative as the family of emotions related to empathy.

Empathy is in some sense prototypical of a fundamentally civic orientation among human beings: an ability to put oneself in the place of another and to feel what she would feel, and act how she might want us to act. In this era of multicultural and multiethnic societies, an understanding of how empathy functions to maintain a sense of civil society among people with very different backgrounds would seem to be essential. The literature on intergroup relations is dark and rife with concepts such as social dominance orientation (SDO), right-wing authoritarianism (RWA), prejudice, in-group favoritism, stereotypes, conformity, representations of war, and other constructs that emphasize the exclusive and closed nature of human groups. But from another perspective, intergroup relations seem to involve as much borrowing as purifying, as much fascination as repulsion, and as much intermixing as exclusion. While it is true that the latter of these pairs is highlighted during violent and oppressive periods, and while it is entirely appropriate to describe the limits to empathy (see for instance, Bar-Tal 2001; Opotow 1994), such an approach cannot describe all that is happening in terms of intergroup and intercultural relations. A more expansive "dual process model" of intergroup relations involves the differential impacts of empathy and authoritarianism, rather than interactions between close cousins SDO and RWA (see Duckitt 2001; Altemeyer 1998). Theorizing about the narrative construction and empathic reception of socially shared systems of historical belief is a first step in constructing theory that weighs equally the light side and the dark side of group and intergroup behavior.

AUTHOR NOTE

The authors wish to gratefully acknowledge helpful comments from Michael Harris Bond, Daniel Bar-Tal, Denis Hilton, Nicole Kronberger, Howard Schuman, Wolfgang Wagner, and James Wertsch on earlier drafts of this chapter.

REFERENCES

Altemeyer, B. 1998. The other "authoritarian personality." In *Advances in experimental social psychology*, vol. 30, ed. M. P. Zanna, 47–92. San Diego, CA: Academic Press.

Al-Zawahiri, A. 2001. *Knights under the prophet's banner.* Casablanca: Dar-al-Najaah Al-Jadeedah.

Anderson, B. 1983. *Imagined communities: Reflections on the origins and spread of nationalism.* London: Verso.

Assmann, J. 1992. *Das Kulturelle Gedachtnis: Schrift, Erinnerung und Politische Identitaet in Fruehen Hochkulturen.* Munich: Beck.

Bal, M. 1985. *Narratology: Introduction to the theory of narrative.* Toronto: University of Toronto Press.

Bandura, A. 2004. Swimming against the mainstream: The early years from chilly tributary to transformative mainstream. *Behaviour Research and Therapy* 42 (6): 613–30.

Bar-Tal, D. 2000. *Shared beliefs in a society: Social psychological analysis.* London: Sage.

———. 2001. Why does fear override hope in societies engulfed by intractable conflicts, as it does in the Israeli Society? *Political Psychology* 22:601–27.

Billig, M. 1993. Studying the thinking society: social representations, rhetoric, and attitudes. In *Empirical approaches to social representations,* ed. G. M. Breakwell and D. V. Canter, 39–62. Oxford: Clarendon.

Blanco, F., and A. Rosa. 1997. Dilthey's dream. Teaching history to understand the future. *International Journal for Educational Research* 27 (3): 189–200.

Branscombe, N. R., and B. Doosje. 2004. *Collective guilt: International perspectives.* Cambridge: Cambridge University Press.

Bruner, J. 1986. *Actual minds, possible worlds.* Cambridge, MA: Harvard University Press.

———. 1990. *Acts of meaning.* Cambridge, MA.: Harvard University Press.

Burckhardt, J. 1979. *Reflections on history.* Indianapolis: Liberty Fund.

Burke, P. 1989. History as social memory. In *Memory: history, culture, and the mind,* ed. T. Butler. Oxford: Basil Blackwell.

Cabecinhas, R. 2006. Identidade e memória social: Estudos comparativos em Portugal e em Timor-Leste [Identity and social memory: Comparative studies in Portugal and East Timor]. In *Comunicação e Lusofonia,* ed. M. Martins, H. Sousa, and R. Cabecinhas. Porto, Portugal: Campo das Letras.

Campbell, J. 1949. *The hero with a thousand faces.* Princeton, NJ: Princeton University Press.

Doise, W. 1986. *Levels of explanation in social psychology.* Cambridge: Cambridge University Press.

Dresler-Hawke, E., and J. H. Liu. 2006. Collective shame and the positioning of German national identity. *Psicologia Politica* 32:131–53.

Duckitt, J. 2001. A dual-process cognitive-motivational theory of ideology and prejudice. In *Advances in experimental social psychology,* vol. 33, ed. M. P. Zanna, 41–113. New York: Academic Press.

Ehmann, B., V. Garami, M. Naszodi, B. Kis, and J. László. Forthcoming. Subjective time experience: Identifying psychological correlates by narrative psychological content analysis. *Empirical Culture and Text Research.*

Eisenberg, N., and J. Strayer, eds. 1987. *Empathy and its development.* Cambridge: Cambridge University Press.

Fitzgerald, J. M. 1988. Vivid memories and the reminiscence phenomenon. The role of self narrative. *Human Development* 31:261–73.

Flick, U. 1995. Social representation. In *Rethinking psychology, ed.* J. A. Smith, R. Harré, and L. Van Langhove, 70–96. London: Sage.

Gerrig, R. J. 1993. *Experiencing narrative worlds.* New Haven, CT: Yale University Press.

Gilbert, D. T. 1991. How mental systems believe. *American Psychologist* 46 (2): 107–19.

Halbwachs, M. 1950/1980. *The collective memory.* New York: Harper and Row.

Hart, M. H. 1992. *The 100: A ranking of the most influential persons in history.* New York: Citadel.

Hein, L., and M. Selden. 2000. *Censoring history. Citizenship and memory in Japan, Germany and the United States.* Armonk, NY: Sharpe.

Hobsbawm, E. 1990. *Nations and nationalism since 1780: Programme, myth, reality.* Cambridge: Cambridge University Press.

Hobsbawm, E., and T. Ranger, eds. 1983. *The invention of tradition.* Cambridge: Cambridge University Press.

Huang, L. L., J. H. Liu, and M. L. Chang. 2004. The double identity of Chinese Taiwanese: A dilemma of politics and identity rooted in history. *Asian Journal of Social Psychology* 7 (2): 149–89.

Jovchelovitch, S. 2002. Social representations and narratives: Stories of the public life in Brazil. In *Narrative approaches in social psychology,* ed. J. László and W. Stainton-Rogers, 47–58. Budapest: New Mandate.

Kennedy, P. M. 1987. *The rise and fall of the great powers.* New York: Random House.

King, M. 2004. *The Penguin history of New Zealand.* Auckland, NZ: Penguin.

Kohl, P. L., and C. Fawcett, eds. 1996. *Nationalism, politics, and the practice of archaeology.* New York: Cambridge University Press.

Kuno, S. 1976. Subject, theme and the speaker's empathy—A reexamination of the relativization phenomena. In *Subject and topic,* ed. C. N. Li, 47–51. New York: Academic Press.

László, J. 1997. Narrative organisation of social representations. *Papers on Social Representations* 6 (2): 93–190.

———. Forthcoming. *The science of stories. Introduction to narrative psychology.*

László, J., B. Ehmann, and O. Imre. 2002. Les représentations sociales de l'histoire: La narration populaire historique et l'identité nationale. In *La mémoire sociale. Identités et représentations sociales,* ed. S. Laurens and N. Roussiau. Rennes, France: Université Rennes.

László, J., O. Vincze, I. Kőváriné Somogyvári. 2003. Representation of national identity in successful historical novels. *Empirical Studies of the Arts* 21 (1): 69–80.

László, J., and O. Vincze. 2004. Coping with historical tasks. The role of historical novels in transmitting psychological patterns of national identity. *SPIEL* 21 (1): 76–88.

LeGoff, J. 1992. *History and memory*. New York: Columbia University Press.

Leung, K., and M. H. Bond. 2004. Social axioms: A model for social beliefs in a multicultural perspective. *Advances in Experimental Social Psychology 36*: 119–97.

Linsroth, J. P. 2002. History, tradition, and memory among the Basques. *History and Anthropology* 13 (3): 159–89.

Liu, J. H. 2005. History and identity: A systems of checks and balances for Aotearoa/New Zealand. In *New Zealand identities: Departures and destinations*, ed. J. H. Liu, T. McCreanor, T. McIntosh, and T. Teaiwa, 69–87. Wellington, NZ: Victoria University Press.

Liu, J. H., and T. Atsumi. Forthcoming. Historical conflict and resolution between Japan and China: Developing and applying a narrative theory of history and identity. In *Meaning in action: Constructions, narratives, and representations*, ed. T. Sugiman, K. J. Gergen, W. Wagner, and Y. Yamada. Tokyo: Springer-Verlag.

Liu, J. H., R. Goldstein-Hawes, D. J. Hilton, L. L. Huang, C. Gastardo-Conaco, E. Dresler-Hawke, F. Pittolo, et al. 2005. Social representations of events and people in world history across twelve cultures. *Journal of Cross-Cultural Psychology* 36 (2): 171–91.

Liu, J. H., and D. Hilton. 2005. How the past weighs on the present: Social representations of history and their role in identity politics. *British Journal of Social Psychology* 44:1–21.

Liu, J. H., B. Lawrence, C. Ward, and S. Abraham. 2002. Social representations of history in Malaysia and Singapore: On the relationship between national and ethnic identity. *Asian Journal of Social Psychology* 5 (1): 3–20.

Liu, J. H., and C. S. Sibley. 2006. Differential effects of societal anchoring and attitude certainty in determining support or opposition to (bi)cultural diversity in New Zealand. *Papers on Social Representations*. http://www.psr.jku.at/frameset.html.

Liu, J. H., M. W. Wilson, J. McClure, T. R. Higgins. 1999. Social identity and the perception of history: Cultural representations of Aotearoa/New Zealand. *European Journal of Social Psychology* 29:1021–47.

Malinowski, B. 1926. *Myth in primitive psychology*. London: Kegan Paul, Trench, Trubner.

Mann, M. 1986. *The sources of social power*. Cambridge: Cambridge University Press.

Marques, J., D. Paez, J. Valencia, and O. Vincze. 2006. Effects of group membership on the transmission of negative historical events. *Psicologia Politica* 32:79–105.

McAdams, D. P. 1993. *The stories we live by: Personal myths and the making of the self*. New York: Guilford Press.

Moscovici, S. 1984. The phenomenon of social representations. In *Social representations*, ed. R. M. Farr and S. Moscovici, 3–70. Cambridge: Cambridge University Press.

———. 1988. Notes towards a description of social representations. *European Journal of Social Psychology* 18:211–50.

Oakes, P. J., S. A. Haslam, and J. C. Turner. 1994. *Stereotyping and social reality*. Oxford: Basil Blackwell.

Olick, J. K. 2003. *States of memory: Continuities, conflicts, and transformations in national retrospection*. New York: Columbia University Press.

Opotow, S. 1994. Predicting protection: Scope of justice and the natural world. *Journal of Social Issues* 50 (3): 49–63.

Paez, D., J. H. Liu, E. Techio, P. Slawuta, A. Zlobina, and R. Cabecinhas. Forthcoming. "Remembering" World War Two and willingness to fight: Sociocultural factors in the social representation of warfare across 22 societies. *Journal of Cross-Cultural Psychology*.

Pennebaker, J. W., D. Paez, and B. Rimé. 1997. *Collective memory of political events*. Mahwah, NJ: Lawrence Erlbaum.

Pennebaker, J. W., J. Rentfrow, M. Davis, D. Paez, E. Techio, P. Slawuta, A. Zlobina, et al. 2006. The social psychology of history: Defining the most important events of world history. *Psicología Política* 32:15–32.

Pew Global Attitude Project. 2006. America's image slips, but allies share U.S. concerns over Iran, Hamas. http://www.pewglobal.org.

Polya, T., J. László, and J. P. Forgas. 2005. Making sense of life stories: The role of narrative perspective in communicating hidden information about social identity. *European Journal of Social Psychology* 35:785–96.

Preston, S. D. and F. B. M. de Waal. 2002. Empathy: Its ultimate and proximate bases. *Behavioral and Brain Sciences* 25 (1): 1–72.

Prince, G. 1987. *Dictionary of narratology*. Lincoln: University of Nebraska Press.

Propp, V. 1968. *The morphology of the folktale*. Austin: University of Texas Press.

Reicher, S., and N. Hopkins. 2001. *Self and nation*. London: Sage.

Ricoeur, P. 1974. The model of the text: Meaningful action considered as text. In *Interpretive social science: A reader*, ed. P. Rabinow and W. M. Sullivan, 73–101. Berkeley: University of California Press.

———. 1991. L'identité narrative. *Revues de Sciences Humaines* 221:35–47.

Rimé, B. 1997. How individual emotional episodes feed collective memory. In *Collective memory of political events*, ed. J. W. Pennebaker, D. Paez, and B. Rimé, 131–46. Mahwah, NJ: Lawrence Erlbaum.

———. 2007. Interpersonal emotion regulation. In *Handbook of emotion regulation*, ed. J. J Gross, 466–85. New York: Guildford.

Schuman, H., and W. L. Rodgers. 2004. Cohorts, chronology, and collective memories. *Public Opinion Quarterly* 68:217–54.

Schwartz, B. 1997. Collective memory and history: How Abraham Lincoln became a symbol of racial equality. *The Sociological Quarterly* 38:469–96.

Shore, B. 1996. *Culture in mind: Cognition, culture, and the problem of meaning*. Oxford: Oxford University Press.

Sibley, C. G., and J. H. Liu. 2007. New Zealand = bicultural? Implicit and explicit associations between ethnicity and nationality in the New Zealand context. *European Journal of Social Psychology*.

Sibley, C. G., J. H. Liu, and S. Kirkwood. 2006. Toward a social representations theory of attitude change: The effect of message framing on general and specific attitudes toward equality and entitlement. *New Zealand Journal of Psychology* 35 (1): 3–13.

Sidanius, J., and F. Pratto. 1999. *Social dominance: An intergroup theory of social hierarchy and oppression*. Cambridge: Cambridge University Press.

Smith, E. R., and D. Mackie. 2005. Aggression, hatred, and other emotions. In *On the nature of prejudice: Fifty years after Allport, ed*. J. F. Dovidio, P. Glick, L. A. Rudman, 361–75. Malden, MA: Blackwell.

Solomon, S., J. Greenberg, and T. Pyszczynski. 1991. A terror management theory of social behavior: The psychological functions of self-esteem and cultural worldviews. In *Advances in experimental social psychology*, ed. M. P. Zanna, 61–139. San Diego, CA: Academic Press.

Southgate, B. 2005. *What is history for?* New York: Routledge.

Spellman, B. A., and K. J. Holyoak. 1993. If Saddam is Hitler then who is George Bush? Analogical mapping between systems of social roles. *Journal of Personality and Social Psychology* 62:913–33.

Staub, E. 1988. The evolution of caring and nonaggressive persons and societies. *Journal of Social Issues* 44:81–100.

Tajfel, H., and J. C. Turner. 1979. The social identity theory of intergroup behaviour. In *Psychology of intergroup relations*, ed. S. Worchel and W. Austin, 33–48. Chicago: Nelson-Hall.

Tilly, C. 1975. *The formation of national states in Western Europe*. Princeton, NJ: Princeton University Press.

Tóth, J., O. Vincze, J. László. 2005. *Representation of the Austro-Hungarian monarchy in secondary school history books. Paper presented at the 14th General Meeting of the European Association of Experimental Social Psychology*, Würzburg, Germany, July 19–23. Abstract, p. 310.

Turner, J. C., M. A. Hogg, P. J. Oakes, S. D. Reicher, and M. S. Wetherell. 1987. *Rediscovering the social group: A self-categorization theory*. New York: Basil Blackwell.

Uspensky, B. A. 1974. *The poetics of composition: Structure of the artistic text and the typology of compositional forms*. Berkeley: University of California Press.

Wagner, W. and N. Hayes. 2005. *Everyday discourse and common sense: The theory of social representations*. New York: Palgrave Macmillan.

Wagner, W., N. Kronberger, and F. Seifert. 2002. Collective symbolic coping with new technology: Knowledge, images and public discourse. *British Journal of Social Psychology* 41:323–43.

Ward, C., S. Bochner, and A. Furnham. 2001. *The psychology of culture shock*. 2nd ed. London: Routledge.

Wertsch, J. V. 2002. *Voices of collective remembering*. Cambridge: Cambridge University Press.

White, H. 1981. The value of narrativity in the representation of reality. In *On narrative*, ed. W. J. T. Mitchell, 1–23. Chicago: University of Chicago Press.

———. 1987. *The content of the form: Narrative discourse and historical representation*. Baltimore: Johns Hopkins University Press.

Wiebe, J. 1994. Tracking point of view in narrative. *Computational Linguistics* 20 (2): 233–87.

Wilson, R. A. 2005. Collective memory, group minds, and the extended mind thesis. *Cognitive Process* 6 (4): 227–36.

Winter, J, and E. Sivan. 1999. *War and remembrance in the twentieth century*. New York: Cambridge University Press.

Wyer Jr., R. S., R. Adaval. and S. J. Colcombe. 2002. Narrative-based representations of social knowledge: Their construction and use in comprehension, memory, and judgment. In *Advances in experimental social psychology*, vol. 34. ed. M. P. Zana, 133–99. New York: Academic Press.

CHAPTER 7

REPRESENTING "US" AND "THEM"

CONSTRUCTING WHITE IDENTITIES IN EVERYDAY TALK

Martha Augoustinos
Damien Riggs

ACKNOWLEDGMENTS

We begin by acknowledging the sovereignty of the Kaurna people, the first nations people upon whose land we live in Adelaide, South Australia. We would also like to acknowledge Lucinda Sale, who conducted and transcribed the focus group interviews.

INTRODUCTION

The beginning of the new millennium has witnessed a resurgence of debates around "race," ethnicity, and multiculturalism in Western liberal democracies. Moreover since September 11, 2001, and the ensuing "War on Terror," these debates have taken on global significance as nations grapple with issues of cultural "difference" and the values that come to define the social identities that cohere around liberal democracies and Islamic nation-states. These debates are profound for understanding the social and political challenges that face the international community, but at the same time, the debates are not new and have always been central to making sense of intergroup social relations more broadly.

How social groups negotiate and acquire identities for themselves, and make sense of the identities of those defined as "other"—what we refer to in this chapter as the "politics of identity"—has always been a central concern of social representations theory as originally formulated by Moscovici (1984). However, it was only until recently that it has attracted serious and sustained attention (for example, Breakwell 2001; Chryssochoou 2000, 2004; Duveen 2001; Howarth 2006; Philogène 1999). In this chapter, we seek to examine how social representations theory can enrich our understanding of the politics of identity and the nature of social relations in Australia, specifically in the relationship between Indigenous peoples and the dominant white majority. Our analysis aims to examine how representations of "us" and "them" and of social group "differences" more broadly are embedded in a dominant historical narrative of colonialism, and how an implicit social Darwinism that, despite its scientific illegitimacy, continues to manifest itself in the public mind. We use this very specific social and historical example to suggest that essentialized representations of social group differences have become reified and objectified ways of making sense of difference, even in the face of scientific claims to the contrary. Thus, despite the proliferation of scientific challenges to the validity of essentialized categories such as "race," such representations have remained resilient in everyday understandings of group difference. As Moscovici (1984, 1988) argues, such representations become so entrenched and objectified that their social and political origins become forgotten. People come to view essentialized representations of difference as "natural" and commonsense ways of perceiving and understanding the social world.

THE CONCEPT OF "RACE": A SOCIAL REPRESENTATION

Throughout the twentieth century, the concept of "race" became entrenched in both everyday and scientific discourse as a taken-for-granted, "natural" way by which to classify people of differing social groups. Essentialist views of "race" emerged and proliferated in the first half of the nineteenth century and held that different "races" constituted fixed and distinct biological entities or species (Richards 1997). European imperialist expansion and colonial rule over Indigenous peoples during this period created the ideal conditions for the proliferation of such essentialist representations not only among the wider populace but also within the reified universe of anthropology, ethnography, and biology, as they were consonant with social Darwinist beliefs about a natural biological hierarchy between what were seen as fundamentally different "racial groups" (Richards 1997). Drawing as it did upon a social context whereby racial differences were understood as central markers of privilege and moral worth (McClintock 1995), social Darwinism served to legitimate the emergence of scientific racism and, in particular, the empirical investigation of biological and psychological "racial" differences. This research enterprise, which came to be known as "race psychology," came to dominate the concerns of U.S. psychologists between 1910 and 1940. However, with the defeat of Nazism, after the Second World War, influential scholarly critiques of scientific racism led to the eventual demise of this research focus.

Indeed, geneticists had begun to discredit the validity of "race" as a scientific category during the 1930s (Cunningham-Burley and Kerr 1999; Richards 1997), but this view that "race" was not a scientifically valid concept was not consolidated until the 1950s. Gannett (2001, SS182) cites the United Nations Educational, Scientific, and Cultural Organization (UNESCO) "Statements on Race" in 1950 and 1951 as marking "a consensus among social scientists and natural scientists that population geneticists had successfully demonstrated that 'race' is a social construct without biological foundation." More recently, following the completion of a draft map of the human genome in June 2000, Craig Venter (Head of Celera Genomics, and chief private scientist involved with the Human Genome Project [HGP]) claimed that his analysis of the genomes of five people of different ethnicities had shown that "there was no way to tell one ethnicity from another," and that, therefore, "race" is not a valid scientific or biological construct. This scientific claim was reaffirmed in February 2001, when the final completion of the human genome was published in both *Science* and *Nature*.

Yet despite these critiques, debate over the scientific status of the "race" concept has continued unabated (Billig 1998). Indeed, even the most recent assertions by human genome scientists that race is a social construct without biological foundation have been treated with skepticism and incredulity by scientists and members of the public alike (see McCann, Augoustinos, and LeCouteur 2004). In psychological research in particular, the concept of "race" continues to be used unproblematically as a "natural kind" variable in ways that reinforce the commonplace view that it is a biological and genetic reality (Tate and Audette 2001). As Hopkins, Reicher, and Levine (1997) have argued, social psychological research is also guilty of perpetuating and reproducing the view that "race" is a natural category that people automatically use to categorize the self and others. Far from being understood as socially constructed and strategically deployed for social and ideological ends, race becomes seen as a "non-problematic 'given' which is . . . somehow inherent in the empirical reality of observable or imagined biological difference" (Hopkins, Reicher, and Levine 1997, 70).

within the social cognition tradition for example, "racial" categorizations are theorized to be similar to other kinds of categorizations, driven by our cognitive and perceptual need to simplify complex sensory information from the social environment. In this way, racial categorization becomes a natural and inevitable human cognitive process, not an ideological and social practice (Augoustinos and Walker 1998). Social categorizations such as "race" are conceptualized as laying the cognitive and perceptual foundations for stereotyping of and ultimately discrimination toward dissimilar others. Hopkins and his colleagues argue that there are disturbing conceptual similarities between this social cognitive approach to prejudice and the "new racism" discourse, both of which construct intergroup differentiation and discrimination as "human," based on a psychological preference for similar others who share the same values and way of life, and a "natural" tendency to prejudge dissimilar others, especially those who are "racially" different (see also Billig 1985).

Thus, the resilience of the construct of "race," despite what is claimed to be scientific evidence to the contrary, is reflected by its entrenched use as a commonsense, "natural" category by which to classify people. In Moscovici's terms (1984, 1988), "race" can be seen to have become a reified and objectified reality through which social group differences come to be understood and explained. That is, "race" has become a social representation. Essentialized categories of difference such as race and gender have a ubiquitous appeal, not only in everyday commonsense understandings, but also in scientific reasoning. Group differences, whether physical or cultural, continue to operate as socially meaningful and relevant sense-making practices. These practices, as we will outline in the following section, typically function to construct a viable dominant group identity that, while founded upon racial categories, nonetheless serves to deny both racism and race privilege.

THE CONSTRUCTION OF A VIABLE DOMINANT GROUP IDENTITY

"Race" and identity have been salient concerns in Australian public life since its colonization by the British around two hundred years ago. As with all nations' histories, Australia's history has been subject to fierce contestation and debate. "Official" traditionalist accounts construct Australia's colonial past as the white settlement of a previously uninhabited land. The doctrine of *terra nullius* had, until overturned by the High Court's *Mabo*[1] decision in 1992 embodied the view in Australian law for nearly two hundred years that pre-European Australia was literally an empty continent. Alternative versions of the European settlement of

Australia have referred to the same historical events as the "invasion" of an already possessed land, inhabited and owned by the Aboriginal peoples who had lived there for thousands of years. This version of history emphasizes the genocide and dispossession of the many Indigenous nations that held sovereignty to the land prior to colonization and the attempts by European invaders to deny this sovereignty. During the last ten years, these contrasting accounts of Australia's history have come to be known euphemistically as "the history wars," a symbolic struggle that has been central to major social debates on Indigenous entitlement to land, reconciliation, and apologizing to Indigenous peoples for past historical injustices.

Most notably, these "history wars" have involved both Indigenous contestations to white hegemony, alongside ongoing attempts by white Australia to assert a valid identity in the face of accounts of colonization. As such, resistances by, for example, the Howard government to calls for an apology to Indigenous peoples, or denials in the High Court of Indigenous land-rights claims, may be seen as examples of the white majority not only attempting to maintain ownership of the land itself, but to also legitimate white identities as separate "from the past"—as founded upon a claim to belonging that is unrelated to acts of white colonial violence. Yet, as we will suggest, such claims may be seen to display a series of anxieties about the ongoing ways in which violence is carried out against Indigenous people in the name of white belonging and white identities.

In an incisive paper on white belonging, Nicolacopoulos and Vassila-copoulos (2004) suggest that white identities demonstrate an "ontological disturbance"—that any claims to belonging by white people in Australia are thoroughly unsettled by the relationship that white people have with Indigenous sovereignty. In other words, and in contrast to "us" and "them" accounts that depict the former as entirely independent of the latter, the "us" of white Australia is always already in a relationship with the "them" of Indigenous people through the ongoing existence of Indigenous sovereignty—which continues to survive despite over two hundred years of white violence (Nicoll 2004). To elaborate, Nicolacopoulos and Vassilacopoulos suggest that in order for those of us who identify as white people to belong, we require the recognition of our "right to belong" at an ontological level.

Yet, if the sovereignty of Indigenous people is denied, there can be no possibility of such recognition for white people by those who would be in a position to recognize us as subjects who belong. As a result, white violence (through various individual and state-sponsored practices) is directed at managing this ontological disturbance, so as to deny the agency of Indigenous people, and thus position the white nation as its own point of recognition—as an a priori sovereign power (as the fiction of *terra nullius* would have us believe). Yet, if we are to understand white identities as founded upon this lack of belonging, or more specifically, as constituted through a lack of any recognition of a "right to belong," then the "ontological disturbance" that white identities are founded upon prevents white people from being in any way other than through anxiety (Riggs 2003). Having said that, there is obviously an uncanny relationship that exists between the foundational lack of white subjectivities and the hegemony of whiteness in this country. The question, then, is how is it that white people continue to benefit from unearned race privilege, despite our rather anxious location in relation to histories of place?

Jacques Rancière (1994) suggests that white anxieties over the lack of a valid claim to belonging are repressed through recourse to spatialization as an identificatory practice. In other words, through the production of a range of discourses that simulate the "settledness" of white national identity in Australia (for example, an emphasis on white "achievements" in relation to war ["the digger"],[2] agriculture ["the pastoralist"],[3] and "overcoming the harsh environment" ["the battler"]),[4] it has been possible for white identities to be shaped through a notion of place and belonging (Moran 2002; Moreton-Robinson 2003). In this way, "settler belonging" is premised on what Probyn (2002, 75), following Spivak, terms "epistemic violence." Such acts work to mask colonial violence against Indigenous people, and thus allow for the rewriting of white history as the "peaceful settlement" of an uninhabited land (see Moreton-Robinson 2004a; Riggs 2004a for more on this in regard to the "history wars" in Australia).

These points about the denial of white violence demonstrate the ongoing connections between the ideologies of *terra nullius* and the identificatory practices of white people. While *terra nullius* may have been challenged as a justification for refusing the land-rights claims of Indigenous peoples, this has not translated into the contestation of *terra nullius* as a social practice that informs white spatialized identifications (Moran 2002). Indeed, such identifications may be understood in many ways as being reinforced by the High Court's verdicts—while the outcomes may be viewed as a step toward recognizing the sovereignty of Indigenous peoples, the verdicts nonetheless serve to enshrine white ways of knowing a priori as being an objective measure of what is classified as place and belonging. Thus, as Moreton-Robinson (2004b) suggests, refusals to recognize Indigenous land rights, both pre- and post-*Mabo*, demonstrate the tight grip that the white nation maintains in regard to defining who can, and who cannot, possess land. Thus, as an ongoing practice of colonization, *terra nullius* continues to exist as an a priori justification for the "settledness" of white identities through the construction of an "us" and "them" binary that posits both the legitimacy and superiority of the former over the latter.

To reiterate our position in this section, our interest in looking at the ways in which white violence functions in the service of white identities is *not* to attribute to individual white people the subject position of "bad white racist," nor is it to suggest that the actions or words of particular white people reflect a stable, internal set of psychological mechanisms. Rather, our intent is to examine some of the commonplace representations, sense-making practices, and turns of phrase that circulate within the white Australian idiom that serve to justify or deny white violence. By understanding these as broad cultural resources that are available to nominal group members (such as white people in Australia), our goal in the following analysis is to highlight how they work in the service of white hegemony.

The analysis thus draws in part upon work in the discursive tradition within critical psychology, which looks at the particular resources that speakers utilize when accounting for racism or race privilege (for example, Augoustinos 2002; Augoustinos and LeCouteur 2004; Wetherell and Potter 1992), but it extends this through the framework of social representation theory by examining how the broader tropes of "us" and "them" function in conjunction with social Darwinist notions of a cultural hierarchy that provides dominant group members with a language through which to account for their identities. Such an approach sees talk not only as a site where dominant discursive resources are put together to formulate arguments or positions on particular issues, but also as a site where we can read a "collective psyche"—where we can see how particular histories are played out in talk. This requires a focus not on idiom or rhetoric per se, but rather on what particular portions of talk may signify to us when located in a broader social context. As such, we examine how social representations of "us" and "them" and of group "differences" between Indigenous and white peoples in Australia have been central to major debates within Australia in the last ten years, and how vestiges of social Darwinism can be identified in everyday talk and reasoning on such matters.

HISTORICAL NARRATIVES AND THE LEGITIMATION OF COLONIZATION

In the analyses that follow below, we demonstrate how white people in Australia anchor their social identities and those of Indigenous peoples in historical narratives of Australia's colonial past that minimize and downplay the history of racism and oppression of the Indigenous minority during the two hundred years of "white settlement," and how this narrative is organized by social Darwinist tropes of a cultural hierarchy of group differences.

The following extracts of talk come from focus group discussions conducted with white university students regarding "race" relations in Australia, and we offer these as examples of everyday talk and reasoning on matters pertaining to social group differences. In these discussions, participants argued that understanding contemporary relations between Aboriginal and non-Aboriginal people, and more specifically, the inequities that Aboriginal people face necessitate a historical analysis of the past. Featuring strongly in the historical narratives that participants offered was a recognizably "traditional" version of colonialist and imperialist discourse (Said 1993) that, while acknowledging that the British "imposed" their "lifestyle" on Indigenous people—and that this lifestyle was in direct conflict with existing Aboriginal social practices—also discounted blame from the British by stressing the "benefits" of European culture and progress.

The lifestyle imposed by the British was invariably described as "culturally advanced" and "superior," while Aboriginal culture was commonly referred to as "primitive." This "clash of cultures," it was argued, inevitably led to a mutual failure of "understanding" between the British settlers and existing Aboriginal communities. Elements of this explanatory account are evident in Extract 1,[5] in which participant "A" draws upon an imperialist discourse of European "progress," "modernity," and "sophistication."

EXTRACT 1

> A: Think too and also when you look at history you look back at the fact that the Aborigines were very very primitive *(Mmm)* and they confronted our culture that was superiorly [*sic*] more advanced, the wheel had been invented and whatnot but the Aborigines hadn't seemed to to advance past that very primitive stage and whatnot *(Mmm)*. Umm, they had sort of had no modern technologies as such as the British had. Like the British had gun powder and alcohol and these things, ahh, I think that was another big problem.

This account of colonization serves to legitimate white violence through the narrative of a "civilizing mission." The extreme case formulation "very very primitive" functions to emphasize the state of Indigenous societies as being "confronted" by what is depicted as a "culture that was superiorly [*sic*] more advanced." Such a "confrontation" is implicitly constructed as necessary in order to address what is referred to at the close of the extract as "another big problem," the problem being that Indigenous people lacked "modern technologies" such as "gun powder and alcohol." This construction of "Indigenous lack" allows the white speaker to ignore the fact that the various "advancements" (for example, gun powder and alcohol) were tools of white violence (such as gun powder and its role in the murder of Indigenous peoples and alcohol in its ongoing role as detrimental to Indigenous communities). The account provided in Extract 1 thus constructs a "good white identity" through both the depiction of Indigenous cultures as "very very primitive," and through the denial of the role that white violence played in the "civilizing mission" (Riggs 2004b; Riggs and Augoustinos 2004).

Such an account of a valid white identity is also achieved through a very specific deployment of "history" as a rhetorical warrant for A's account. The formulation "when you look at history" appeals to factuality and gives the account the status of neutrality and objectivity. Thus it is not just A who says that Aboriginal people were "very very primitive," but rather it is "history" itself that "proves" this—A merely provides a factual and unproblematic description. The representation of Aboriginal people as undeveloped and primitive is further instanced by the deployment of the "facts"—that Indigenous people had failed to develop the wheel and possessed "no modern technologies." The Aboriginal society is thus contrasted with British culture, which is represented as "superior" and more technologically advanced, and with which A claims identification by the use of the indexical pronoun "our." In this way, A not only provides a representation of "them," but at the same time constructs an identity for his own in-group identity as a member of the dominant non-Indigenous majority ("us").

EXTRACT 2

In Extract 2, another participant, J, draws on a "clash of cultures" repertoire to account for the dispossession of Aboriginal people by invoking the "nomadic" nature of their lifestyle. The lack of permanent architecture in forms recognizable to Europeans provides an explanatory account as to why Aboriginal people purportedly lacked the moral basis for legitimate ownership claims. Note that the cited absence of villas, towns, and cities in this extract is similar to the citing of the wheel, gunpowder, and alcohol as constituting technological difference (and superiority) in the previous extract. The deployment of "concrete examples" of what is depicted as Western technological superiority (emphasizing modernity and progress) serves in these arguments to position Aboriginal cultures (which are depicted as nomadic, unsettled, and primitive) as inferior—or "beneath"—Western culture.

This extract,[6] like the previous one, functions to establish a cultural hierarchy between Indigenous peoples and the British:

> J: That was partly thing to do with their lifestyle being nomadic because they didn't actually build towns and villas, they didn't build any sort of solid sort of ahh cities or whatever (syll syll) they moved around they didn't have a lot to sort of claim when we got here. There wasn't like a a city which they could say this is *ours* like you're not coming in here or whatever they were a, they didn't have anything to hold onto I guess.

Not only does this extract function to establish a hierarchy between Indigenous people and the British, but also it serves to reify this hierarchy through a construction of ownership as tied to particularly white, Western values. Such a construction may be seen as serving the purpose of maintaining a focus on an imagined past within which Indigenous people were "nomadic" and "didn't have anything to hold onto." This focus on the past serves two functions: it legitimates the present context in Australia whereby white Australians claim ownership on the basis of "illegal possession" (Moreton-Robinson 2003) by preserving the fiction of *terra nullius,* and it denies the ongoing agency of Indigenous people who have continued to resist invasion and dispossession. Thus the notion of not having "anything to hold onto" implicitly constructs Indigenous people in the present as likewise having nothing to hold into, which flies directly in the face of successes in regard to land-rights claims and the ongoing critiques that Indigenous people make of white privilege (Moreton-Robinson 2000).

EXTRACT 3

The following extract of a conversation between participants M and J provides an example of how participants delicately managed discussions about Aboriginal responses to colonization and, ultimately, to a dominant European lifestyle. Here we see an account of the violence committed against Indigenous people as a result of colonization that denies such violence by depicting it in terms of an Aboriginal "failure" to adapt. Again, the accountability of Aboriginal people was emphasized by setting up Aboriginal people as one part of a contrast pair, in opposition to other (more recently arrived) ethnic groups, whose differential success in "fitting" in with Australian society was stressed.

While the previous extracts implicitly suggest that the "problems" faced by Indigenous people in the present have resulted from a failure to adapt (usually glossed as a consequence of differing "lifestyle" preferences), the following exchange[7] makes this explicit:

> M: Well I think it it gets back to the lifestyle situation though? The fact that those other ethnic communities can come in and tend to fit in and—
> J: —Yeah, that's right.
> M: They've sort of got the European-type lifestyle which is not a lot different and ours particularly now we're becoming a lot more multicultural where I think the Aboriginal umm that was the problem is that they, we, wouldn't fit with, it wasn't a good fit *(Mmm)*.

M claims factual status for the adaptability of "other ethnic communities" arriving in Australia and goes on to provide an explanatory account for this degree of being able to fit in terms of similarity of lifestyle and the increasing multiculturalism of mainstream Australian society (that "we" are becoming). Moreover, J offers independent agreement for this explanation ("Yeah, that's right"). In contrast, the case of the Aboriginal "fit" is described as "*the* problem," and M attributes responsibility for this problem across a self-correcting "they versus we" binary, prior to settling with the vague phrase, "it wasn't a good fit." This vagueness again distances the speaker from a particular position while keeping open the possibility that either or both sides of the pair ("they" versus "we," or Aboriginal people versus nonIndigenous Australians) are accountable for the putative failure to fit.

Extract 3 also affords the participants the opportunity to construct themselves neither as "Aboriginal" nor as members of "other ethnic communities," but rather as members of the dominant group who neither has "problems" with adapting nor has to attempt to "fit in." As such, the white participants are able to claim for themselves an unproblematized identity through the category "ours" that neatly sidesteps both the fact of colonial violence and the forcible nature through which "other ethnic communities" are expected to assimilate within the white Australian nation. In this sense, what is depicted as a relatively polite account of "them," and "their" various attempts at fitting in may instead be read as an active attempt at maintaining the space between "us" and "them" so that the former are seen as rightful claimants to the national space.

A construction of Indigenous people as having no "continual contact with their land" is used by the participants in Extract 4 as another means of accounting for the legitimacy of white identities.

EXTRACT 4

As we will see in the next extract, by constructing Indigenous people as no longer being "full blood,"[8] Indigenous people are implicitly constructed as being "just another Australian"—thus suggesting that they should be treated the same as white Australians. Yet at the same time, Indigenous peoples are positioned as being the sole occupiers of the category "race." As can be seen in Extract 4,[9] the "conflict" of Indigenous land claims is positioned as resulting from Indigenous people's "problematic racial identity."

> M: So in between killing them off they'd dilute what was left and they would bring them up with all the cultures like our ideas and ideologies and . . .
> B: Part of the problem is we don't really have any true Aboriginals anymore they're all half caste or quarter caste that's where you get problems because they've got this conflict "I am Aboriginal but I have a white parent or I come from a slightly white background" and then you get this confusion.
> M: We don't have any true Australians either we're a multi-cultural nation—so aren't we all Australians?"
> J: So there's been a concerted effort to assimilate?
> B: Ohh yeah.
> J: Yeah 'cos you don't see that many full bloods at all.

The positioning of Indigenous people as being part of a "multicultural nation"—"so aren't we all Australians?"—works to deny ongoing histories of colonization, and thus positions land claims as unjustified and as intentional threats to the harmony of the "multicultural nation." The claim that "we don't really have any true Aboriginals anymore" problematizes contemporary Indigenous identities by constructing two contrasting categories: "true Aboriginals" and thus, implicitly, "false Aboriginals." In this way, the legitimacy of Indigenous identity claims (and by implication, land claims) is rendered suspect. This "confusion" over identity is moreover located within Indigenous people themselves ("*they've* got this conflict . . . confusion"). The speakers, in contrast, are able to claim for themselves an unproblematic location within the category "all Australians," one that ignores the violence through which the category "Australian" is constituted.

Of course, it is important to recognize here a moment when the white participants *do* acknowledge acts of colonizing violence. Thus M begins her turn in Extract 4 by saying, "So in between killing them off." Here, M is clearly stating what she knows or is aware of about colonization—that it involved genocide. Yet, as we have suggested in the previous paragraph, this statement leads into a statement about "bring[ing] them up with all the cultures." In this way, while M does indeed acknowledge colonizing violence, she negates this acknowledgment in many ways through the implicit assumption that "killing them off" was a part of the "civilizing mission" to "bring them up with all the cultures." Statements such as those made by M signal the inherent difficulty that the participants appeared to face in talking about colonizing violence without resorting to explaining it away with clarifying follow-up comments.

EXTRACT 5

Another way in which anxieties over white identities are managed is evident in Extract 5 in the positioning of white people as victims of unfounded Indigenous land claims. As can be seen in this extract, white talk about Indigenous land claims centers on stereotypical constructions of Indigenous peoples as "abusing the system," thus implicitly working to both avoid the topic of colonization, and thereby legitimating the "concerns" of white Australians.

> A [in regard to *Mabo*]: You just have to be careful . . . a backlash . . . in the sense that not too many people get very upset that "why should they being having all these handouts" in a sense.
>
> J: If they're going to abuse it, particularly if they abuse it then if it comes up again that . . . well people will say "what are you going to do with it, last time . . . alcohol and what ever . . . you've abused your position."
>
> A: There is a fine line between them being compensated and them taking advantage of their position. A lot of Anglo-Australians would umm are sort of are concerned about, they feel they are taking advantage; they're given much more than they need, umm whereas where it may be true that what ever percentage of them.

In this extract,[10] constructions of "us" and "them" also work to problematize Indigenous claims to identity and land. Thus, "Anglo-Australians" are seen in Extract 5 as being "upset [that] they [Indigenous people are] having all these handouts," and as believing that Indigenous people are "taking advantage; they're given much more than they need." Such constructions work to position Indigenous people as "taking advantage," rather than as being compensated for the impact of colonization. Thus, as A suggests, "there is a fine line between them being compensated and them taking advantage of their position." Statements such as these work to position white people as blameless for Indigenous disadvantage (indeed, Indigenous people are seen as having money thrown at them—as being privileged), and to suggest that there are not implicit advantages to being recognized as white in Australia.

In this extract, we can therefore see some of the ways in which the advantages that white people hold simply by being white are repressed, and instead projected onto Indigenous people, who are characterized as receiving "all these handouts." By expanding our focus to the historical contingencies of white advantage, it is possible to understand such acts of projection as maintaining whiteness (and specifically white privilege) as an unspoken category. Anxieties over land claims may thus be read as anxieties over the challenging of white privilege and white identities. When white dominance is exposed as a historically located (rather than a priori) network of power relations, then the hegemony of white systems of representation is unsettled.

EXTRACT 6

The following and final extract[11] makes explicit the ways in which such anxieties over land-rights claims generate enactments of white fear:

> M: Something the media failed to bring out—the sort of aid—you've been given all this chunk of land and that it was sort of "save the back-yards" kind of mentality and a lot of people got scared . . . the truth of the matter was that unless they had continual contact with their land they didn't have a claim under that decision so I think that people failed to realise that and that scared a lot of people.
>
> A: Umm and I was surprised 'cos I guess you read about but . . . a friend I do have that's fairly close is doing law and actually he's manning some case against the housing trust or whatever but in amongst all that he you know was telling me about some group that was about to make a claim on Adelaide and it really freaked me out this is bullshit.
>
> B: [laugh]
>
> J: They've already claimed part of Brisbane, haven't they a claim.

The enactment of white fear as a response to the "Indigenous threat" (in the form of land claims) is exemplified by A, who suggests, "claim on Adelaide . . . really freaked me out." M's suggestion that there is a "save the backyards kind of mentality" refers to the ways in which the white nation purports to "live in fear" of Indigenous people who will come in and take "our" land. This fantasy of the "dangerous Other" (Elliot 1996) is actually an incisive comment on the sentiment of white belonging in Australia, as it demonstrates the fear held by white Australians that acts of repression will fail, and hence reveal the anxiety of white belonging. These anxieties show not that Indigenous people threaten the white nation in the ways that the participants in these extracts would suggest, but rather that white belonging is always already threatened by the very presence of Indigenous people, and by the fact that they carry sovereignty and ontological belonging in ways that cannot be extinguished by white claims to the contrary.

DISCUSSION

Of particular interest in the first three extracts we presented are the recurring and interrelated metaphors around which participants organized their talk. The first of these is the familiar imperialist metaphor of hierarchy (itself symbolizing progress) that relies on a set of spatial dichotomies—above versus beneath, advanced versus backward—that serves to position Aboriginal culture as beneath British or European culture. We see this spatial metaphor in Extract 1 in which Aboriginal culture is referred to as "very very primitive" in comparison to European culture, which is described as superior and "more advanced." This hierarchy metaphor is also implicitly used in Extract 2 in which the absence of Western examples of modernity and civilization (solid buildings and cities) is used to confer upon Aboriginal cultures an inferior status. As Lakoff and Johnson (1980) argue, this up-down spatial or "geographic" metaphor is both integral to Western notions of status and social hierarchy and also historically contingent in its development with European colonization (Foucault 1980). Moscovici and Hewstone (1983) have emphasized how the use of graphic metaphors in this way helps to make abstract and complex notions culturally accessible and concrete, in this case having to do with history, culture, and social group inequalities. The metaphor of a hierarchy is used here to objectify and essentialize a set of complex social relations between a dominant and dominated group, a metaphor that also provides an explanatory framework to account for these social relations. As Moscovici has emphasized, it is through this process of objectification and reification that social representations are generated.

Another prevalent and related metaphor was that of "fit." Aboriginal people are represented as having failed to fit with and adapt to an advanced and dominant culture. This is explicit in Extract 3, when M constructs Aboriginal "problems" primarily as "it wasn't a good fit" and contrasts what is depicted as an Aboriginal "failure" to adapt with other ethnic communities who "tend to fit in." These metaphors of hierarchy, fit and adaptation, are reminiscent of social Darwinism, which posits the existence of an evolutionary hierarchy of discrete biological groups. Although participants in this study did not make explicit references to discrete biological groups, nor did they mobilize racial typologies in their talk, they nonetheless did frame their talk around notions of a *cultural* hierarchy. Aboriginal people were not only constructed as culturally different from the British, but also as culturally inferior. Indigenous people and the specific social problems and inequities they experience in contemporary Australian society were represented largely in social Darwinist terms as problems of fit and adaptation to a culturally superior culture. In the same way that beliefs in a biological hierarchy of groups functioned to rationalize and legitimate inequities between dominant and dominated groups during the first half of the twentieth century, the notion of a cultural hierarchy today serves the same functions and continues to reproduce essentialist accounts of difference that reside in culture rather than in biology.

As Essed (1991) and Barker (1981), among others, have argued, the replacement of a biological hierarchy between groups with that of a cultural hierarchy is one of the defining characteristics of contemporary forms of modern racism. Although notions of "race" and racial difference have been transformed over time to rely less on biological framings, remnants of these representations persist in ordinary sense-making practices to account for group differences and in representations of "us" and "them." Old representations resurface as new ones become anchored to already existing and familiar modes of understanding. In the same way Philogène (1999) has noted that despite the replacement of the social category "black American" with "African-American" in the United States as a widely accepted and normative way of referencing this category of people, this new social representation, with its emphasis on ethnicity rather than "race," has not completely replaced existing representations and practices. Likewise, Walker (2001) suggests that old and new forms of racism coexist, and that this coexistence of old and new forms of representation is indicative of the ambivalence that characterizes intergroup relations in contemporary liberal democracies.

In the final three extracts, the projection of threat onto Indigenous people, and the corollary denial of white violence, is accomplished in multiple and often contradictory ways. In the first three extracts, Indigenous people are positioned as the "them" to the "us" of white Australia. Yet in the final three extracts, Indigenous people are positioned as no longer being "full blood," the suggestion being that Indigenous people should consider themselves to be "Australians" like everyone else. Such contradictions work to manage Indigenous land claims by positioning them as unjustified and illegitimate (in that everyone should have the same access), but simultaneously as being made by a group of people who are a threat to the white nation. Thus, Indigenous people are a threat in that they "unsettle the settler" (the dominant majority) via land claims (through focusing on the specter of colonization), yet Indigenous people are also positioned as passive recipients of government policies (such as assimilation, welfare, and so on). It is through these multiple positionings that white violence is managed—the construction of Indigenous people as "a threat" works to mask whiteness and its relation to colonization, while the construction of Indigenous people as always already subjugated works to manage this "threat" by reasserting white superiority.

As may be seen in the final three extracts, subjective investments in whiteness are managed in many ways. The talk examined here demonstrates how the "anxiety of whiteness" circulates in white people's talk about Indigenous land rights. Most obviously, there were attempts at projecting unsettling events onto Indigenous peoples. Rather than adequately acknowledging complicity in histories of oppression (as opposed to acknowledging colonization as M did in Extract 4 by referencing "killing" and then backing down from it by turning the focus to other issues), the white participants positioned themselves as "objective observers" of history. We would suggest that this demonstrates some of the social practices that constitute subjective investments in whiteness in Australia, and the ways in which this draws attention to what we have termed elsewhere the "psychic life of colonial power"—a set of resources that circulate for repressing histories of white violence (Riggs and Augoustinos 2005).

CONCLUSIONS

As we have suggested throughout this chapter, an account of white identity that is established through the categories of "us" and "them" establishes the following three things: a) it allows white Australians to justify their sense of belonging or ownership as "defended territory," b) it disavows or represses the fact of Indigenous sovereignty and the inability of the white nation to actually overwrite it, and c) it legitimates white identities as the province of "good people" who hold no relationship to ongoing histories of white violence. Underpinning this account of white identity is the logic of social Darwinism, and in particular the notion of cultural hierarchies and essentialized racial categories. Hence the participants variously engaged in the reification of racial categories so as to prop up their own privilege as dominant group members. At the same time, however, they wielded racial categories *against* Indigenous peoples through a focus on notions of "blood," "loss of culture," and the category of "true Aboriginals." Thus the construction of "us" and "them" categories serves two competing functions: to create a distinction between white and Indigenous Australians that privileges the values of the former, and to deny the claiming of this distinction *by Indigenous people* when it is used as a warrant for land rights and compensation. In this sense, definitions of categories of "us" and "them" are tightly held by white people in order to deny alternate representations or accounts.

Understanding how the politics of identity function in Australia is thus important in its potential for contributing to the destabilization of white hegemony. Social representations theory contributes to this by affording us an understanding of how particular representations of dominant group members circulate, and how they are deployed in the service of white hegemony. We have shown how an objectified and essentialized representation of a cultural hierarchy anchored in old and discredited social Darwinist notions of biological hierarchy is a pervasive way in which majority group members accomplish this. Our analysis has also engaged with recent suggestions in the field of social representations theory to incorporate analyses of "power, dialogue and resistance in the development and circulation of representations" (Volklein and Howarth 2005, 448). By focusing on how the white participants wielded racial categories that themselves are formed within particular power relations, and on how such categories are formulated and circulated within everyday conversation, we have contributed to an understanding of white identities that goes beyond simply recounting their existence, and that instead provides a means to both interpreting and resisting their normative location.

As such, we suggest that challenging white hegemony requires more than simply either acknowledging the existence of racism or denying the validity of racial categories; as we suggest at the beginning of this chapter, there is a long history of doing precisely these two things, yet as our participants have demonstrated, racial categories continue to function in the service of white privilege. Instead, what is required is a sustained analysis of how racism functions through racial categories in the representations of *both* "us" and "them." Focusing solely on the latter will always run the risk of ignoring how dominant group members construct their own identities, and attributing racism to marginalized group members through a focus on social inequities that is primarily connected to marginalized identities. A focus on the ways in which particular social representations work in the service of dominant group identities may offer one means to challenging what is often a failure to speak about the identity work undertaken by dominant group members.

NOTES

1. The doctrine of *terra nullius* was legally overturned in 1992 following a land claim by Torres Strait Islander Eddie Mabo against the Queensland government. The High Court of Australia ruled in this case that an inherent *right* of native title—or Indigenous ownership of land—existed where formerly none had been acknowledged.
2. Australian slang for solider.
3. Australian slang for farmer.
4. Australian slang for a hard worker.
5. The extract is from Augoustinos, Tuffin, and Sale, 1999.
6. Ibid
7. Ibid.
8. We use this term because it is deployed in participants' talk. The reader should be aware that such terms are highly offensive to Indigenous communities, and the use of such terms is in no way supported by the authors.
9. The extract is from Augoustinos, Tuffin, and Sale, 1999.
10. Ibid.
11. Ibid.

REFERENCES

Augoustinos, M. 2002. History as a rhetorical resource: Using historical narratives to argue and explain. In *How to analyse talk in institutional settings: A casebook of methods,* ed. A. McHoul and M. Rapley, 137–47. London: Continuum International.

Augoustinos, M., and A. LeCouteur. 2004. Apologising to Indigenous Australians: The denial of white guilt. In *Collective guilt: International perspectives,* ed. N. Branscombe and B. Doosje, 552–609. Cambridge: Cambridge University Press.

Augoustinos, M., and I. Walker. 1998. The construction of stereotypes in social psychology. From social cognition to ideology. *Theory & Psychology* 8:629–52.

Barker, M. 1981. *The new racism.* London: Junction.

Billig, M. 1985. Prejudice, categorization and particularisation: From a perceptual to a rhetorical approach. *European Journal of Social Psychology* 15:79–103.

————. 1998. A dead idea that won't lie down. *Searchlight*, July. http://www
.searchlightmagazine.com (accessed March 20, 2005).

Breakwell, G. 2001. Social representational constraints upon identity. In *Representations of the social: Bridging theoretical traditions*, ed. K. Deaux and G. Philogène, 271–84. Oxford: Blackwell.

Chryssochoou, X. 2000. Multicultural societies: Making sense of new environments and identities. *Journal of Community and Applied Social Psychology* 10:343–54.

————. 2004. *Cultural diversity: Its social psychology*. Oxford: Blackwell.

Cunningham-Burley, S., and A. Kerr. 1999. Defining the "social": Towards an understanding of scientific and medical discourses on the social aspects of the new human genetics. *Sociology of Health & Illness* 21:505–16.

Duveen, G. 2001. Representations, identities, resistance. In *Representations of the social: Bridging theoretical traditions*, ed. K. Deaux and G. Philogène, 257–70. Oxford: Blackwell.

Elliot, P. 1996. Working through racism: Confronting the strangely familiar. *Journal for the Psychoanalysis of Culture & Society* 1:63–72.

Essed, P. 1991. *Understanding everyday racism*. London: Sage.

Foucault, M. 1980. *Power/knowledge: Selected interviews and other writings, 1972–1977*, ed. C. Gordon. Brighton: Harvester.

Gannett, L. 2001. Racism and human genome diversity research: The ethical limits of "Population Thinking." *Philosophy of Science* 68:479–92.

Hopkins, N., S. Reicher, and M. Levine. 1997. On the parallels between social cognition and the "new racism." *British Journal of Social Psychology* 36: 305–29.

Howarth, C. 2006. Race as stigma: Positioning the stigmatised as agents, not objects. *Journal of Community and Applied Psychology* 16:442–51.

Lakoff, G., and M. Johnson. 1980. *Metaphors we live by*. Chicago: University of Chicago Press.

McCann, P., M. Augoustinos, and A. LeCouteur. 2004. "Race" and the Human Genome Project: Constructions of scientific legitimacy. *Discourse & Society* 15:409–32.

McClintock, A. 1995. *Imperial leather*. New York: Routledge.

Moran, S. 2002. As Australia decolonizes: Indigenizing settler nationalism and the challenge of settler/Indigenous relations. *Ethnic and Racial Studies 25*: 1013–42.

Moreton-Robinson, A. 2000. *Talkin' up to the white woman: Indigenous women and feminism*. St. Lucia, Australia: University of Queensland Press.

————. 2003. I still call Australia home: Indigenous belonging and place in a white postcolonizing society. In *Uprootings/regroundings: Questions of home and migration*, ed. S. Ahmed, C. Castañeda, A. Fortier, and M. Sheller, 131–49. Oxford: Berg.

————. 2004a. Indigenous history wars and the virtue of the white nation. In *The ideas market: An alternative take on Australia's intellectual life*, ed. D. Carter, 219–35. Melbourne: Melbourne University Press.

————. 2004b. The possessive logic of patriarchal white sovereignty: The high court and the Yorta Yorta decision. *Borderlands e-journal* 3 (2). http://www .borderlandsejournal.adelaide.edu.au/vol3no2_2004/moreton_possessive.htm (accessed June 15, 2005).

Moscovici, S. 1984. The phenomenon of social representations. In *Social representations,* ed. R. M. Farr and S. Moscovici, 3–69). Cambridge: Cambridge University Press; Paris: Maison des Sciences de l'Homme.

————. 1988. Notes towards a description of social representations. *European Journal of Social Psychology* 18:211–50.

Moscovici, S., and M. Hewstone. 1983. Social representations and social explanation: From the "naïve" to the "amateur" scientist. In *Attribution theory: Social and functional extensions,* ed. M. Hewstone, 98–125. Oxford: Blackwell.

Nicolacopoulos, T. and G. Vassilacopoulos. 2004. Racism, foreigner communities and the onto-pathology of white Australian subjectivity. In *Whitening race: Essays in social and cultural criticism,* ed. A. Moreton-Robinson, 32–47. Canberra: Aboriginal Studies Press.

Nicoll, F. 2004. "Are you calling me a racist?" Teaching critical whiteness theory in indigenous sovereignty. *Borderlands e-journal* 3. http://www.borderland sejournal.adelaide.edu.au/vol3no2_2004/nicoll_teaching.htm (accessed October 9, 2006).

Philogène, G. 1999. *From black to African American: A new social representation.* Westport, CT: Greenwood-Praeger.

Probyn, F. 2002. How does the settler belong? *Westerly* 47:75–95.

Rancière, J. 1994. Discovering new worlds: Politics of travel and metaphors of space. In *Traveller's tales: Narratives of home and displacement,* ed. G. Robertson, M. Mash, L. Tickner, J. Bird, and B. Curtis, 175–91. London: Routledge.

Richards, G. 1997. *"Race," racism and psychology: Towards a reflexive history.* New York: Routledge.

Riggs, D. 2003. Repressing a privileged location: Exploring the uncanniness of white belonging in Australia. *Analysis* 12:97–112.

————. 2004a. Understanding history as a rhetorical strategy: Constructions of truth and objectivity in debates surrounding Windschuttle's "fabrication." *Journal of Australian Studies* 82:37–49.

————. 2004b. Benevolence and the management of stake: On being "good white people." *Philament: A Journal of the Arts and Culture* 4.

Riggs, D., and M. Augoustinos. 2004. Projecting threat: Managing subjective investments in whiteness. *Psychoanalysis, Culture & Society* 9:216–24.

————. 2005. The psychic life of colonial power: Racialised subjectivities, bodies and methods. *Journal of Community and Applied Social Psychology* 15:461–77.

Said, E. W. 1993. *Culture and imperialism.* London: Vintage.

Tate, C., and D. Audette. 2001. Theory and research on "race" as a natural kind variable in psychology. *Theory and Psychology* 11:495–520.

Volklein, C., and C. Howarth. 2005. A review of controversies about social representations theory: A British debate. *Culture and Psychology* 11:431–54.

Walker, I. 2001. The changing nature of racism: From old to new? In *Under-standing prejudice, racism, and social conflict*, ed. M. Augoustinos and K. Reynolds, 24–42. London: Sage.

Wetherell, M., and J. Potter. 1992. *Mapping the language of racism: Discourse and the legitimation of exploitation*. New York: Columbia University Press.

CHAPTER 8

"IT'S NOT THEIR FAULT THAT THEY HAVE THAT COLOUR SKIN, IS IT?"

YOUNG BRITISH CHILDREN AND THE POSSIBILITIES FOR CONTESTING RACIALIZING REPRESENTATIONS

Caroline Howarth

WITHIN THE REALMS OF THE ACADEMY, the dynamic and multiple nature of racism is fiercely debated; symbolic, institutional, cultural, localized, global, new, old, neocolonial, gendered, blatant, and subtle (Back and Solomos 1996; Durrheim and Dixon 2004; Leach 2005; Omi and Winant 1986; Pettigrew & Meetens 1995; Sears 1988) are all terms used in making sense of the ways in which racism adapts itself to the changing contours of the societies we inhabit and research. As a social psychologist informed by Serge Moscovici's (1961/1976, 2000) theory of social representations, a central concern of mine in the study of racism is *how is racism understood in the everyday?* How is racism made sense of? Does its contested nature enter into "ordinary" experiences? Does new racism (Leach 2005) for example, have significance in our commonplace discussions about "race" and racism? Furthermore, as a social psychologist concerned with the impact of racism on the identities of children and teenagers, I examine how young people make sense of racism. How do they explain its operation and its consequences in their lives?

A more pressing issue, I suggest, is how racism is *problematized* in the everyday. How is it challenged by young people who experience it and witness it in the contexts of school, media, and community, for example?

In what ways can children and young people negotiate, navigate, and contest its significance and rupture its hold over the ways in which we make sense of ourselves and make sense of each other? Consider the quote in the title of this chapter (from a nine-year-old white British research participant): "It's not their fault that they have that colour skin, is it?" What does this question do? Does it ride on the dynamics of racism that fix difference on the skin of the Other and construct such difference as something "bad," something "at fault," or does it problematize society's racism and so reveal support for and allegiance to those targeted by racism? In many ways it does both, as the tag "is it?" questions the taken-for-grantedness of racist discourses and so could be said to disrupt, if momentarily, the hold of racism on social cognition and identity.

As Reicher notes, "it is one thing to provide a sophisticated under-standing of structural forms and cultural/ideological products. But how do these then translate into forms of behaviour that either reproduce or challenge existing social forms?" (2004, 941). In the field of racism, stud-ies and theories have attended principally to the social, psychological, and sometimes institutional *reproduction* of racism, and so have neglected the social, psychological, and institutional conditions of resistance in the face of racism (Hook and Howarth 2005). I suggest that we need to look for moments and spaces of resistance when and where racist discourses are held up, disrupted, and contested. To do otherwise would naturalize and objectify racism as an impermeable and predetermined aspect of our ongoing realities (Howarth 2006a).

If contemporary social psychology is to make a useful and original contribution to the analysis of racial categorization in the everyday, we need to explore the ways in which *representations of race* become prob-lematic, contested, and rejected in everyday sense making, talk, and action. This is not to imagine some idealized world where we can dismiss the grasp of racism over collective memories (Riggs and Augoustinos 2005), spatial arrangements (Durrheim and Dixon 2005), institutional-ized practices (Howarth 2004) or subjectivities (Hook and Howarth 2005)—a utopian and politically dangerous vision, as Ahmed (2004) warns us. As Gilroy points out, while racism "involves a mode of exploita-tion and domination that is not merely compatible with the phenomena of racialized differences but has amplified and projected them in order to remain intelligible, habitable, and productive" (2004, 33), it is imperative that we explore the ways in which the underlying logic of racism is also made *unintelligible, uninhabitable*, and *nonproductive*.

Mama's account of psychology and "race" points to the ways in which the discipline has marginalized the experiences and perspectives of those racialized and so-produced homogenizing and acritical accounts of racism. She calls for a comprehensive examination of the possibilities for personal change, agency, and transformation in the relationship between racism and identity. She explains that "racism can be seen as texturing subjectivity rather than determining black social and emotional life. Put another way, race is only ever one among many dimensions of subjectivity and it never constitutes the totality of an individual's internal life. Even where racial contradictions feature a great deal in people's history and experience, the fact they are responded to by personal change means that they are not an omnipresent force acting on passive victims" (1995, 111–12).

Social representations theory is a valuable tool for the study of racism precisely because it addresses the dialectic between representation and identity, and so focuses on possibilities for agency, resistance, social change, and transformation (Howarth 2006b). Social representations and social identities must be seen as two sides of the same coin. In positioning ourselves in relation to others—that is, in asserting, performing, or *doing* identity—we reveal our perspective on the world and our ways of seeing and constructing the world, or our social representations. And just as identities tie us to particular communities of others and simultaneously highlight what is individual and unique about us, representations carry traces of our collective histories and common practices while revealing the possibilities of resistance and agency. The relationship between social representations and social identities becomes more complex, more fraught, and sometimes more damaging in relationships and contexts that are racialized. Representations that *race* particular power relations, communities, bodies, practices, and ways of knowing impact social identities in ways that may damage identities, lower self-esteem, and limit the possibilities of agency, community, and humanity.

In this chapter, I discuss the relationship between representation, identity, power, and resistance in experiences of racism in a predominantly white primary school in southeast England. While it is recognized that identity and esteem can be damaged by racist representations, my research demonstrates how children and young people find innovative ways to problematize racism, disrupt its gaze, and so rupture its hold over their own identities. The psychological damage of racism is then an important but partial aspect of the complex connection between power, representation, and identity.

As the primary focus of my research, I examine how we may privilege, negotiate, and contest the racializing representations that inform, spoil, and remake our multiple identities. This shows how we are actively involved in challenging racism, reconstructing representations of differ-ence, and so redefining the possibilities of identity and community. The chapter concludes with a critical discussion of the possibilities for agency in challenging representations that *race*.

USING SOCIAL REPRESENTATIONS THEORY TO
INFORM THE RESEARCH DESIGN AND ANALYSIS

Social representations theory (Moscovici 2000) is primarily about the social, psychological, historical, and ideological dynamics of the produc-tion and reproduction of knowledge—particularly knowledge that relates to the social categorization, differentiation, and identification of social groups and communities. The theory locates knowledge systems not only in what we say and write, in text and talk, but also in what we, individu-ally and collectively, *do*—in terms of social practices, cultural traditions, and institutionalized norms (Howarth 2006c; Jovchelovitch 2001).

Social representations researchers, therefore, may examine the inter-play between different systems of representations (Wagner, Duveen, Verma, and Themel 2000), look at whose interests are at stake in pre-serving certain systems of knowledge (Jovchelovitch 1997), and reveal the possibilities for critique and contestation (Howarth 2004). Social repre-sentations enable people to know "who they are, how they understand both themselves and others, [and] where they locate themselves and oth-ers. . . . There is no possibility of identity without the work of represen-tation" (Jovchelovitch 1996, 125; Howarth 2002a). To my mind, these aspects of the theory make it extremely useful in the study of racism and anti-racist strategies. Verkuyen and Steenhuis have also commented on the value of the theory, particularly in the study of children's *active* and *collaborative* meaning making of social and cultural relations. For social representations researchers, "cognition is seen as embedded in historical, cultural and sociorelational contexts. Cognitions are not purely individ-ual constructions but are greatly influenced by the kinds of beliefs in the child's environment. The construction of meaning is seen as a social process, and meanings as social products. Common understandings are being created and recreated through interaction and communication between individuals and groups" (2005, 661).

What the theory offers the study of racism is an explicit focus on the social dynamics of "race," that is, the collaborative, social, and ideological construction and reconstruction, negotiation, and contestation of repre-sentations and practices that *race*. This is precisely what I examine in this research: children's social representations of racism and the possibilities of resisting racism in one particular, but very ordinary, context—a white majority primary school in southeast England.

These issues are relatively under-researched in schools—especially in primary schools (Connolly 2000). What appears missing from much educational research is an analysis of how pupils and teachers themselves make sense of, debate, and challenge discourses and practices at school (Sewell 1997). In addition, research often focuses on the ways in which racism is experienced in "obviously" multicultural and heavily racialized contexts—where "race" is literally seen on the bodies of nonwhite children and their communities (Gaine 1987). The issues explored tend to be the institutionalization of racism (see Cole 2004; Gillborn 1995), the disproportionate numbers of black pupils appearing in exclusion and discipline statistics (for example, see Blair 2001; Howarth 2004) and the failure of (white) teachers and schools to meet the needs of black and other ethnic minority pupils (see Majors 2001). In contrast, predominantly white contexts with predominantly white bodies are constructed and often researched in ways that make racializing discourses and practices less visible. I would argue that it is as important to study the operation of racism in "white" spaces precisely to make visible the racializing and racist discourses and practices of whiteness that those of us[1] invested in whiteness often seek to minimize (Riggs and Augoustinos 2005). However, as Ahmed (2004) points out, whiteness is generally only invisible to those not subjected to its essential racism. In the research presented here, young black and Asian children had no problem identifying the marginalizing and stigmatizing dynamics of whiteness and racism operating in their school. As social representations theory would predict, it is precisely these contexts where "race" and racism are less visible, less debated, and less controversial that racializing and racist representations are most hegemonic, "fossilized," and hence have their most power (Moscovici 1984).

A predominantly white school committed to developing anti-racist policies makes good sense as a research location not only in terms of ease of access, but also in terms of understanding the tenaciousness and vitality of racism in all contexts. For here—where teachers reject the existence of blatant forms of racism, where many children explain that racism "is not allowed," and where some parents assert that racism is "not an issue"—racism can be seen to operate in subtle and sometimes not-so-subtle but rather systematic forms in the children's friendship patterns and experiences of bullying and discipline procedures.

Pupils across all year groups (eight to twelve years old) were invited to participate in the research.[2] Two or three friendship pairs volunteered from each year group, with an approximately equal numbers of girls and boys (see Table 8.1). Although white British children made up 97 percent of the school population, the selection of children ensured that the sample was equally representative of white children and nonwhite children: That is, there were eleven white British children (eight English and three Irish or Scottish), six Southeast Asian students (describing themselves as Bangladeshi, British-Pakistani, Pakistani, Indian, British-Muslim, and Muslim), and five children with mixed heritage from other countries such as Colombia, Italy, Lebanon, Portugal, Spain, Trinidad, as well as the British Roma community. While this is a diverse sample, it is important to remember that, as the school is predominantly white, the nonwhite children stand out as such in their class.

Social representations theory highlights the dynamic and reactive nature of representation that develops, supports, or challenges different positions and associations in different contexts. Hence it demands an approach to methods that foreground dialogue, debate, and agency. Furthermore, given the age of the children in the study (eight to twelve years), and given the topic of racism—which many children find abstract, difficult to discuss, upsetting, provoking, or guilt-inducing (Eslea and Mukhtar 2000)—the nondirective research methods of vignettes, storytelling, and drawing were chosen to elicit stories from the children that reflect their experiences and emotions. In order to explore how "race" and racism are made sense of, I sought to position children as "active participants in the situational and interactive construction of distinctions and understandings" (Verkuyen and Steenhuis 2005, 677) relating to "race" and racism.

To promote argumentation and critique in discussions, children were placed in friendship pairs in order to invite discussion and debate of the same experiences from multiple perspectives (see David, Edwards, and Alldred et al. 2001; Morrow 1999). Claire (2001) finds that children are more reserved both on their own and in focus groups, and that the presence of friends as "trustworthy others" is more likely to "permit disclosures of confidential material" (9) and differences of opinion. I sought to encourage these differences so as to highlight the connections between identity and representation and, hence, the role of agency and subjectivity in the collaborative production of knowledge while enabling the children to accept differences of opinion and contradictions.

In order to position the children as "knowers and actors, as opposed to objects of the research" (Pole, Mizen, and Bolton 1999, 46), I encouraged them to tell their own stories of experiencing, witnessing, or enacting racism by relating to them stories about racist bullying constructed from

Table 8.1   Participant details

Friendship pairs[3]	Ethnicity (as defined by school)[4]	Ethnicity (as defined by participant)	Age	Sex	Year
Thomas	White Asian (has Indian heritage)	White	8	M	4
Richard	White British	British	8	M	4
Catherine	White British	English	8	F	4
Laura	White British	British	8	F	4
Chelsea	Other	Portuguese, Lebanese, and English	10	F	5
Sophie	White British	Italian-English	10	F	5
Garth (Preferred to be interviewed alone)	Roma	Gypsy	10	M	5
Matthew	White British	British	9	M	5
John	White British	British	9	M	5
Lizzie	White British	Irish and English	10	F	6
Amina	White British	British	11	F	6
John 2 (Preferred to be interviewed alone)	Pakistani	Muslim	10	M	6
Jessica	Bangladeshi	British-Bangladeshi	10	F	6
Cathleen	Bangladeshi	British-Bangladeshi	10	F	6
Tonia	Pakistani	British-Muslim or British-Pakistani	12	F	7
Kelley	White British	British	11	F	7
Sharon	White British	Irish and Scottish	11	F	7
Jane Frank	White British	Scottish and English	11	F	7
Frank	Other	Spanish and Trinidadian	11	M	7
Bob	White British	English	11	M	7
Tak	Other	Colombian and English	11	M	7
Mark	Bangladeshi	Bangladeshi	11	M	7

previous pilot research at the school[5] (see Box 8.1). Drawing worked particularly well in this regard and, with storytelling, gave the students a tangible means of anchoring and objectifying an abstract concept such as racism.[6]

Box 8.1

Story to read to pairs:
>Faranaz was not very happy at school. There were some others in her class who were always picking on her. They made fun of her name and her accent. One lunchtime they started calling her nasty names. Sarah, who was her best friend, stood up for her and told the other girls to go away. This made Faranaz like Sarah even more as she thought this was very brave.

Questions to ask about story (prompts, not necessarily in this order):
>Why did the other children pick on Fanaraz?
>What kind of names do you think they used?
>How would you feel if you were Faranaz? What would you do?
>How would you feel if you were Sarah? What would you do?
>How would you feel if you had picked on Faranaz? What would you do?

Questions to ask to elicit stories and drawings:
>Have you ever seen anything like this at school?
>Has anyone ever been mean to you like this? How did it make you feel?
>Have you ever been mean like this to other children? How did it make you feel?

Elicit story and drawing

Storytelling or vignettes can uncover both the *social* and *individual* aspects of representations as they elicit the social or "cultural norms about a specific situation" (Barter and Renold 2000, 310) as well as "individuals' perceptions, beliefs and attitudes to a wide range of social issues" (Hughes 1998, 384). Narratives allow for the organization and sense making of experiences, particularly those experiences that are difficult, through the objectification of abstract concepts that facilitates new connections and counterarguments. Narrative not only enables dialogic sense making and communication, but it also promotes different ways of connecting with each other, and thus common identity and a sense of community. As Claire (2001) states, narrative is "at the heart of the construction of identity. The stories we tell are 'who we are.' They hold the meanings of our experiences, the judgments we make" (11).

The stories and drawings placed children at the center of the research process by seeking to reconstruct their experiences, capturing both their voices and representations and foregrounding their own subjective meanings (Young and Barrett 2001). It enabled children to represent and communicate their experiences freely, and created an informal dynamic between the children and myself that I hoped would foster trust and thus the disclosure of sensitive material, giving the children control over what to say and when to divulge personal experiences (Barker and Weller 2003).

A critical social psychological study of racism needs to explore the possibilities for *problematizing* racism (Howarth and Hook 2005). Arguably, children could be inclined to do this within the dynamics created by a formal research encounter where there is an acceptance of the school rules on racism, as well as established social conventions and the presence of a (white) adult.[7] Hence the context was constructed to elicit anti-racist views and a rejection of discriminatory behavior. The strategies the children used in their resistance against racism are explored in the remainder of this chapter.

Contesting Racial Categories: Disrupting Racism?

The analysis reveals three dominant ways of representing "race": "race" as real, "race" as imposed, and "race" as contested. While there are some significant age- and gender-related differences, as developmental psychologists would predict (Aboud and Amato 2001; Fishbein 2002), all children used all three representations to different degrees in positioning themselves in the racialized relations of inclusion and friendship at school. "Race" was most often constructed as "real"—as visually obvious in the way the Other is seen (marked by black and brown skin), and so difference is made tangible, essential, and nonnegotiable.

In the short story, there is no reference to either Faranaz's or Sarah's visual appearance. However, for most children who drew a picture from this story, one difference was very clear: skin color (though there was one exception that will be discussed below). Take this picture from Jane (Scottish-English, aged eleven):

Figure 8.1

The dialectic of sameness-difference is clear here, as Jane has depicted the girls as very similar in stature, hairstyle, and clothes with the only—albeit very obvious—difference being skin color. Difference, as the children described, is visually evident and so naturalized and unproblematic. At the same time, children *did* problematize this version of "race" and reveal how racialized difference is something constructed and imposed on them through associations to foreignness, danger, and contagion. Sophie (Italian-English, aged ten), explained the following:

> *Caroline* [interviewer]: So is there racism in this school?
> *Sophie*: Yeah—lots. Lots yeah. The English people, yeah—like "look at you—smelly," or "you are really ugly." And when they touch someone they will "oooh! I touched her! I need to wash my hands!" And all that stuff. It's like no one wants to sit next to them or anything. Also—like they don't want to get into trouble.

Here "race" is imposed through a racist gaze that constructs blackness or brownness as different, as ugly, as dirty, and as trouble. Children gave various stories that illustrated the operation and power of this representation in their experiences at school, in sports, and in the community in general. Here, in this picture by Mark (Bangladeshi, aged eleven), he shows us how he has experienced racist abuse at a birthday party barbecue as a child shouts, "You black!" and an adult demands he "get out of here":

Figure 8.2

Hence there are two competing representations of "race": it is either something that is understood as "real"—in that it can be seen, touched, and even caught from the Other—or it is something that is constructed, imposed, and deeply hurtful. Both these representations are discussed in detail elsewhere (Howarth 2009). Here, I describe the ways in which the children problematized and rejected the significance and power of racism. In these accounts that contest "race," we see these two representations at play.[8]

Very evident in all of the children's accounts was the claim that racism affected relationships and interactions at school. Take this discussion between Mark (Bangladeshi, aged eleven), and Tak (English-Colombian, aged eleven). After we discussed what they like about the school, I asked,

> *Caroline*: So what don't you like about this school?
> *Mark*: The bullying—people calling us nasty names—like "coloured" or "Paki." People pick on us because of this [*he touches his arm, indicating that his skin is brown*]. That makes me feel bad.
> *Caroline*: How do you feel Tak?
> *Tak*: I just want to be like everyone else. I want to be white, I wish I could rub this off—
> *Mark*: If I was white, people wouldn't pick on me and I wouldn't get into trouble. If I was white, people wouldn't notice me.
> *Tak*: And the teachers should do something about it.
> *Caroline*: What do the teachers do about it?
> *Tak*: They treat it like anything else—like calling someone fat, or four-eyes. Look, people call me fat, people call me Paki. It is not the same thing.
> *Caroline*: Ok. Why not?
> *Tak*: Fat is just me, it's here (he touches his stomach), fat is my body. My body doesn't feel these things. If they call me Paki—it's all of me—and my family too. It's everything—my mum, my home, I don't know how to explain. It hurts. It hurts me a lot more.

Shocking as this is, there were many accounts similar to this, pointing to the tangible and damaging reality of racism in these children's lives. Not only does racism limit friendship patterns at school, but it also impacts children's sense of belonging, identity, and esteem. Racism was presented as an almost mundane feature of everyday encounters that penetrates how people see one another and themselves. Despite this salience, children found many ways to problematize racism and its operation at school. Their collaborated strategies included the following:

- contest the ideological construction of difference
- highlight the "stupidity" of racists and the contradictions of racism

- develop protective and inclusive friendship networks and claims to commonality
- expose the invisibility of whiteness and reject white identities
- produce the self as an agent not object in racialized networks of power

The ideological construction of difference was contested by challenging the significance of racism, describing how it is superficial and "only on the outside" (Mark, Bangladeshi, aged eleven). In rejecting racialized difference, children proposed "alternative narratives" (McKown 2004, 610) that asserted connection and commonality with their peers, saying, "I am *not* different. I am like everyone else" (Frank, Spanish-Trinidadian, aged eleven) and "We are all the same really" (Amina, white British, aged eleven). This shows how children are actively involved in challenging racism, reconstructing representations of difference, and so redefining the possibilities of identity and community.

Many of the children developed an individualistic account of racism in which racism exists "because some people are really, really, really, really, really stupid!" (Tonia, British-Pakistani, aged twelve). Like "race" itself, racism is seen as somehow inscribed in the body or the mind of the racist, and it is so illogical that it is only people who are "'dumb" who could be seduced by the contradictions of racism.[9] Take this exchange between Matthew and John (both white British, aged nine) and myself (Caroline):

Matthew: Some people are racist, not all.
Caroline: So why do you think that some people are racist?
John: Because they don't like the other type.
Matthew: I think they are stupid. And ignorant.
Caroline: And ignorant?
Matthew: They are like ill—and they may they have a special something inside their body probably—and that makes them do that, or they are probably drunk or something like that.

Matthew appears to be more reflective and critical of racism than John (this may be due to the fact that he himself has experienced a lot of name-calling over his "ginger" hair). While racialized differences are constructed as real by John—evoking a systematic classification of human "types"—Matthew constructs the racist as someone who cannot make sense of things logically. Other children in the study, mostly children who had experienced racism themselves, characterized racists as "mad" and "stupid," by saying, for example, that they should be in a "mental asylum" (Mark, Bangladeshi, aged eleven). There is a trace of this in Catherine's (white British, aged eight) picture: she explained that the bullies "look

Figure 8.3

stupid" (see Figure 8.3). When I asked why they were dressed differently from Faranaz and Sarah, she answered,

> *Catherine*: They look stupid! They won't wear the school uniform. They are stupid and do not go to school.

Similarly John 2 (Muslim, aged ten) explains,

> *John 2*: You just think—how many lessons have you had before telling you that racism is wrong, racism is wrong, but they don't understand it. Six- and seven-year-olds can understand it, but some adults can't understand it. Adults can say things about skin color, or "you come from another country," how they look like and all that. I don't know why. It's stupid! It does not make sense.

With much passion and anger, the children highlighted the contradictions of racism, often pointing to the fact that otherness, difference, and visible blackness or brownness are simultaneously feared and desired (as theorists such as Fanon, du Bois and Hall have long recognized). For instance, they pointed to the fact that black and brown skin signals difference, and yet many white people do not like being "all white and pale" (Frank, Spanish-Trinidadian, aged eleven). Similarly, when discussing the impact of racism, Tonia (British-Pakistani, aged twelve) says,

> *Tonia*: I just think—there is one thing that REALLY gets me about it—is all people who are white—they love going into the sun and getting a tan to make themselves brown. And then they want to make fun of black people, and they are brown! It's stupid!

Not only did the children point to the fact that brown and black skin is desired but they also recognized that otherness itself can be a quality envied by white people. Thomas (who describes himself as white and "looks" white while having some Indian heritage, aged eight), in discussion with Richard (white British, aged eight) and myself, for example, asserts that people are jealous of the attention that difference attracts as follows:

> *Caroline*: Okay, Richard, why do you think that the other children picked on Faranaz?
> *Richard*: Cos she is a different color because that sounded like an Indian name and her accent—and being different really.
> *Caroline*: So if someone speaks differently—why do other children pick on them?
> *Richard*: Cos they are different.
> *Caroline*: But why pick on them?
> *Thomas*: Maybe because they are jealous! Because they get all the attention because they are different.

Highlighting the contradictions of racism can be seen as a way of contesting representations and practices that *race*. Some children, such as Tonia (British-Pakistani, aged twelve), gave many examples of these; for instance, she described how white audiences admire black celebrities in film, music, and sport, such as Ashley Cole and Will Smith, but "don't like anyone on the street who is black." Many of the boys commented on the operation of racism in football and said that it was "unfair" (Frank, Spanish-Trinidadian, aged eleven). Here is a picture from Bob (English, aged eleven) depicting a miserable looking black footballer play in front of a sea of white faces (and a McDonalds "I'm loving it'" advertisement).

For other children, an understanding of the constructed nature of "race" and the inherent tensions and inconsistencies in racist discourses is less obvious and comes out in discussion only after explicit challenges either from myself or the other participant. Take this discussion with Amina (white British, aged eleven) and Lizzie (Irish-English, aged ten). From an early stage in the interview, they asserted that some children are "picked on" by racists simply because "they are different" and have different cultural practices, in relation to dress and food, for example, as follows:

Figure 8.4

> *Amina*: Well loads of people picking on someone because they were dif-
> ferent or their skin color is different. Or they can't wear the certain
> clothes that you are meant to.
> *Lizzie*: Yeah, some people pick on them because they are not wearing the
> clothes that they should wear. You look at them and judge them, and
> just hate them because of that and don't get to know them.

Difference is quite obvious for them at this point: it is visually apparent and defined by (dominant white) social conventions. Racism appears
as "the fault" of the Other as other cultures are seen to maintain different
social and cultural practices. The interview continues with much discussion on racism and bullying at school when I pressed both girls to take the
perspective of the other (Mead 1972) and imagine how it is to be seen as
different and so "hated." They told me stories and drew pictures of their
own experiences: Lizzie experienced prejudice related to her Irish heritage
and Amina had a friend with a "funny accent" who was bullied. At the
end of the interview, about an hour later, I ask them if there was anything
they would like to add.

> *Caroline*: Okay, is there anything else you would like to say about this?
> *Amina*: Bullies do it because they have a great sense of power. They like
> their own power and control—and they are afraid of other people—
> especially other people who are different.

Caroline: So, different? How are they different?

Amina: They are different—because [pause], well they are. [pause] They look different, they wear different clothes, they EAT different food. They are different. But it doesn't matter. We are all the same really.

Lizzie: Those are just small things, it doesn't matter what you eat. Anyway, I like their food. Everyone likes curry, and that's different. And pizza, that's not English, but we like that. That's Italian.

The dichotomy "us" and "them" ("their food"; "we like that") is still apparent. However, difference is beginning to appear more complex and less transparent. Difference may be inferred in different foods, though we "all" enjoy these—so we may all be involved in the practices of claiming difference and claiming commonality. What we begin to see, albeit fleetingly, is that there is a clear dominant social representation of difference (where some people simply "are" different) that does not fit completely with their own experiences and subjective understandings—as the representation "doesn't matter" and "I like their food."

Representations of difference and commonality are also apparent in the children's friendship networks and claims to inclusion and belonging. Some more straightforward examples of children protecting themselves against racism were "sticking together" and "sticking up" for one another. Cathleen and Jessica (both British-Bangladeshi, both aged ten gave examples of this. On every visit to the school over a period of four months, I observed that these girls were only ever in each other's company. After discussing the short story, Jessica said that Faranaz and Sarah are "best friends," just like she and Cathleen. I asked,

Caroline: Okay—so you two are best friends?

Cathleen: Yes—and we always stick up for each other. We don't need anyone else to stick up for us.

Caroline: So what do you do?

Jessica: We just make each other feel better.

Caroline: And do you say anything to the other children?

Cathleen: No—because that will make it more worse.

Caroline: So have you ever seen anything like that happen? [pointing to the text of the story I have read them]

Jessica: Yes—but not now, not recently. But there was this time when Melissa pulled my hair down to the ground and was horrible to me. She called me a "blackie."

Caroline: And what happened?

Jessica: She told a lot of lies and I told the truth. But we both got bad bookings—and I did nothing at all. It was her fault and what she said was bad. And Cathleen made me feel better.

The picture that Cathleen and Jessica drew together (as they did not want to draw separate pictures, a fact quite revealing in itself) also emphasizes commonality and similarity. Unlike all the other pictures of Sarah and Faranaz, here they are almost identical:

Figure 8.5

Difference, so apparent to the other children, is not visible here. An implication is that, for them, difference does not matter, or perhaps *should* not matter. While Jessica and Cathleen found it easy to relate to each other and care for each other through their shared experiences of racism, it was apparent that many white children in the school also challenged systems of exclusion and difference through their friendship with nonwhite children. White children who were racialized through white minority ethnicities (such as Greek or Irish) or through their friendships with black and Asian children also found ways to connect with those racialized and to reject racism. Take this quote from Catherine (white British, aged eight) who has witnessed this herself:

> *Catherine*: Like there is this boy in our class—people always say to him— "errrr I don't want to touch you"—and he is a bit dark.
> *Caroline*: So people are horrible to him?
> *Catherine*: No—not everyone—there is another boy—Patrick he is always playing with him and he is not dark. Other people will pick on him but Patrick plays with him. Patrick is Irish and is picked on a lot because of the way he talks.

Children who have experience with racism and other forms of prejudice (being Irish, having "ginger" hair, being fat) recognize a common bond and develop friendships through these shared experiences. Mark (Bangladeshi, aged eleven) and Tak (English-Colombian, aged eleven), whom we met earlier in this chapter, were close friends and described many experiences of "sticking up" for each other. They discussed how they collaborated in ways of inverting racist discourses and using these against the racializing Other. They said, for instance,

> *Caroline*: So have you been horrible like that, or racist ever?
> *Tak*: Yeah—if someone was to say "oh you black, you have been left in the oven for too long," we go—"oh you are so white cos you are um, made up with white chocolate." But I have only said that about four times or something.
> *Mark*: We will stick up for each other.

There were various references to chocolate in the study. Kelley (white British, aged eleven), for example, observes that some of her friends "get called things like 'you chocolate face,'" and in Matthew's (white British, aged nine) picture, a very sad looking child is being called "chocolate head":

Figure 8.6

As we have seen, there were also examples of calling white people "white chocolate." This is interesting as it does not necessarily work to simply reject a racialized connotation. It could be seen to demonstrate the fixity of the racist gaze and the impossibility of stepping outside of its frameworks (Ahmed 2004). It could also be seen as a way of proposing connection, a commonality—for the racialized Other is often depicted as "chocolate colored"—and so if the white Other is seen as "white choco-late" rather than asserting difference, this affirms an essential sameness. As Richard (white British, aged eight) emphasizes, "underneath, we are all the same." So Tak (English-Colombian, aged 11) may in fact be asserting a connection to the white children who call him "chocolate head," and so very subtly disrupting a racist dichotomy. There is not a clear answer to what these pieces of talk "do" in any definite sense in terms of maintain-ing or rejecting racist representations. What is important is that they throw up these questions and contradictions, and so work in ways that unsettle and destabilize racializing and racist associations and stereotypes. They may offer new possibilities in terms of asserting identity, connec-tion, and humanity—and propose new ways of being seen.

Evident in the children's remarks on "white chocolate" is an attempt to subvert the racializing discourses that make whiteness invisible for many. While few children in the study in fact used the label "white," children who had experienced racism and their white friends found ways of bringing whiteness into focus. Here, for example, Kelley (white British, aged eleven, close friends with Tonia, British-Pakistani, aged twelve) comments,

> *Kelley*: Because Sharon is white, and Tonia does not make fun that she is white or anything—so Sharon should not make fun that Tonia is a dif-ferent color to her.

It is significant that white children such as Kelley in the study asserted connections with children seen as Other as a way of rejecting racism—and also minimizing the possibility that they could be positioned as racist themselves. Some children who appeared to have close friendships with racialized children tried to minimize or remove their associations with whiteness and implicitly assert their connections with other cultures and places. Catherine (white British, aged eight), for example, said that she preferred holidays in Africa to holidays in England. Lizzie (Irish-English, aged ten), as we saw earlier in this chapter, told me that she liked "differ-ent" foods such as pizza and curry. Some children criticized white skin, saying that "it makes your teeth look all yellow" (Chelsea, Portuguese-Lebanese-English, aged ten) and "it's too pale" (Frank, Spanish-Trinidadian, aged 11). Another critique of whiteness was to highlight white histories of oppression and violence, saying, for example, that "the white people always treat the black people like slaves" (Chelsea, Portuguese-Lebanese-English, aged ten).

Whiteness was uncomfortable for some of the children—it was some-thing that had to be negotiated and possibly rejected. For Kelley to claim whiteness would be to claim a difference that would maintain the representations of exclusion and othering that she rejects. Hence her only option is to reject whiteness altogether as follows:

> *Tonia*: I really like being brown. I like my skin—it is like an everyday tan. Spring, summer, autumn, winter—I will be brown. Even if I went to Antarctica I would still have a tan! White people just go red! I would not like to be red. I like being brown.
> *Kelley*: I wish I was brown.

Just as Kelley rejects her own position in a racializing binary, Tonia challenges the unspoken assumption that white skin is "better." In doing so, she highlights the operation of racializing representations, rejects the privilege of whiteness, and claims a proud identity as brown. This could work to unsettle the ideology of racism that positions her as victim of racializing ways of constructing social relations, so Tonia reproduces herself as *agent* not *object* of racialized networks of power. Rather than being objectified as a racial other, she takes delight in criticizing white skin and positioning herself as essentially, permanently, and *happily* brown. Unlike Tak and Mark, she states that she really likes being brown and does not wish to be white, and she does not want to avoid the racializing gaze and remove her otherness; rather, she confidently asserts it and so challenges dominant representations that *race*. Opportunities like this may be limited, but they provide important occasions for us to position and reposition ourselves as agents of representations "about us" and so demand that we are recognized as we see ourselves.

THE POSSIBILITIES FOR AGENCY

A psychological reality of "race" is that the racialized Other becomes an object to him- or herself (Howarth 2006c). As Du Bois (1989) explains, the racialized other develops a double consciousness—a consciousness imposed by racializing representations and a consciousness of self that extends beyond and challenges these stereotypes. The racialized Other can be so fixed by the representations of the racializing Other, and therefore the symbolic violence of these representations is that they constrain the dialectics of self, impose limiting versions of self, and so deny humanity, agency, and liberty.

"Race" is made an object as the racialized Other is fixed and dehumanised (Hall 2000). As "shared representations penetrate so profoundly into all the interstices of what we call reality that we can say that they constitute it" (Moscovici 1998, 245), representations produce "extremely concrete and real consequences" (Jovchelovitch 2001, 177). Thus representations of "race" are real in that they constitute a reality for these children: they cannot simply opt out of categories, discourses, and representations that race. As Fanon's own experiences of the racist gaze demonstrate so powerfully, these children also spoke of the imposition of difference.

To conclude here on the depressing note of the impossibility of moving beyond racist discourses and of the psychological violence racism inflicts on all of us would do no service or justice to the stories told here. These stories, spoken by very young children, speak to another world, another possibility and demand that we as social researchers provide a functionally useful account of agency, resistance, and transformation in the face of racialized difference. Social representations theory, as a *radical* social psychological perspective, is useful here, for it allows us to consider how racializing representations are not only anchored in histories of white privilege, oppression, and violence but it also allows us to explore "those social processes through which novelty and innovation become as much a part of social life as conservation and preservation" (Duveen 2000, 7). What is valuable here is the emphasis on re-presentation as an active, collaborative social and psychological project—something *we do* in partnership with or in reaction against others (Howarth 2006b).

Seeing re-presentation as a collaborative project highlights our agency as the represented Other and reveals our collective roles in the production and contestation of difference, its significance and its social, psychological, and ideological consequences (Moloney and Walker 2002). These are the issues that social representations theory brings forward, and they are the ones that I have focused on in discussing the children's understanding of racism. This invites discussion as to what a critical social psychology of racism might look like, foregrounding questions of recognition, relationship, contestation, agency and, fundamentally, hope.

The stories given here show that while children feel the inescapability of the racializing gaze, they also find ways to resist this, and so to detach themselves from the images imposed on them. In doing so, they produce counterimages, propose connections with the Other, and so produce their identities again—as *agent* not *object* in the resistance of racism. Their accounts show how they attempt to problematize racism, disrupt its gaze, and so rupture its hold over their own identities.

While it is true that representations can constrain and limit the possibilities of agency and connection, this is only part of the story. It is true that children in my research spoke of wanting to be recognized and wanting to belong in a way that racializing relations of power do not often allow, but they also spoke of anger, resistance, and strategies to undermine the technologies of racism. What is important is that they threw up questions and contradictions, and so worked in ways that unsettle and destabilize racializing and racist representations. Their strategies of resistance, collectively negotiated and performed, offer new possibilities in terms of asserting identity, connection, and humanity—and so propose new ways of being seen.

As Moscovici has stated, "individuals and groups, far from being passive receptors, think for themselves, produce and ceaselessly communicate their own specific representations and solutions to the questions they set themselves . . . which have a decisive impact on their social relations, their choices" (1984, 16). We saw this clearly in this study, as the children took up and worked out their own ways of making sense of the institutionalized dynamics of racial categorization and racism. In other words, we saw how they negotiate social representations of racialized difference and come to position themselves within racialized networks of power and influence at school. This demonstrates how social representations inform the collaborative processes of identification, the "othering" of particular groups, the objectification of racialized others, and, most crucially, the problematization and rejection of representations and practices that *race*.

ACKNOWLEDGMENTS

I would like to thank Derek Hook, Chris Sonn, Anna Rastas, and Gail Moloney for their very helpful feedback on earlier drafts of this chapter. I would also like to thank Ama de-Graft Aikens for her advice on the methodology used here. I am indebted to the staff and children at the school where this research was carried out for giving their time and stories so generously. Special thanks to Elizabeth and Sarah.

NOTES

1. It is essential to challenge an "us" and "them" racialized dichotomy in which "we" speak from a positioned of white institutionalized authority about "them," our nonwhite Other "subjects" of research. However, it is also important to expose my own positioning and privilege within such institutionalized and racialized relations as a white female academic. Being white (and female, mid-thirties with an Antipodean accent—a product of British parents and my early childhood years spent in Kenya, Fiji, Australia, and Papua New Guinea—living in the local area) no doubt informed the ways in which research participants saw and positioned me and so had an impact on how they spoke about racism in the study. For a longer discussion on the impact of researcher identity in research on racism, see Back and Solomos (1993) and also Howarth (2002b).
2. As is particularly important in research with young children (David, Edwards, and Alldred 2001; Hurley and Underwood 2002), I sought their informed

consent by stressing the fact that they did not have to participate and could leave the research encounter at any point. If they appeared distracted, unsettled, or uncomfortable, I reminded them that they could leave. No child took this option, though one interview was significantly shorter than the others (20 minutes as opposed to between 55 and 125 minutes) as, I suspect, one of the participants was uncomfortable disclosing his experiences of racism.

3. Pupils volunteered to be part of the research. They were asked to volunteer in pairs—though two boys asked to be interviewed alone, which I agreed to. Pupils all choose a pseudonym.

4. I have made two slight changes to protect the children's identity. For example, I could have changed French to German if there was only one French child in the school.

5. The pilot research consisted of a series of observations across all year groups, including break times, playground activities, and informal discussions with staff and pupils over a period of three months. The purpose of this was to familiarize myself with the school, its ethos, and the pupils.

6. All sessions were conducted in English, tape recorded, and transcribed by the author.

7. Furthermore, my deliberate decision to problematize any comments made by children that could have been read as racist would have made it even more difficult for this kind of remark to be made. Following Connolly (2000), I would signal disagreement and disapproval, attempt to reveal contradictions in their argument, and expose their own points of connection and identification with racialized others. This was to highlight the argumentative nature of their and my talk, as well as to limit the possibility that the research encounter could be a space where racist comments were accepted unproblematically (in the name of conducting so-called "objective" research).

8. In the following quotes, the children's names are pseudonyms that they chose themselves. The ethnicity given is how they defined themselves (which was sometimes different from school definitions; see Table 8.1).

9. Archer and Francis (2005) also find that children explain racism as a product of cognitive immaturity—something that "a few silly people are" (400). This echoes certain intellectualized versions of racism in which racism is represented as the property of certain individuals (Leach 2002). We must accept that scientific accounts of racism filter into and shape commonsense notions of racism (McKown 2004). Hence it is important to challenge academic accounts that individualize racism and so divert attention away from its institutional, historical, and cultural constitution. For a fuller discussion of the consequences of such, see Howarth (2006b).

REFERENCES

Aboud, F., and M. Amato. 2001. Developmental and socialization influences on intergroup bias. In *Blackwell handbook of social psychology: Intergroup processes*, ed. R. Brown and S. Gaertner, 65–85. Oxford: Blackwell.

Ahmed, S. 2004. Declarations of whiteness: The non-performativity of anti-racism. *Borderlands* 3 (2). http://www.borderlandsejournal.adelaide.edu.au.

Archer, L., and B. Francis. 2005. Constructions of racism by British Chinese pupils and parents. *Race, Ethnicity and Education* 8:387–407.

Back, L., and J. Solomos. 1993. Doing research, writing politics: The dilemmas of political intervention in research on racism. *Economy and Society* 1:178–97.

———. 1996. *Racism and society.* London: Macmillan.

Barker, J., and S. Weller. 2003. Never work with children?: The geography of methodological issues in research with children. *Qualitative Research* 3:207–27.

Barter, C., and E. Renold. 2000. "I wanna tell you a story": Exploring the application of vignettes in qualitative research with children and young people. *International Journal of Social Research Methodology* 3:307–23.

Blair, M. 2001. *Why pick on me? School exclusion and black youth.* Stoke-on-Trent, England: Trentham Books.

Brah, A. 1996. *Cartographies of diaspora: Contesting identities.* London: Routledge.

Claire, H. 2001. *Not aliens: Primary school children and the citizenship/PSHE curriculum.* Stoke-on-Trent, England: Trentham Books.

Cole, M. 2004. "Brutal and stinking" and "difficult to handle": The historical and contemporary manifestations of racialisation, institutional racism and schooling in Britain. *Race, Ethnicity and Education* 7:35–56.

Condor, S. 1998. Race stereotypes and racist discourse. *Text* 8:69–91.

Connolly, P. 2000. Racism and young girls' peer-group relations: The experiences of South Asian girls. *Sociology* 34:499–519.

David, M., R. Edwards, and P. Alldred. 2001. Children and school-based research: "Informed consent" or "educated consent." *British Educational Research Journal* 27:347–65.

Du Bois, W. E. B. 1989. *The souls of black folk.* New York: Bantam.

Durrheim, K., and J. Dixon. 2004. Attitudes in the fiber of everyday life: The discourse of racial evaluation and the lived experience of desegregation. *American Psychologist* 59:626–36.

———. 2005. Studying talk and embodied practices: Toward a psychology of materiality of "race relations." *Journal of Community and Applied Social Psychology* 15:446–60.

Duveen, G. 2000. Introduction: The power of ideas. In *Social representations: Explorations in social psychology,* ed. S. Moscovici, 1–17. Cambridge: Polity.

Eslea, M., and K. Mukhtar. 2000. Bullying and racism among Asian schoolchildren in Britain. *Educational Research* 42:207–17.

Fishbein, H. D. 2002. *Peer prejudice and discrimination.* Boulder, CO: Westview.

Gaine, C. 1987. *No problem here: A practical approach to education and race in white schools.* London: Hutchinson.

Gillborn, D. 1995. *Racism and anti-racism in real schools.* Buckingham, England: Open University Press.

Gilroy, P. 2004. *After empire: melancholia or convivial culture?* London: Routledge.

Hall, S. 2000. The spectacle of the "other." In *Representation: Cultural representation and signifying practices*, ed. S. Hall, 223–90. London: Sage.

Hook, D., and C. Howarth. 2005. Future directions for a critical social psychology of racism/antiracism. *Journal of Community and Applied Social Psychology* 15:506–12.

Howarth, C. 2002a. Identity in whose eyes? The role of representations in identity construction. *Journal for the Theory of Social Behaviour* 32:145–62.

———. 2002b. Using the theory of social representations to explore difference in the research relationship. *Qualitative Research* 2:21–34.

———. 2004. Re-presentation and resistance in the context of school exclusion: Reasons to be critical. *Journal of Community and Applied Social Psychology* 14:356–77.

———. 2006a. How social representations of attitudes have informed attitude theories: The consensual and the reified. *Theory and Psychology* 16:691–714.

———. 2006b. Race as stigma: Positioning the stigmatised as agents, not objects. *Journal of Community and Applied Social Psychology* 16:442–51.

———. 2006c. A social representation is not a quiet thing: Exploring the critical potential of social representations theory. *British Journal of Social Psychology* 45:65–86.

———. 2009. "I hope we won't have to understand racism one day": Researching or reproducing "race" in social psychological research? *British Journal of Social Psychology* 48(3): 407–26.

Howarth, C., and D. Hook. 2005. Towards a critical social psychology of racism: Points of disruption. *Journal of Community and Applied Social Psychology* 15:425–31.

Hughes, R. 1998. Considering the vignette technique and its application to a study of drug injecting and HIV risk and safer behaviour. *Sociology of Health and Illness* 20:381–400.

Hurley, J., and M. Underwood. 2002. Children's understanding of their research rights before and after debriefing: Informed assent, confidentiality and stopping participation. *Child Development* 73:132–43.

Jovchelovitch, S. 1996. In defence of representations. *Journal for the Theory of Social Behaviour* 26:121–35.

———. 1997. Peripheral communities and the transformation of social representations: Queries on power and recognition. *Social Psychological Review* 1:16–26.

———. 2001. Social representations, public life and construction. In *Social representations: Introductions and explorations*, ed. K. Deaux and G. Philogène, 165–82. Oxford: Blackwell.

Leach, C. 2002. The social psychology of racism reconsidered. *Feminism & Psychology* 12:439–44.

———. 2005. Against the notion of a new racism. *Journal of Community and Applied Social Psychology* 15:432–45.

Majors, R. 2001. *Educating our black children: New directions and radical approaches*. London: Routledge.

Mama, A. 1995. *Beyond the masks: Race, gender and subjectivity.* London: Routledge.

McKown, C. 2004. Age and ethnic variation in children's thinking about the nature of racism. *Journal of Applied Developmental Psychology* 52:597–617.

Mead, G. H. 1972. *On social psychology: Selected papers.* Ed. A. Strauss. Rev. ed. Chicago: University of Chicago Press.

Moloney, G., and I. Walker. 2002. Talking about transplants: Social representations and the dialectical, dilemmatic nature of organ donation and transplantation. *British Journal of Social Psychology* 41:299–320.

Morrow, V. 1999. If you were a teacher, it would be harder to talk to you: Reflections on qualitative research with children in school. *International Journal of Social Research Methodology: Theory and Practice* 1:297–314.

Moscovici, S. 1961/1976. *La psychanalyse, son image et son public.* 2e éd. entièrement refondue. Paris: Presses Universitaires de France.

———. 1984. The phenomenon of social representations. In *Social representations,* ed. R. M. Farr and S. Moscovici, 1–84. Cambridge: Cambridge University Press.

———. 1998. The history and actuality of social representations. In *The psychology of the social,* ed. U. Flick, 209–47. Cambridge: Cambridge University Press.

———. 2000. *Social representations.* Cambridge: Polity.

Omi, M., and H. Winant. 1986. *Racial formation in the United States: From the 1960s to the 1980s.* New York: Routledge and Kegan Paul.

Pettigrew, T. F., and R. Meetens. 1995. Subtle and blatant prejudice in Western Europe. *European Journal of Social Psychology* 10:57–75.

Pole, C., P. Mizen, and A. Bolton. 1999. Realising children's agency in research: Partners and participants? *International Journal of Social Research Methodology* 2:39–54.

Reicher, S. 2004. The context of social identity: Domination, resistance and change. *Political Psychology* 25:921–45.

Riggs, D., and M. Augoustinos. 2005. The psychic life of colonial power: Racialised subjectivities, bodies and methods. *Journal of Community and Applied Social Psychology* 15:461–77.

Sears, D. O. 1988. Symbolic racism. In *Eliminating racism: Profiles in controversy,* ed. P. Katz and D. Taylor, 53–84. New York: Plenum.

Sewell, T. 1997. *Black masculinities and schooling: How black boys survive modern schooling.* Stoke-on-Trent: Trentham Books.

Verkuyen, M., and A. Steenhuis. 2005. Preadolescents' understanding and reasoning about asylum seeker peers and friendships. *Applied developmental psychology* 26:660–79.

Wagner, W., G. Duveen, J. Verma, and M. Themel. 2000. "I have some faith and at the same time I don't believe"—Cognitive polyphasia and cultural change in India. *Journal of Community & Applied Social Psychology* 10:301–14.

Young, L., and H. Barrett. 2001. Adapting visual methods: action research with Kampala street children. *Area* 33:141–52.

CHAPTER 9

CONCEPTIONS AND MISCONCEPTIONS

SOCIAL REPRESENTATIONS OF MEDICALLY ASSISTED REPRODUCTION

Iain Walker
Pia Broderick
Helen Correia

INFERTILITY AND ITS TREATMENT IS A SOCIAL ISSUE in most Western countries. As many as one couple in seven will have difficulty becoming pregnant when they want to. Medical interventions to assist reproduction have developed rapidly over the last four decades so that it is now possible for many couples to become pregnant when once they would have remained childless. Many such interventions rely on the use of donated sperm, eggs, or embryos. Along with the rapid development of new medical technologies, there is now a sizable industry of counselors working in the area (Burns 1993; Daniels 1993), and legislation and policy to control the fertility industry exist in many states and countries, including Australia (Broderick 2005a, 2005b). Academics have turned their attentions to studies of the stresses experienced by people undergoing medically assisted reproductive technology (MART) procedures (for example, Edelman, Connolly, and Bartlett 1994; Wasser 1994), of the wisdom of telling a child of the circumstances of its conception (for example, Broderick and Walker 1995; Daniels and Taylor 1993; Savage 1995), and of the gender politics involved (for example, Abbey, Andrews, and Halman 1991; Haimes 1993). MART technologies, perhaps especially when they involve donated gametes and embryos, raise many psychological, social, legal, ethical, and political dilemmas. Infertility and the technologies used to overcome it are public issues as well as private concerns.

MART technologies have developed so swiftly that the community, as well as the community's "experts," such as ethicists, counselors, psychologists, and politicians, have struggled to understand their meaning and implications. There are probably several "understandings" of MART, each embodying different constellations of values, beliefs, attitudes, knowledge, and self-interests. These different forms of understanding have real consequences, especially for those undergoing, or seeking to undergo, MART treatment, and for any children born as a result of such treatment. Thus, the medical community has one form of understanding; psychologists, counselors, and other mental health professionals in the area have another understanding; donors of sperm, eggs, and embryos have a different understanding; and the community at large has yet another understanding, or perhaps no understanding at all. Different forms of understanding have different consequences. Almost no research is available that documents or analyzes these different forms of understanding and their consequences. This chapter describes briefly three studies we have conducted, using social representations theory as the theoretical framework.

Social representations theory (SRT) provides an account of the structures and processes of social thought. SRT is a theory of "social thinking" (Augoustinos, Walker, and Donaghue 2006). It has been used to document and analyze community understandings of, for example, health and illness (Herzlich 1973), mental disorders (de Rosa 1987; Jodelet 1991), human rights (Doise 2001), biotechnology (Durrant, Bauer, and Gaskell 1998; Wagner et al. 2001), and organ donation (Moloney Hall, and Walker, 2005). Purkhardt (1993) describes social representations (SRs) as "environments of thought," simultaneously constituting social reality and determined by human action and interaction. SRs are symbolic, prescriptive, dynamic, and autonomous systems of thought. Not only do they arise from and through human action and interaction, but they also enable communication and interaction by providing common, shared systems of meaning and rules of interaction. Furthermore, SRs demarcate and identify groups, direct socialization, and make the unfamiliar familiar and the new, the bewildering, and the threatening understandable (Augoustinos, Walker, and Donaghue 2006).

This last feature of SRs—making the unfamiliar and the strange familiar and understandable—occurs through two processes. *Objectification* is the process whereby what is unfamiliar, strange, or abstract is made concrete and is summarized iconically. Some researchers suggest that concepts are often objectified by becoming attached to the core, or "figurative nucleus," of an SR (Abric 1993). Whereas objectification "transforms the intangible into something real" (Purkhardt 1993, 15), *anchoring* makes the unfamiliar meaningful. The unfamiliar is anchored by being classified and compared with what is already familiar and accessible. This often involves naming and classification.

SR theory distinguishes between the *reified* and the *consensual* universes. The former is the domain of expertise (usually, but not necessarily, the world of science), where thinking is typically in a logical and rational form. The latter is the domain of everyday thinking, of common sense. Expert knowledge is transformed, represented, and appropriated in the consensual universe; knowledge in the reified universe is distilled and made more accessible as it is translated into the consensual universe. The distinction between these two universes has been challenged (see Purkhardt 1993), and it is more reasonable to understand the relationship between the two as bidirectional and coconstitutive rather than unidirectional and separate.

The area of MART is an ideal one in which to examine identity and representation. The area involves the rapid development and introduction of new technologies that have a direct and significant impact on a great number of people (infertile couples, their friends and families, and, of course, the children born through the use of such technology), as well as an indirect effect on contemporary social consciousness. These new technologies are unfamiliar, and often threatening. They come from the abstract, reified world of science, and often appear bewildering to many people.

In MART, the processes of translation from the reified to the consensual universes, of objectification and anchoring, are all easily evident. The medical and scientific (expert) communities have created a vast body of knowledge, techniques, and language to facilitate reproduction for people for whom it would normally not occur. Many of the activities and achievements of these experts have received sensationalized coverage in the popular media. The ways in which the nonexpert community understands the medical techniques are informed and limited by the ways in which expert information is distilled by the media. Knowledges in the consensual and reified universes are, in this case, quite different. However, the "commonsense" knowledge of the medical practitioners themselves is also likely to influence their own beliefs, understandings, and behaviors. The form of understanding in the consensual universe is apparently iconic and abbreviated. Thus, "IVF" (in vitro fertilization) is a label applied to many different techniques, all of which are undifferentiated in the consensual universe. "Test-tube baby" is a name used to refer to the product of the technique, tying that product (child) to the method of its production (falsely, too, since test tubes are not literally used). Furthermore, different groups (counselors and infertile couples) involved in MART technologies appear to have different and conflicting understandings of the meaning of the procedures (Broderick and Walker 1995; Walker and Broderick 1999a, 1999b).

It can be seen, then, that MART is one area in which the processes of constructing SRs are clearly evident. We now present a brief overview of three different studies, each of which examines aspects of SRT in the domain of MART.

STUDY 1: GENEALOGY OF A NEW TERM

A striking theme in the literature concerning psychological issues related to the diagnosis and treatment of infertility—mostly written by counselors, social workers, and psychologists—concerns the psychological and emotional dangers faced by children conceived using donated genetic material. These children are assumed to be doomed to a sense of "genealogical bewilderment," a "lack of biological identity or sense of rootlessness" that "is accompanied by a sense of not belonging with other people, of being different or of not being a 'whole person'" (Winkler and Midford 1986, 44). Such children will not understand where they have come from, what their place is in their world, and who their families really are. This genealogical bewilderment is assumed to result in identity dilemmas, emotional disturbance, a sense of instability and uncertainty, and general unhappiness with life.

Our systematic investigation of the origin, acceptance, and usefulness of this concept of genealogical bewilderment in medically assisted conception using donation revealed a number of surprises as follows:

  the concept was first proposed about 50 years ago;
  it was first used to explain issues in a small specific clinical sample of
      adoptees;
  it has little empirical basis;
  it gathered momentum as an explanation for the cause of difficulties
      suffered by adoptees, particularly as laws regarding information
      access were relaxed in many Western countries during the
      1960s and 1970s;
  it has become an uncritically accepted "fact" that children will be
      psychologically damaged because of it.

Our investigation also suggests that couples and individuals conceiving children using donated gametes or embryos have been inadvertently misled by counselors regarding the dangers of genetic unrelatedness, and in fact their children are unlikely to suffer the emotional disturbances described as a result of their use of donated genetic material.

TRACING THE CONCEPT IN ADOPTION

The term "genealogical bewilderment" first appeared in print in 1964 (Sants 1964). Sants was at the University College of North Wales, Bangor, when he incorrectly attributed the first use of the term to E. Wellisch, twelve years earlier, in 1952. Both psychiatrists, Wellisch and Sants worked together in a child guidance clinic in Bexleyheath in Kent. In 1952, Wellisch published a letter in *Mental Health* in which he draws "*attention to the observation that lack of knowledge of their real parents and ancestors can be a cause of maladjustment in [adopted] children*" (41). But he does not use the term "genealogical bewilderment" in that letter, and it seems more likely that Wellisch and Sants discussed the issues Wellisch refers to in his letter to the journal, and Sants coined the term later, based on both discussions with Wellisch and the ideas expressed in Wellisch's letter.

In his letter, Wellisch talks about the need to identify genealogy to develop "complete body image" (presumably identity), and states that the intimate relationship between one's own body image and that of genetic relatives, "real [genetic] parents and other members of . . . [the] family," is essential to the development of the complete "body image": *Knowledge of and definite relationship to his genealogy is therefore necessary for a child to build his complete body image and world-picture. It is an unalienable and entailed right of every person. There is an urge, a call in everybody to follow and fulfil the tradition of his family, race, nation, and the religious community into which he was born. The loss of this tradition is a deprivation which may result in the stunting of emotional development*" (Wellisch 1952, 41). Wellisch uses the concepts of genetics and genealogy interchangeably to refer to genetic relatedness. However, "genealogy" is a socially constructed bond between people linked as a family, while "genetic linkages" are clear consanguineal links between people who may or may not be family connected in any traditional social manner. This confusion persists in the literature, and is at the basis of therapeutic recommendations by counselors.

Wellisch's initial position that "lack of knowledge of their real parents and ancestors can be a cause of maladjustment in children" *(1952, 41)* is fairly cautious, but Sants (1964) moves to a more definitive and absolute concept, accompanied with greater certainty of this state being apparent in *all* children in particular circumstances: "A genealogically bewildered child is one who either has no knowledge of his natural parents or only uncertain knowledge of them. The resulting state of confusion and uncertainty, it will be argued, fundamentally undermines his security and thus affects his mental health" *(133)*. Sants also expands the concept from its initial basis in clinical cases to include potentially the whole population. He writes, "Genealogically bewildered children may be found in any family where one or both of the natural parents is missing, step-children, foster children, those reared by one natural parent in the absence of the other, most commonly the illegitimate children of married mothers. These children all have in common at least one unknown parent" *(133)*. Being genealogically bewildered then evolves to become the explanation for all one's personal problems: "The preoccupation (with finding the real parent) amounts to an obsession in that genealogically deprived children feel that all their troubles would be solved by a solution of this one" *(Sants 1964, 133)*.

By 1975, genealogical bewilderment (Sorosky, Baran, and Pannor 1975) was asserted as one of the four categories of psychological difficulties in adopted individuals. At this point, genealogical bewilderment had become an established "fact," along with "disturbances in early object relations, complications in the resolution of the Oedipal complex, and prolongation of the 'family romance' fantasy".

A few isolated voices opposed attributing blame for emotional difficulties experienced by adoptees to genealogical bewilderment. Humphrey and Humphrey (1986) report distinct differences between those adoptees with a compulsion to search for and meet their birth parents and those for whom background information is generally sufficient to satisfy their curiosity. The former group tends to show some evidence of personality problems and disturbed family relationships, or "adverse" factors in their adoptive history (early death of an adoptive parent, marital conflict, unexpected birth of a child), while the latter group reports a more satisfactory home life and better self-image. Humphrey and Humphrey (1986) conclude that "it is primarily where family relationships are disturbed, or in some other way unsatisfactory, that the syndrome of genealogical bewilderment is likely to arise" (139).

TRACING THE CONCEPT'S TRANSLATION INTO MEDICALLY ASSISTED CONCEPTION WITH DONATION

Translating the concept of genealogical bewilderment from adoption into medically assisted conception with donation weakens it even further, but regardless of the lack of empirical evidence, it is used by counselors to support arguments for disclosure of the use of donated genetic material and to avoid the psychological damage inflicted by "secrets."

There are three reasons, listed below, why genealogical bewilderment has become so well accepted in medically assisted conception with donation, each of which illustrates the formation of a social representation to accommodate the strange and unfamiliar, posed by the new reproductive technologies.

1. There was no "model" for practitioners and clients to use in understanding what is happening in medically assisted conception with donation. The model provided by adoption was seized, in the absence of any other model, as the basis for anchoring and understanding the new technologies.
2. The one similarity between adoption and MART with donation (genetic unrelatedness) overrode all major differences between the two. The need to anchor on *something* apparently led to incompatibilities with that anchor being ignored and glossed over, presumably because no better anchor was available, or because alternatives (such as organ donation) were politically or socially unacceptable.
3. The emphasis on the distinction between "real" or "natural" parents and "adoptive," or "social," or "psychological" parents established by Wellisch and Sants allowed the analogy between adoption and medically assisted conception using donation to flourish.

So it became generally "understood" among counselors that adoption and medically assisted conception with donation are very similar, and as the idea that genealogical bewilderment, in the context of causing damage to adoptees, continued to gain momentum and acceptance in adoption, it became uncritically accepted that it would have the same role in children born through donation.

In 1986, twenty-two years after Sants's initial discussion of the concept, two papers were published that inextricably linked adoption, having children as a result of donation, and genealogical bewilderment. One was a paper by Humphrey and Humphrey (1986). Although both authors had worked in adoption for many years, the impetus for the 1986 paper came from a large number of couples they had counseled who had requested the use of donated sperm to overcome male infertility, as well as the 1984 publication of the UK Warnock Committee Report on Human Fertilization and Embryology (Warnock 1984). Although they reject the inevitability of genealogical bewilderment, they assume uncritically that the use of donated gametes is analogous to adoption. At the same time, in Australia, Winkler and Midford (1986), both psychologists, uncritically adopted and used Sants's concept. They argue that it is essential for adoptees to have genetic knowledge about their heritage; they confidently confuse the concepts of genetics and genealogy, with no reference to the existing genealogy of the adoptive family; and they argue that a lack of biological knowledge of heredity has substantial negative effects on the psychological functioning of many adoptees.

They argue strongly for open discussion of birth circumstances in adoption, conception involving donation, and new birth technologies, simply because "it is hard to escape the feeling that secrecy following AID [artificial insemination by donor], IVF, and other unusual technologies will result in problems later in the child's life" (45). This "feeling" is backed by just one empirical source, Triseliotis's 1973 UK study of the experiences of adoptees. But their paper is notable for the use of a device that has gained great acceptability in the relevant literature in the absence of empirical data: the evocative and emotive personal testimony of one woman's emotional trauma over her lack of sense of identity due to her conception using donated sperm.

These highly emotive personal testimonials have become a common device to support the need for full disclosure of genetic origins, and they are now found in both the adoption and medically assisted conception literature, with the concept of genealogical bewilderment assuming greater importance with the publication of each new account. Daniels (1987, 1988, 1993) uses the device to good measure in clearly implicating the single fact of genetic unrelatedness to the father for all the child's problems. This understanding, that lack of genetic knowledge is to blame for all personal problems, not only misleads infertile couples and individuals wanting to use donation as to the potential for psychological damage to any potential children, but it also ensures that any other clinical issues for the individuals portrayed will not be attended to and resolved.

A recurring theme in Daniels's writing is that any privacy sought by potential or actual parents in medically assisted conception with donation is seen as dysfunctional and evidence of repressing emotion, and therefore not normal. Inevitably, the fact that most parents indicate that they will not inform their children of the donation used in their conception (Broderick and Walker 2001) leads commentators such as Daniels to argue for the "rights of the child" to protection against genealogical bewilderment, so full disclosure becomes a moral issue, precisely because lacking knowledge of one's genetic origins is assumed to impede identity development and promote psychological disturbances.

A 1990 interview study of a small number of people in the United Kingdom who had been told they were conceived using donor sperm found that this group expressed surprise that their parents had kept the issue secret for so long. They all reported enjoying life and feeling happy to be alive. None regretted being conceived through donor insemination; they were in fact pleased to feel that their parents had wanted a child so badly. None were "overly curious" about the donor, and they did not have a feeling of lack of identity about themselves, or a sense of being unsure about who they were (Snowden 1990, 82).

So far, we have seen how a term coined to help understand a few clinical cases in adopted children has been coopted to refer to all adopted children, and then to all children conceived through the use of donated gametes. This position is then used to inform therapeutic practices advocating for "openness." The next step in the genealogy of the genetic bewilderment concept is for it to underpin legislative and policy change.

The first and most sweeping change in the world regarding access to information in the case of children conceived using donation was made by the Swedish government in 1985. Under new legislation, it became mandatory for all genetic origin information to be exchanged. In its report to the Swedish government, the committee stated, *"The committee finds viable reasons for applying—as has been done by the British adoption researchers McWhinnie and Brandon—to the AID children the research results and experiences with regard to adopted children's need of obtaining knowledge about their origin"* (Sverne 1983). At its core, the Swedish legislation is concerned with protecting children conceived from donated gametes from genealogical bewilderment, and in so doing, institutionalizes full disclosure to children. No new evidence was presented to suggest that genealogical bewilderment was even an issue for these children. In fact, in classic circular fashion, the Swedish government sources cite UK, U.S., and Canadian sources about the dangers of genealogical bewilderment for these children, and in subsequent publications and reports, the Swedish review is then cited to argue for the dangers of genealogical bewilderment in the United Kingdom, the United States, and Canada.

At this point, genealogical bewilderment as a concept had reached a new peak of respectability and acceptability, from its genesis in the 1950s as a suggested explanation for emotional problems in some adopted children, through its gradual acceptance as "the" explanation for all problems in these children, adolescents, and adults, to its passionate acceptance in the area of medically assisted conception with donation, to its role as the centerpiece of a national government's legislation—all in the space of twenty-one years. As a result of the Swedish legislation, and still in the absence of supporting evidence, this national precedent has been authoritatively cited in support of changes in comparative legislation in Australia, New Zealand, the United Kingdom, and Canada (Broderick 2005a, 2005b).

The evolution and uncritical acceptance of the concept of genealogical bewilderment has resulted in wide-ranging implications for legislation wherever medically assisted conception with donation is used, as well as broad implications for the meaning in our societies of what it is to be a "parent," and indeed what it is to be "normal." The social and moral challenges posed by a burgeoning medical technology that severed the link between genetic relationship and genealogy have been responded to by anchoring understanding of that new technology in an extant (though flawed) model. That anchored understanding has then been used as a springboard for the development of the therapeutic policy and legislative frameworks that have worked to reify the original connection between conception using donated gametes and adoption.

STUDY 2: ACCESS TO REPRODUCTIVE TECHNOLOGIES BY SINGLE WOMEN AND LESBIANS

In February 2000, a forty-year-old woman from the state of Victoria, Australia, challenged a Victorian fertility clinic's decision to deny her treatment on the basis that she was single. In a Federal Court, John McBain, the gynecologist from whom she sought treatment,[1] argued that Victoria was breaching the federal Sex Discrimination Act (1984) by denying services on the basis of marital status, as legislated in the Victorian Infertility Treatment Act (1995). In July 2000, the Federal Court ruled in her favor.

Following this landmark decision, John Howard's federal government said that it would amend the Sex Discrimination Act to allow states to restrict access to MART to heterosexual couples. This statement was followed by intense public discussion throughout August and September 2000, yielding hundreds of articles and opinion pieces from journalists and the public about the legitimacy of MART access by single women and lesbians.

Social representations develop within a social and public sphere (see Jovchelovitch 2001). In this public space, members of a community have access to social knowledge and systems of ideas with which they have the potential to engage, interpret, explore, and communicate. Decisions about MART, particularly the legal ruling in 2000, are portrayed within the very public and social sphere of the media. Further, it is a public space in which social actors not only have the opportunity to access information, but also to interact through such means as opinion pieces and letters to the editor.

The purpose of the current study (for a full account of the study, see Correia, Broderick, and Walker 2006) was to identify the social representational content and processes involved in community understandings of single-mother and lesbian parenthood, specifically in response to potential legislative decisions about access to MART in Australia.

The data consisted of 180 letters to the editor and 2 editorials in 2 newspapers, 1 national and 1 statewide, that were published during August and September 2000 following the decision in *McBain v. State of Victoria*. Letters were selected for analysis if they mentioned the case or referred to issues surrounding the topic, such as MART and nontraditional family structures. Thematic analysis was used to identify representations and relevant concepts used to discuss issues related to access to MART from the newspapers. Themes and issues were first identified within the content of the letters. This involved identifying items of interest found in the letters, taking into consideration the words used, and the context in which they occurred. Focusing particularly on content, such as arguments and opinions that were discussed in relation to access to IVF and MART, these items were sorted into possible themes. Each letter was then reassessed in relation to the potential themes to minimize the loss of data. These themes were then assessed in terms of their relationship with each other, such as whether they contrasted with other themes, or whether they could be grouped into larger thematic categories.

The published letters focus on a broad range of issues in relation to the *McBain v. State of Victoria* case and the prime minister's subsequent announcement regarding access to IVF. Interestingly, the acronym "IVF" is used throughout letters to represent MART practices in general and, in keeping with the nature of the social representation, will be used in describing the data, even where the specificity of the term may be misunderstood. About two-thirds of all letters oppose lesbians and single women having access to IVF. Regardless of valence, though, the letters are overwhelmingly centered in the construct of the "family."

Many letters are grounded in an iconic, concrete image of the family as a mother and father with children. This prototypical characterization assumes elevated importance by its association with other frames of reference. These include

definitions of the family as "natural";
the importance of the father within the family;

the rights of the child to both a father and a mother;
and the natural family as "good."

However, some letters draw upon competing representations of "family," defined, for example, by loving and caring bonds between adults and children. These letters are usually positioned relative to the dominant iconic representation, presumably because they may not be understood without the anchoring context provided by the dominant representation.

The association of the family with the "natural order" automatically confers a special status on some and excludes others. Because it is "the natural order of things" for children to be conceived by a man and a woman, there is a "natural," necessary role for the father in constituting a family, and children have a "natural right" to both a mother and a father in their family. Technologies that disrupt this natural order, and legislation that allows lesbians and single women access to such technologies, are therefore a violation of the natural order and thus must be opposed (see also Kronberger and Wagner, Chapter 10, this volume). The effect, of course, is to deny lesbians and single women the possibility of having children (see also Clarke 2001; Stanworth 1987).

Some of the letters display strong, outright hostility toward lesbians, obviating the need for subtle or indirect exclusion. These letters all feature a particular depiction of lesbians as "man-haters," violent, and unstable, noting that their "choice" to live a "homosexual lifestyle" automatically denies them a role in "creating life." These letter writers do not merely rely on representations of the family to communicate ideas of what constitutes a "family," but also integrate other relevant representations, such as ideas about lesbians and lesbian relationships, to negotiate the boundary of the representation of the "family."

Depictions of the family as consisting of a mother, father, and children are often associated with the notion of "goodness." In this, the traditional family is viewed as the standard by which a good home is measured. The father's role is seen as positive and necessary. Children would be denied this in lesbian or single-mother families. Allowing lesbians and single women access to IVF undermines the "ideal" family.

Another means used by letter writers defining the family as "good" is through associating the family with religion and morality. This is contrasted with the decay of moral values associated with divergence from traditional family structures. In particular, homosexuality is associated with "moral bankruptcy," thereby defining homosexual relationships as a poor environment for children. This religious disapproval is also reported by Clarke (2001) as an argument against gay and lesbian parenting.

These moral depictions do not go unchallenged, though. Other writers identify "love" and "commitment" as defining good parenting. Others dispute representations of homosexuality as "bad." And some directly challenge the assertion that traditional families alone provide moral foundations for upbringing.

Letters that oppose lesbian and single women having access to IVF emphasize the iconic image of a traditional family and hence define family by form or structure. Letters challenging this emphasize function instead, arguing that the provision of love and support to children does not exclude single women or lesbians as parents, and that associating "family" with positive function associates it even more closely with "goodness" than does the traditional definition.

In conclusion, representations of the family and of IVF serve to influence judgments about who ought to have access to IVF procedures. The family, and conception, is valorized as a natural process that inherently includes men and the children's right to both a mother and a father. This representation excludes lesbians and single women from the right to reproduce using MART (and arguably through any other means, too). Additionally, lesbians are further excluded from "family" by their identification as "man-haters," violent, unstable, and immoral. Lesbians and single women are also seen to be exercising control over their reproductive potential by "choosing" their "lifestyle," and hence are seen as categorically different from heterosexual couples who are experiencing infertility.

Particular mention should also be made of the way in which emerging representations were introduced and developed. In order to dispute the traditional representation of family, letter writers had to base or anchor their disputations in that traditional representation; that is, they could not pronounce their position *in vacuo*. Notably, many describe their own personal experiences, or those of close others, in order to rebut the orthodoxy from an unchallengeable position. In this, they act in a manner similar to the expert authors described in Study 1, who rely upon personal anecdotes to buttress the concept of genealogical bewilderment. The blending of personal experience with public debate helps anchor abstract moral debate in daily experience, thus making the genesis and adaptation of a social representation more "real."

Social representations are not defined by consensus, but rather are dynamic systems in which change may be fuelled by the contribution of personal experience to the public domain. In addition, this particularly emotive topic makes salient beliefs about access to IVF and MART procedures that are negotiated through a network of social representations. In the process of social communication and debate in an attempt to understand the various "realities" as described by Jovchelovitch (2001), individuals access and make use of various representational systems. In this case, in understanding who should have access to IVF in order to create a family, representations of lesbians and homosexuality become important in negotiating representations of family.

Although representations of the family and IVF serve to limit access to IVF to heterosexual couples, emerging representations of the family and IVF, defined by positive values, do not exclude single women and lesbians in their access to such procedures. These emerging representations may signify a change in defining the family. It may be that representations based on form—on concrete images of a mother, father, and child—are more easily recognized than functional representations of the family based on abstract values such as love, support, and commitment. However, through the identification of personal experiences, such abstract concepts may become objectified, opening a path for the development of emerging representations of family that include nontraditional parenting structures.

STUDY 3: FOCUS GROUP DISCUSSIONS

Study 1 traced the origins and gradual acceptance of the concept of genealogical bewilderment and showed how acceptance of the concept relies on social representational processes rather than any scientific evidence. The concept is now widely and uncritically accepted to the point at which it underpins legislation and policy in various countries. Study 2 examined public debate in letters to the editor relating to discussion following a court decision allowing lesbians and single women access to MART. These letters are predominantly opposed to such access, mostly because it violates representations of the family and the natural order. The third study analyzes how people talk *in interaction* about MART. In doing so, it brings us incrementally closer to social thinking in action. The aim of this study was to identify and document different understandings of MART, how those understandings might influence a hypothetical decision to use or not to use MART, and how those understandings might influence how people react to others who use MART (a full report of the study is presented in Broderick and Walker 2003).

The data came from transcripts of three focus-group discussions involving university students. Groups were comprised of both women and men, and younger and older participants. The discussions were semi-structured to probe

1. whether and how participants related the use of donated gametes in MART to adoption,
2. what participants thought about MART procedures and whether or not they thought they would use such procedures if they found themselves unable to conceive on their own,
3. what participants' attitudes were toward people who have used MART procedures and to children born through the use of MART.

As in Study 2, transcripts were analyzed thematically. The discussions were wide ranging, but we focus here only on two primary themes.

The theme of "nature," "natural order," and "natural process" was strongly evident as a core organizing principle of the focus-group discussions. This relates closely to the first dominant organizing theme to emerge in the letters to the editor analyzed in Study 2, which was the "natural order of things." From this core principle followed many features, such as the role of the father and the right of the child to a mother and father, which together can be taken to constitute the social representation of "family."

Conception and reproduction were seen as natural processes that most people can accomplish without assistance or intervention. Using MART was seen as unnatural, as "meddling with nature." This was used by many people to justify their opposition to MART. Failure to conceive "naturally" was seen by some as an example of natural selection. The use of donated gametes was additionally viewed as "unnatural," and hence objectionable, because it disrupts the "natural relationship" between parent and child. It is also noteworthy that those people who spoke in favor of MART also relied on notions of "nature," but asserted simply that nature just "needs a little bit of help."

The second theme to emerge from the focus-group discussions was the idea of a natural linkage between parents and children, of a genetic bond. This was used by participants to support an analogy between conception using donated gametes and adoption. The idea of adoption was never challenged or opposed. In fact, its very incontrovertible acceptance seemed to be part of the reason why the use of donated gametes in MART could be understood in terms of adoption. This parallel allowed participants to then apply the same distinctions to both cases. Thus, participants often distinguished between "birth" or "natural" parents and "adoptive" parents, without questioning the status of "parent" in either case. Similarly, participants talked of "biological" parents and "psychological" or "social" parents when discussing the case of reproduction using donated gametes. Again, the status of "parent" was not discussed, and neither was the adjectival qualification of "parent."

This second theme functions in the same way as the association of the "family" with the "natural order" that was observed in Study 2. The "natural order" there was defined as a unit comprising children and the man and woman who conceived those children. Here, this is extended, so that the relationship between the man and woman, on the one hand, and the children, on the other, is assumed properly to be defined by a genetic or biological tie. In Study 2, violations of the "natural order" justified excluding lesbians and single women from accessing MART. Here, this is extended to deny any sort of technological intervention to those people, regardless of their sexual orientation or marital status. Common across the two studies is a reliance on a tacit understanding of the "natural order." This is used generatively to create attitudes about issues that participants had probably not thought much about before. Relying on this tacit understanding *allows* participants to be able to talk about the issues at hand; without it, they would be rendered mute. However, a consequence of this reliance is the exclusion of some people from technologies that would allow them to conceive a child when otherwise they would be unable to do so.

CONCLUSION

In summary, the brief description of the focus-group discussions shows considerable consistency with the analyses of the development of the concept of genealogical bewilderment and of the letters to the editor written in response to a court decision allowing lesbians and single women access to MART. All three cases show how unfamiliar technologies come to be understood through anchoring discourse to an already accepted representation. Furthermore, there is a broader representational context in which this anchoring process occurs. MART procedures, perhaps especially when they use donated gametes and embryos, constitute an unfamiliar threat to established understandings of the world, challenging orthodox assumptions about the genetic constitutions of genealogy and about the nexus between individual and family identity and biological relationships. MART is understood, or comes to be anchored to, already established understandings of adoption. The broader context for all this is the presumed "natural order of things." This powerfully but tacitly conditions and valorizes all else. A consequence of the "natural order" premise is that it affords a justification for disallowing some groups of people access to MART procedures. Although most people in Studies 2 and 3 seized the opportunity to display prejudice and discrimination justified by higher (nonbigoted) principles, some showed no compunction about displaying openly hostile and discriminating views about groups of other people.

The sense of personal identity is, for most people, intimately and inextricably tied to their genealogy. The importance of genealogical ties is often invisible, and only becomes apparent when the ties that normally bind the self to family and ancestry are challenged. Recent advances in medically assisted reproductive medicine allow the biological links between a child and his/her family to be altered but all the nonbiological links to remain. Across the studies presented in this chapter, we conclude generally that traditional understandings of family are strongly tied to biological relatedness; that sections of the public, and significantly the helping professionals working with people undergoing MART, understand the donation of gametes to be akin to adoption; that opposition to medically assisted conception procedures is based on strong but tacit beliefs about Nature and God's will; and that opposition to lesbians' (and others') access to medically assisted reproduction procedures is also couched in the language of Nature and God's will to avoid the opprobrium of being unjust and discriminatory.

NOTE

1. Although the clinic was withholding treatment in compliance with state legislation, the clinic joined the woman's legal action seeking redress on the basis of federal legislation.

REFERENCES

Abbey, A., F. M. Andrews, and L. J. Halman. 1991. Gender's role in responses to infertility. *Psychology of Women Quarterly* 15:295–316.

Abric, J. C. 1993. Central system, peripheral system: Their functions and roles in the dynamics of social representations. *Papers on Social Representations* 2:75–128.

Augoustinos, M., I. Walker, and N. Donaghue. 2006. *Social cognition: An integrated approach.* 2nd ed. London: Sage.

Broderick, P. 2005. Disclosure and child development: What we think we know, what we really know, and what we need to know. *Invited paper presented for the American Society for Reproductive Medicine Mental Health Professional Group Annual Meeting Postgraduate Course "Counseling couples about collaborative reproduction: Ethical, cultural and psychological dimensions of parenthood following ART."* Montreal, Quebec, October 15–16.

Broderick, P. 2005.. Lessons from down under: Can behavior be legislated? Invited paper presented for the *American Society for Reproductive Medicine Mental Health Professional Group Annual Meeting Postgraduate Course: "Counseling couples about collaborative reproduction: Ethical, cultural and psychological dimensions of parenthood following ART."* Montreal, Quebec, October 15–16.

Broderick, P. and I. Walker. 1995. Information access and donated gametes: How much do we know about who wants to know? *Human Reproduction* 10:101–4.

———. 2001. Donor gametes and embryos: Who wants to know what about whom, and why? *Politics and the Life Sciences* 20:29–42.

Broderick, P. and Walker, I. 2003. The birth of understandings: Social representations and medically assisted conception. A paper presented at *The Third Talk-In-Interaction Conference: Talking Health. Rockingham, WA, December 15–17.*

Burns, L. H. 1993. An overview of the psychology of infertility. *Psychological Issues in Infertility* 4:433–54.

Clarke, V. 2001. What about the children? Arguments against lesbian and gay parenting. *Women's Studies International Forum* 24:555–70.

Correia, H., P. Broderick, and I. Walker. 2007. Access to reproductive technologies by single women and lesbians: Social representations and public debate. In submission.

Daniels, K. R. 1987. Semen donors in New Zealand: Their characteristics and attitudes. *Clinical Reproduction and Fertility* 5:177–90.

———. 1988. Attitudes to donor insemination and IVF—a community perspective. *New Zealand Social Work Review* 1:4–10.

———. 1993. Infertility counselling: The need for a psychosocial perspective. *British Journal of Social Work* 23:501–15.

Daniels, K. R. and K. Taylor. 1993. Secrecy and openness in donor insemination. *Politics and the Life Sciences* 12:155–70.

de Rosa, A. 1987. The social representations of mental illness in children and adults. In *Current issues in European social psychology*, vol. 1, ed. W. Doise and S. Moscovici, 47–138. Cambridge: Cambridge University Press; Paris: Editions de la Maison des Sciences de l'Homme.

Doise, W. 2001. Human rights studied as normative social representations. In *Representations of the social: Bridging theoretical traditions*, ed. K. Deaux and G. Philogène, 96–112. Oxford: Blackwell.

Durrant, J., M. W. Bauer, and G. Gaskell. 1998. *Biotechnology in the public sphere: A European sourcebook.* London: Science Museum.

Edelman, R. J., K. J. Connolly, and H. Bartlett. 1994. Coping strategies and psychological adjustment of couples presenting for IVF. *Journal of Psychosomatic Research* 38:355–64.

Flament, C. 1994. Consensus, salience and necessity in social representations: Technical note. *Papers on Social Representations* 3:97–105. http://www.psr.jku.at/PSR1994/3_1994Flam1.pdf (accessed November 20, 2002).

Haimes, E. 1993. Issues of gender in gamete donation. *Social Science and Medicine* 36:85–93.

Herzlich, C. 1973. *Health and illness: A social psychological analysis.* London: Academic Press.

Humphrey, M. and H. Humphrey. 1986. A fresh look at genealogical bewilderment. *British Journal of Medical Psychology* 59:133–40.

Jodelet, D. 1991. *Madness and social representations.* New York: Harvester Wheatsheaf.

Jovchelovitch, S. 2001. Social representations, public life, and social construction. In *Representations of the social: Bridging theoretical traditions,* ed. K. Deaux and G. Philogène, 165–82. Oxford: Blackwell.

Moloney, G., R. Hall, and I. Walker. 2005. Social representations and themata: The construction and functioning of social knowledge about donation and transplantation. *British Journal of Social Psychology* 44:415–41.

Purkhardt, S. C. 1993. *Transforming social representations: A social psychology of common sense and science.* London: Routledge.

Sants, H. J. 1964. Genealogical bewilderment in children with substitute parents. *British Journal of Medical Psychology* 37:133–41.

Savage, O. M. N. 1995. Secrecy still the best policy: Donor insemination in Cameroon. *Politics and the Life Sciences* 14:87–88.

Snowdon, R. 1990. The family and artificial reproduction. In *Philosophical ethics in reproductive medicine,* ed. D. R. Bromham, M. E. Dalton, and J. C. Jackson, 70–185. Manchester: Manchester University Press.

Sorosky, A. D., A. Baran, and R. Pannor. 1975. Identity conflicts in adoptees. *American Journal of Orthopsychiatry* 45:18–27.

Stanworth, M. 1987. Reproductive technologies and the deconstruction of motherhood. In *Reproductive technologies: Gender, motherhood, and medicine,* ed. M. Stanworth, 10–35. Minneapolis: University of Minnesota Press.

Sverne, T. 1983. *Children conceived by artificial insemination.* Stockholm: Government of Sweden.

Triseliotis, J. 1973. *In search of origins: The experiences of adopted people.* London: Routledge and Kegan Paul.

Wagner, W., N. Kronberger, G. Gaskell, N. Allum, A. Allansdottir, S. Cheveigne, U. Dahinden, et al. 2001. Nature in disorder: The troubled public of biotechnology. In *Biotechnology 1996–2000: The years of controversy,* ed. G. Gaskell and M. Bauer, 80–95. London: National Museum of Science and Industry.

Walker, I., and P. Broderick. 1999a. The psychology of assisted reproduction, or psychology assisting its reproduction? *Australian Psychologist* 34:38–44.

———. 1999b. Challenges to the reproduction of misunderstanding. *Australian Psychologist* 34:221–28.

Warnock, M. A. 1984. *Report of the Committee of Inquiry into human fertilisation and embryology.* London: Department of Health and Social Security.

Wasser, S. K. 1994. Psychosocial stress and infertility: Cause or effect? *Human Nature* 5:293–306.

Wellisch, E. 1952. Children without geneology: A problem of adoption. *Mental Health* 13:41.

Winkler, R. C., and S. M. Midford. 1986. Biological identity in adoption, artificial insemination by donor (AID) and the new birth technologies. *Australian Journal of Early Childhood* 11:43–48.

CHAPTER 10

INVIOLABLE VERSUS ALTERABLE IDENTITIES

CULTURE, BIOTECHNOLOGY, AND RESISTANCE

Nicole Kronberger
Wolfgang Wagner

INNOVATION AND RESISTANCE TO TECHNOLOGICAL CHANGE AND IDENTITY

One of the most frequently mentioned quotes in social representations literature is Serge Moscovici's claim that the "purpose of all representations is to make something unfamiliar, or unfamiliarity itself, familiar" (1984/2001, 37). This short quote not only highlights the importance of sense-making activities but also implies the active role of social actors in understanding their worlds: the familiar is always familiar to *somebody*, and there is no familiarity in itself. Consequently, Moscovici concludes, a social representation of an object tells more about a group's identity than about the nature of this object. Social representations denote what "the group thinks of itself in its relationships with the objects which affect it" (Durkheim 1895/1982, 40; cf. Moscovici and Vignaux 1994/2001, 158). Our membership in social groups constrains the ways in which we come to understand an object, and conversely, by positioning oneself with regard to an object and by the style we communicate about it, we ascertain our belonging to a particular group of people, and simultaneously distance ourselves from others (cf. Duveen and Lloyd 1986). "Just as the water level in communicating vessels changes when the content is altered at only one point, the act of categorizing an object similarly places the individual in his or her rightful place, like a bilateral lever arm whose axis is fixed in the social field common to both" (Wagner and Hayes 2005, 207; cf. Clémence 2001; Harré and van Langenhove 1999).

Although there is some disagreement about whether a social representation is prior to identity or whether identity is prior to a social representation (see Brewer 2001; Duveen 2001; Breakwell 2001; Zavalloni 2001), in the present context, it might suffice to assume a mutual interdependence of the two concepts. While identities may constrain the representations that social groups enact, the emergence of new social objects necessitates a restructuring of existing identities.

In the following, we set out to review some of our work on social representations of modern biotechnology, exploring the link between identities, representations, and identity politics. Thinking about this technology in terms of being a father or mother, for example, determines what is thinkable and communicable, but at the same time, the new technology and its emerging potential change our understanding of what it *means* to be a parent. Biotechnology and its proximal effects on everyday life in the domains of food and medicine can be seen as an innovation that challenges what is taken for granted and that needs to be "symbolically coped with" by social actors (Wagner, Kronberger, and Seifert 2002). Studying this rupture therefore invites exploring the question of *what the group thinks of itself in its relationship to the object*. What understandings of oneself come to the fore in an attempt to confront the new technology? What identity categories—explicitly or implicitly—are being chosen in order to make sense of the new technology? Thereby, we delimit our analysis to the question of the role identity plays in the context of *resistance* to technopolitical rationality, that is, in the context of skepticism toward and opposition to modern biotechnology and its applications. As it turns out, resistance to different biotechnological applications allows insight into different identity-relevant processes.

New technologies, particularly those that address life and nature, can cast doubt on long-held assumptions on our fundamental categories of self-understanding, and consequently can represent a threat to taken-for-granted identities. Biotechnology has implications for our thinking about nature as well as about the existing social and moral order. In the following, we address such identity threats by analyzing resistance to biotechnological applications involving living beings such as animals and humans; more precisely, we consider the examples of cross-species gene transfer and human reproductive cloning. But ruptures to symbolic orders need not always threaten already existing identities. On the contrary, ruptures may also trigger the collective coconstruction of *new* identities. To illustrate this, we will consider the example of resistance to genetically manipulated (GM) food in Austria during the late 1990s. Change and innovation does not always lead to insecurities about identities but may also foster an emerging sense of shared identity. In our analyses, we draw both on the social representations perspective that takes us back to the *meaning* and the *content* of categories that people consider relevant for their self-understandings in communicating about the new technology (Duveen 2001), and on a *rhetorical social identity perspective* (Reicher 2004; Reicher et al. 2006) that allows for insight into the flexible ways of category use in everyday discourses.

MONSTERS: THE CHALLENGE TO NATURAL-KIND IDENTITIES

The categories we use to define and understand ourselves are under constant change. Sometimes new categories emerge and replace old ones, sometimes the boundaries of categories shift, and sometimes categories, under the same label, gain new meanings. Topics such as whether slaves or women count as "citizens," whether nobility is relevant for social interaction, or what it means to be a child or a parent are subject to historical and cultural variation. Technological innovation is one of the many sources that can stimulate such change in category meaning and its communicative use.

While social and artifact categories are easily subject to historical change, natural categories are much less so. Natural objects such as animals and plants have been with us for all the eons of humankind's existence, and it is therefore no surprise that perceiving and categorizing them is a process that involves universal cognitive mechanisms barely flavored by local and cultural spices. Animal categories, for example, follow a logic that is different from artifact categories such that animals cannot be robbed of their animalness, which is analytically prior to their being a cat, a carp, or a swallow (cf. Atran 1990; Donnellan 1962). Hence, living-kind categories are grossly opposed to artifact categories.

Living kinds are categories referring to objects that usually are thought of as existing independently of human behavior: we can easily imagine a world full of snakes and fish, even if humans do not exist. Here, category membership is assumed to rest on some underlying nonobvious structure, a so-called "essence" (Ahn, Kalish, Gelman et al. 2001). In psychology, "essence" is understood as a placeholder term that stands for a "subsurface" entity that is causally responsible for observable features of members of a kind. The term "essence" allows for the assumption of deep-seated properties even if people do not know exactly what these properties are. While it was the representation of "blood" in premodern societies, nowadays, essence is increasingly understood in terms of genes and the genome. *Artifact categories*, in contrast, refer to objects that cannot be thought of as existing independently of humans; there is no existence of chairs or cars in a world without humans. Human artifact categories are things that come into existence by way of human action and thus reflect human needs and desires. Objects in the artifact category share properties of function and form, but there is no underlying essence to determine their identities. There is no underlying nature of chairs or pencils as there is "fishness" or "humanness."

The essence underlying natural kinds endows their exemplars with an inalienable identity. Essentialist understandings present differences as profound, sharply defined, and fixed, obscuring the ways in which they are ambiguous and changeable (Medin and Ortony 1989). While human artifacts are more arbitrary, natural kinds are understood as nonoverlapping, mutually exclusive categories; it is impossible to be a fish and a bird at the same time, but a table can also serve as a chair. Being a member of a natural kind entails a persisting identity over time that cannot be altered. For example, a fish cannot become a mouse. A chair, on the other hand, can—at least in principle—be taken apart and the parts reassembled as a table; an artifact's functional identity is alterable.

Thinking in terms of natural-kind identities implies the assumption of a stable, well-ordered universe of natural beings. Modern biotechnology, however, represents a challenge to our classification systems in that it turns naturally occurring objects such as plants, animals, or human beings into technologically fabricated artifacts. The technology allows transcending natural-kind categories by transferring and mixing genes of different natural-kind beings, thereby treating living beings as if they were artifacts and creating creatures that not only grow from within but are also made and designed according to human will. Nature is perceived to become *designed nature*, making it difficult, if not impossible, to distinguish natural-kind beings from artifacts. This leads to a "category crisis" in which all the things we "know" about categories of beings become dubious knowledge: natural-kind identities no longer can be assumed to be unalterable and nonoverlapping, and artifacts no longer are as predictable and controllable as we might want them to be.

This crisis of categories and identities calls for processes of collective symbolic coping in order to come to terms with the new technology (Wagner, Kronberger, and Seifert, 2002). They make use of symbolic resources that allow a reframing of social objects (cf. Zittoun et al. 2003). One such symbolic resource we found when analyzing media and focus group data on modern biotechnology was the "monster" theme: naming unclassifiable kinds as monstrous is a way of coping that gives the "betwixt-and-between" a label and allows for inferences regarding what to expect from such beings. As shown in pictorial material in newspapers such as cartoons or drawings, the monster is typically related to characterizations of the unpredictability of artificial creations (Wagner et al. 2006). As with the Frankenstein theme, the monster even turns against its creator; in any case, monstrous identity is related to a considerable degree of danger and typically is met with fascination and fear at the same time (cf. Cohen 1996).

We investigated coping with this category crisis in a series of experimental studies (Wagner, Kronberger, Nagata, and Sen, forthcoming). The psychological advantage of thinking in terms of "essences" is, as previously mentioned, that treating living beings as having an innate and nonobvious basis allows drawing inferences about category membership and the characteristics distinguishing it from other categories; a fish, for example, being characterized by its specific essence of fishness, can be expected to look like a fish and to behave like a fish (in other words, to swim and so on). Genetic hybrids matching the genome of different beings, in contrast, no longer allow for such category-based assumptions. One way of symbolically coping with such unclassifiable beings is to label them as "monstrous," that is, to set them apart from natural beings by evaluating them as significantly more dangerous, ugly, and impure than the parent animals.

Our experimental design involved first rating two natural animals on a number of adjective polarities and then using the same polarity scale to rate the genetic hybrid resulting from a genetic combination of the two natural animals. Our results show that hybrids indeed are imagined to be significantly more dangerous and more frightening than the original animals. Monstrosity is perceived highest for hybrids resulting from genetic combinations across kinds (mixing fish with birds is perceived to result in more monstrous hybrids than mixing one kind of fish with another, for example), and it is also higher for hybrids from parents with mismatched capabilities than it is when the parents' capabilities are for roughly the same habitat and activity (for example, swallow-penguin hybrids, combining two kinds of birds but mismatching the associated capabilities of flying and swimming). The results hold for Austrian, Indian, and Japanese adults, and across a wide range of animal kinds, including humans.

The findings show that modern biotechnology represents a challenge to very basic representations of what it *means* to be a natural living being in contrast to an artifact, or an "unnatural" living being. This affects our image of animals as well as humans and our understanding of what

constitutes their identity. In our studies, genetic human-animal combinations, either when animals were imagined as having received some
human genes or when humans were imagined as having received animal
genes, were judged as highest on monstrosity and could least be categorized. Their identity as human beings was utterly destroyed once their
natural essence was perceived as having been violated by a technological
intervention (Rozin 2005; Wagner et al. forthcoming). In a similar vein,
xenotransplantation and, to a lesser degree, ordinary organ transplantation had similar effects on perceived identity (Kronberger et al. 2001;
Moloney and Walker 2002; Wagner et al. 2001). In this realm, and in
contrast to the social world, a person's identity as a natural being does not
allow degrees of membership, but rather is a "yes-no" characteristic
endowed by an imagined essence of humanness.

The perception of genetic hybrids—whether their parents are animals
or humans—as monstrous excludes them from any ordinary category.
Thereby, an animal's or human's identity as a natural being collapses and
becomes a nonidentity that lacks any fixing in the cultural universe.
Attributing monstrosity is a way to deal with the hardly thinkable: the
violation of the inviolable essence, identity and natural-kind membership. In the following, we show that the identity confusion resulting from
interfering with essences is not only cognitively vexing but also has considerable implications for our assumptions about the social and moral
orders we take for granted.

HUMAN ARTIFACTS: HUMAN IDENTITY IN DANGER

In a globalized world where risks and benefits are no longer narrowly cir-
cumscribed in time and place (Beck 1986), the notion of "we as
humankind" becomes an important social category. This is especially
true for modern biotechnology that can be applied to humans themselves. Thereby, basic assumptions of our Western understanding of
what it means to be human, of our core ideas about human identity and
humanness, become questioned (Habermas 2001). On one hand, questions arise about the boundaries of the category "human." For example,
are the entities being used in embryonic stem-cell research human beings
or not? Are human clones full-blown human beings or are they something else? On the other hand, questions on what it *means* to be human
gain relevance: does being genetically determined still allow one to
understand oneself as a free and autonomous human being? As shown in
the foregoing section, humans are a special case of natural kinds in which
the thought of artifact identities is especially disturbing, as is illustrated

by our analysis of lay-group discussions[1] on the issue of human reproductive cloning (Kronberger 2007).

The application of reproductive cloning has created a lot of attention
in the media and in science fiction, but it is not (yet) a reality. Widely
rejected as morally unacceptable, reproductive human cloning can be
considered a projection screen on which to analyze sense-making
processes of the yet unknown. Everyday discussions on human cloning
frequently are centered on the implicit or explicit question of whether a
clone is a human being or not, thus asking for the clone's identity on the
one hand and implications for the self-understanding of "normal" human
beings on the other hand. That this ambiguity arises at all is a sign that
the categorical status of the clone as human is in limbo. Again, the opposition of natural-kind categories and artifacts becomes relevant: the clone
is seen to be at the same time a human being and a human artifact, a dignified being and a product or commodity. In the focus-group discussions,
clones are depicted as "commodities" that "should at the same time be
treated very differently from products" (Nerlich, Clarke, and Dingwall
2000, 232).

An important implication of categorization is the possibility of going
"beyond the information given" (Rothbart and Taylor 1992); categories
are "inference rich" resources (Hutchby and Wooffitt 1998). Category
membership allows for the deduction of further information about an
exemplar. One aspect of the deductive potential of a category is that it
allows for information on how to *relate* to an object. Being a member of
the human category suggests being treated in specific ways and not being
treated in others: human rights apply to humans, animal rights to animals, while machines may be used as any other artifact.

Category membership not only allows deducing morally acceptable
and unacceptable forms of relating; it also offers a basis for rhetorically
justifying social practices and behaviors. When human clones are construed both as human beings and as artifacts, the inferences drawn from
such categorizations not only lead to cognitive confusion but also and
above all to *relational ambiguity*: being depicted as a human being versus
as a product or commodity implies grossly different forms of relating.
Clones construed as human beings must be granted human rights, while
clones as products and commodities can be owned, bought, sold, and
used to fulfill desired purposes; clones as products or commodities are
attributed a functional identity similar to the other artifacts. The relational ambiguity is reflected in a number of images, metaphors, and symbols: human clones are construed as "human animals," "human robots,"
"fighting or working machines," as "designer babies," "living spare-part

stores," or "copied life," and references are made to slavery, the Nazi atrocities, and eugenics. The recognition of the clone's intrinsic worth becomes endangered and replaced by functional value, for example, as a working or fighting machine or as a living spare-parts store that provides organs when needed. All the examples highlight a denial of human status and dignity to a social group.

In the discussions, this lack of social recognition in the form of degradation, commoditization, and making instrumental use of human beings quickly aroused strong moral concern: the emerging images capture the two forms of dehumanization described by Haslam (2006)—animalistic and mechanistic dehumanization—and concern the humanistic self-understanding of humans as free, equal, and dignified beings. This self-understanding represents the backbone of our modern moral identities. While identities in premodern societies were taken for granted because they were due to social hierarchies and social roles, in modern societies, human identity depends on the social recognition of human dignity (Berger 1973; see also Marková 2000). Misrecognition by others is felt as harm, oppression, and as not being granted humanness; the search and struggle for social recognition has become a trademark for modern identity. If genetically designed and cloned human beings depend upon the instrumental intentions of others, the reasoning goes, it is near impossible for one to maintain a self-image as a free and autonomous human being.

Fantasies by our focus-group discussants also played with ideas of new social groups, such as "human designers" opposed to "human products." People easily can deploy such new categorical thinking and also are fascinated with exploring both associated meanings as well as projected relationships between such groups: clones can be thought of as mass-produced robotic slaves but also as super-humans and elites; the question soon becomes an issue of intergroup relations characterized by problems of social dominance, power, and oppression. Category membership, identity definition, and moral implications go hand-in-hand. At the same time, however, people are appalled by the idea of such developments, and in most discussion groups, it does not take long for social reprimand to occur, re-establishing the moral status of the clone as a full-blown human being (Kronberger 2007). In contrast to issues of personal choice, the recognition of human dignity is not merely an attitude that can change on a whim but instead a basic commitment that provides a source of identity as a modern Western citizen. What kind of people are we becoming if we allow "humans-as-products" to exist?

Worries about "designed" human life not only pop up in relation to reproductive human cloning but also in other applications of modern

biotechnology. Issues such as embryonic stem-cell research, preimplanta-
tion diagnostics, and genetic testing arouse similar concerns, although
certainly not as unanimously as in the case of reproductive cloning.
Again, core questions revolve around the issues of human identity and
human dignity: are embryonic stem cells to be seen as full-blown human
beings, as so-called "pre-embryos" (as not-yet embryos) or as just a bunch
of cells? What does it mean for the self-understanding of a child if it was
selected on the basis of its genetic makeup? And what do the new possibilities mean for the self-understanding of parents? For example, female
respondents in our group discussions were afraid of being forced to "produce" perfect offspring, noting, "It would be crime then, if a child were
born with some damage." The new phenomenon of children going to
court against both parents and doctors because of "wrongful birth"
indeed is a sociomoral consequence of the new technological possibilities
(Lübbe 1993). Rather than being biased, holding actors responsible for
their deeds is a socially rational thing to do, even if some of the new forms
of accusation may sound horrifying. Lawyer Lori B. Andrews (1999), for
example, reports a case in which a California appellate court stated in
dicta that a child with a genetic defect could bring suit against her parents
for not undergoing prenatal screening and aborting her. New possibilities
may go hand-in-hand with new decisions to make and changed understandings of what it means to be a parent.

In this context, categories and identities are not only a *description* of
the experiential world but also are *future-oriented projects*: "social identities are not simply perceptions about the world as it is now but arguments
intended to mobilise people to create the world as it should be in the
future" (Reicher et al. 2006, 53). Identities not only reflect what we are,
but are *identity-projects* on what we would like to be in the future (Reicher
2004). This understanding focuses on the rhetorical function of identity
projects and investigates how successful such endeavors are in mobilizing
other social actors. As has been shown with regard to reproductive human
cloning, people not only are cognitively confused about how to understand human clones (as full-blown human beings or artifacts), but they
also actively engage in putting forward specific identity projects. Driven
by the question "what kind of people do we want to become?" such projects are matters of argument. Although the *human being project* in these
discussions is contested by a *human artifact and animal project*, the first is
more successful in mobilizing group participants: in the end, virtually all
groups agreed on a version construing human clones as full-blown
human beings.

YOU ARE WHAT YOU EAT:
GM FOOD AND AN EMERGING IDENTITY AS RESISTANCE

When it comes to GM food, representations about natural kinds and artifacts hardly play an important role. Although social representations of
nature determine assumptions concerning the controllability or uncon-
trollability of consequences following the interference with nature
(Wagner et al. 2001), the idea of transgressing the boundaries of different
plants does not arouse identity concerns in the same way as it does with
animals or humans. Crossbreeding has been with us for a long time, and
the supermarket shelves are full of ever-changing varieties of new combinations. In the context of GM food, identity issues gain relevance in a different way.

The debate about GM food in Austria highlights identity projects in
relation to resistance and public mobilization. Agricultural and food
applications of modern biotechnology are met with strong public resistance in Austria, and *de facto* Austria has been a GM-free zone until today
(2007). Such resistance cannot exclusively be explained by safety concerns, perceived utilities, and risk considerations. Rather, resistance to
GM food in Austria is also associated with concerns about regional and
cultural identity. Based on the analysis of both group discussions with the
Austrian public and political and economic initiatives, we came across an
identity project that represents Austria as a country that is highly concerned with high-quality agricultural produce; the central metaphor
employed is the representation of "Austria as Europe's delicatessen store,"
a metaphor that—as an identity project—allowed for a liaison of a broad
range of social groups and their arguments against GM food (Grabner
and Kronberger 2003).

The first GM consumer products entered the European market in the
1990s. The imports of the first genetically manipulated crops from the
United States in November 1996 lead to massive public and nongovern-
mental organization (NGOs) protests on a European level. GM soybeans
had been mixed with conventional soybeans, thereby precluding labeling
as GMO-free. This was perceived as an infringement on the right to
choose by consumer and environmental organizations, and the event
resulted in massive mobilization of the public in most of the European
Union (EU) member states. Austria played a special role since it was the
first country within Europe to witness such public mobilization
(Torgersen et al. 2002). Until 1996, there was no noticeable public or
media interest in genetic engineering in Austria. The first Austrian release
of genetically manipulated organisms in 1996, however, happened without official permission. This illegal release triggered an immediate

response by NGOs and the mass media, resulting in considerable pressure on the Austrian authorities and the biotechnology industry. The authorities responded with a ban on the import and agricultural use of Bt-maize despite the European Commission's market approval (thus deliberately violating EU regulations). A referendum in April 1997 calling for a moratorium on agricultural applications and patents came to be the second most successful of its kind.[2] With nearly 21 percent of the electorate subscribing, it was the most successful initiative carried by NGOs but not officially supported by any established political party.

The identity project of a GM-free Austrian delicatessen store also played an important role for our group discussions conducted in 1999 and 2000. Thereby, organic farming served as a central example for illustrating Austrian identity. With its strong organic farming sector, the reasoning as follows was that Austria could be an exemplary case to show that it is better to live without GM food:[3]

> CF: If there are no GM products grown here, then we don't have GM food in the Austrian food production <exactly> and I think, if Austria would do that, then it would have an incredible market all over the world, because there are people like us everywhere, isn't it, then we would be Europe's delicatessen store <mhm>, and this would be a great chance for our agriculture.
>
> AF: That's what we see with organic farming, that's the same, here we are ahead. <yes!> [MOTHERS; words in angle brackets signify interjections by others]

Organic farming emerges as a counterpoint to industrialized agriculture, *and* "people like us" are depicted as gourmets shopping for the best quality. In contrast to countries like Italy or France, where food also is of high importance for national identities, the Austrian identity is not constructed around typical dishes or ways of preparation but rather around traditional and ecological ways of agricultural production (such as highland farming or organic farming). By contrasting GM food with organic food and by describing a GM-free Austria as a "delicatessen store," GM products are implicitly construed as low-quality produce. Organic food is repeatedly depicted as an identity marker through which the purchase of GM food signifies a lack of care for quality.

> JF: I mean, I don't have much money neither, but I say: what I eat, that's what I am, isn't it? [MOTHERS]

Green biotechnologies, perceived to be the opposite of high quality, are furthermore associated with industrialization, globalization, and Americanization, consequently represent a dimension for comparing "people like us" with others. As demonstrated in the following quote, GM food is construed as a diffuse threat connected to broader concerns about the dilution of traditional, regional, and local identities:

> YM: And this is the beautiful thing about human beings, their uniqueness, isn't it? This is what makes us special. Otherwise we could go to McDonald's everyday and dress all the same.
> VF: That's horror but that's where it will end, I mean, all those cultures degenerate, those food cultures, I mean, and the kids in Moscow look like those in America. Everything will be the same. And I don't think that's good. And if this goes on like this it will become extremely boring in this world, I guess.
> XM: Will be like that with us as well.
> YM: Yes, maybe not boring but grey.
> VF: Yes, grey, everything is going to be grey.
> XM: Yes, we already look like Europeans. In the past we looked like Tyroleans and Austrians, or Italians, and there also were Slavs, but today? [INNSBRUCK II]

The implicit demarcation from other groups mainly occurs on an international level, by pointing to conflicts of interest between national awareness for quality and international demands for industrialization and globalization. For the public, the latter leads to food cultures such as in the United States, captured in the concern with "McDonaldization" and Americanization, a development that is met with strong skepticism and framed in contrast to "groups like ours *as follows*":

> AM: I really believe that groups like ours do not exist in America. . . . Because, that you find eight people who are against GM food.
> IF: Is that like that? Do we have eight people here being against it? [laughter]
> CF: But this was not the criterion for participation in the discussion! They only said that it is about biotech. [HIGHER EDUCATED]

The identity construction of Austria as a "GM-free delicatessen store" is intuitively convincing for a majority of the public and was taken up by actors in the political and economic domain at the time of the referendum. Interestingly, on a regional level, the opposition to GM food unified rather than juxtaposed the public and economic initiatives. This unexpected liaison caused Austrian supermarkets to take several actions. Until today, they successfully introduce new organic product lines, and

campaign with "GM-free" logos as proof of high quality instead of positively labeling GM products, as is the case in other countries. They also
indicate the personal names and addresses of farmers and butchers on
agricultural products. This indication of local or regional origin seems to
meet a desire for safety, transparency, and identifiable proximity that is
missing with industrialized and globalized food production.

The representation of Austria as a high-quality delicatessen store both
offers a possibility for identification and a way for the country to demarcate itself from less quality-concerned groups. Interestingly, the choice of
this identity category is *not* some local or regional identity; rather, it is the
category of "we as Austrians," the national identity. People speak as
Austrians, unified by their concerns for local and regional variety, tradition, and quality. It is a highly successful identity project that enabled the
mobilization of a number of groups: the organizing team of the referendum included such diverse groups as animal-rights activists, the mountain
farmers' organization, environmental protection groups, and a Catholic
consortium concerned with ecosocial issues. As "identity entrepreneurs"
(Reicher 2004, 935) the organizers of the referendum succeeded in putting forward an identity offer that a broad range of social groups were
willing to join and that allowed for a combination of ethical concerns
about interference with nature, anxieties about health and ecological consequences, and regional worries both in a cultural and economic sense.
This in turn ensured the support of diverse groups. An example of a local
economic initiative that supported the GM-critical referendum was a
consortium of butchers who campaigned under the label of "butchers'
morals." These butchers appealed in a number of advertisements to the
public to trust in their regional, GM-free, high-quality produce.

It should be noted that the identity project of a technology-critical
GM-free Austria[4] was not uncontested. An alternative identity project
was advanced both in the group discussions and from the side of industry
and the scientific community, placing emphasis on an Austrian identity
as an attractive business and technology site. The Austrian authorities in
the aftermath of the 1996–97 mobilization were confronted with highly
contradictory claims: on the one hand, the European Union demanded
compliance with its regulation, and industry and the scientific community warned that Austria would fall back technologically; on the other
hand, NGOs warned the government of following EU regulations against
the public's will. Austria upheld the ban, while the commission failed to
enforce its regulation.[5] To date, the issue has not been resolved.

What is noticeable from a theoretical point of view is that identification with a social category (such as Austrian) does not tell anything about

its consequences. All the social actors refer in one way or another to a shared Austrian identity, which makes the discourse about the meaning of identity "a focus of furious controversies" (Reicher 2004, 937). There are as many versions of Austrian identity involved as there are possible futures. The fact that the national category and not the European or some regional identity became relevant has to do with rhetorical and strategic reasons. On one hand, the national identity provides a large enough canopy to cover a broad front of resisting groups. On the other hand, it is specific enough to distinguish the groups from others and their concerns. The national identity, with its symbols and history, also offers a repertoire of rhetoric means that are efficient in creating persuasiveness. Interestingly, the adversarial identity entrepreneurs often make reference to the same examples, symbols, or historical events (such as Austria's joining the European Union, for example) in order to make a case for their point of view. These argumentative means, however, are ensnared in very different identity narratives and lead to divergent conclusions.

THE ASSUMPTION OF FIXED IDENTITIES IN AN EVER-CHANGING WORLD

In the preceding sections, we reviewed a number of studies on modern biotechnology from the angle of an identity perspective. The different aspects and examples on public resistance to modern biotechnology highlight that the rupture to the symbolic order caused by the new technology can on the one hand, challenge existing identities but on the other hand, also trigger "identity politics" resulting in the formation of new "identities for resistance."

The findings of our experiments on cross-species gene transfer show that people tend to categorize animals and human beings as if they had an immutable natural-kind identity, defined by an intrinsic "essence," and that they tend to perceive exemplars crossing category borders as monsters bereft of identity. Ruptures to everyday common sense, such as the introduction of modern biotechnology and its new possibilities, not only lead to new social representations but also highlight the structure of *pre-existing* everyday conceptions. The change of well-tried categorizations and identities creates feelings of unease and a degree of resistance. Lay reasoning about genetic hybrids is characterized by assumptions on what it means to hold a natural-kind identity: it is, and should be, a stable, nonoverlapping identity that gives orientation on what to expect from such a being.

In a world of constant flux, our categories are under constant change but at the same time, people tend to treat these categories as if they were immutable and fixed, as evidenced by the following quote: "Even if categories change over time, they must always be seen as fixed at any specific point in time. What we need to address, then, is not simply flexibility, but the combination of flexibility with the conviction that wherever we happen to be is where we always have been and always will be" (Reicher 2004, 926). Biotechnology is disturbing in that it makes obvious that fixity cannot even be assumed for our most basic categories. One way of symbolically coping with this troubling message is to label the unclassifiable as monstrous; this gives the out-of-order a specific place in a symbolic order while leaving untouched the customary categories of the natural and the artificial.

But how can we explain this longing for fixity in a world of flexibility and change? Of course it is much harder to orient oneself in a world in which everything is flexible and nothing can be taken for granted. Assuming fixity in this sense provides an illusion of stability; category change should only happen when our categories no longer reflect the demands of our surrounding world. Categories, furthermore, also *serve to legitimate social relations*, and as such, they must be seen as necessary rather than as contingent (Reicher 2004). The lay discussions on reproductive cloning presented earlier in this chapter highlight the implications of a switch between identity categories for social and moral action. Clones are given very different positions in our social worlds and moral orders depending on whether they are fantasized as human being or as a product and commodity. Although being "only" fantasies on a not (yet) existing reality, the discussions illustrate that the attribution of human status is by no means a matter of course; an identity project defining clones as human beings is contested by other identity projects that construe a clone's identity in dehumanized ways. This finding illustrates that social actors are by no means passive members of their categories; rather, they are engaged in an active coconstruction of possible futures.

A "rhetorical social identity perspective," as Reicher et al. (2006; see also Reicher 2004) suggest, is a fruitful complement to a social representations approach in highlighting that identities are not only about being but also about becoming; there is both a perceptual and a rhetorical dimension to categories. Similar to the social representations approach, this perspective aims at bridging the levels of the social and the individual: while individuals certainly are confronted with existing identities and their cultural meanings, they also can—as identity entrepreneurs—advance and coconstruct identities in the making. This view emphasizes communication, social activity, and agency. The specific choice of categories for understanding the self and others no longer appears as an automatic reaction to specific contexts, but rather must be seen as involving a strategic dimension. As such, identity projects are intended to mobilize the in-group and to mitigate challenges posed by others. The Austrian example of public mobilization in the context of GM food in the late 1990s can be considered a showcase illustrating how different groups participate in the collective coconstruction of a highly successful identity project and how shared meanings of categories open the way to collective action. The emerging identity offer managed to draw diverse concerns together under one banner and it mobilized considerable parts of the public to show resistance against GM food.

The conception of identity projects as strategic efforts also opens the way to ask what makes such projects successful. "Success in realizing one project over another depends on imposing one version of identity over all other versions. That is, the very contingency of identity requires that it be presented as non-contingent, as self-evident, as not one version among many but as the only possible version" (Reicher 2004, 938). The assumption of category fixity, hence, is also functional from a rhetorical point of view. Identity offers typically are justified by culturally significant symbols, examples, and metaphors, and by making reference to historical events that are used with the intention to give authenticity to proposed claims. Especially in times of cultural and technological change, when our symbolic order is being challenged and new social representations emerge, it is likely that a number of controversial identity projects will compete for predominance. Thereby, the meanings of categories may remain under dispute for a long time, gain new meanings, or disappear altogether. The troubled researcher who gets worried about such flexibilities and endless contextual variation may be consoled by a final claim of the rhetorical approach to social identity: for a healthy democracy, the continuous questioning of the terms of identity and their meanings is not only normal, but also vital.

NOTES

1. The analyses of the present study are based on data that were, in part, gathered within an international research project (LSES: "Life Sciences in European Society"). For an overview on the project, see Gaskell and Bauer (2001). Nine discussions with approximately seven participants each were conducted in different regions of Austria. Besides considering socioeconomic characteristics such as educational level, sex, and age, sampling also aimed at maximizing perspectives on the topic by inviting a group of mothers,

farmers, prospective economists, and people with an explicit interest in the topic (exhibition visitors). The data were analyzed on the basis of a procedure suggested by Bohnsack (2000).

2. The referendum called for a ban on the production, import, and sale of GM food and agricultural products, a ban on GMO releases (including animals, plants, and micro-organisms), and a ban on patenting any living beings. Medical applications were excepted from the referendum.

3. Eight focus groups with a total of fifty-four participants were conducted from July 1999 through January 2000 in Vienna, Innsbruck, and Linz. Group participants' names were replaced by a combination of capital letters that were selected randomly and an F (female speaker) or M (male speaker) respectively (for example, AM, BF). Utterances of the female interviewer are introduced by the title "IF."

4. Austria also opted out of nuclear power in a referendum in 1978. Since then, there has been no energy produced in nuclear power plants in Austria. Although it was only a slight majority that voted against nuclear power in that referendum, the collective memory of the event is highly important for the discussion on biotechnology. The groups interpret the developments in other countries after the Chernobyl accident as justifying the position taken by the Austrian public as early as in 1978. In retrospection, the reasoning goes, the public's will turned out to be right, and the referendum turned out to become a "focusing event" (Birkland 1998) in the collective memory.

5. As Torgersen et al. (2001) explain, the developments in the aftermath of the 1996 mobilization in other European countries and on the EU level contributed to some kind of normalization of the Austrian debate; in a retrospective view, Austria could even be seen as a "forerunner." Caused by policy shifts in major European countries like France, the United Kingdom, and Germany, the EU adopted policy positions much closer to what had always been the (comparatively critical) Austrian stance. From 1998 on, several European countries banned previously approved GM products. In 1999, the EU Commission issued a de facto moratorium until the directive 90/220 was revised, thereby giving retrospective legitimacy to the Austrian ban. In 2000, the EU even adopted the "precautionary principle" as a rule for decision making, a principle that Austria always had cited in defending contested decisions. The tendency of converging Austrian and European views is also found on the level of public perception. In a 1996 Europe-wide representative survey on attitudes toward biotechnology (the Eurobarometer 46.1), the Austrian public showed more negative attitudes toward "green" biotechnology than most other countries (Wagner et al. 1998); later comparable Eurobarometer surveys showed that the Austrian public remained skeptical but that, on the whole, the views of other European countries became considerably more negative with regard to this topic (Gaskell et al. 2001; Torgersen et al. 2001).

REFERENCES

Ahn, W.-K., C. Kalish, S. A. Gelman, D. L. Medin, C. Luhmann, S. Atran, J. D. Coley, et al. 2001. Why essences are essential in the psychology of concepts. *Cognition* 82 (1): 59–69.

Andrews, L. B. 1999. Genetic predictions and social responses. In *Life science. Ars Electronica* 99, ed. G. Stocker and C. Schöpf, 16–17. Vienna: Springer.

Atran, S. 1990. *Cognitive foundations of natural history—towards an anthropology of science.* Cambridge: Cambridge University Press.

Beck, U. 1986. *Risikogesellschaft. Auf dem Weg in eine andere Moderne* [Risk society. On the way to a different modernity]. Frankfurt: Suhrkamp.

Berger, P. 1973. On the obsolescence of the concept of honour. In *The homeless mind*, ed. P. Berger, B. Merger, and H. Kellner, 78–89. Harmondsworth, UK: Penguin.

Birkland, T. A. 1998. Focusing events, mobilization and agenda setting. *Journal of Public Policy* 1 (1): 53–74.

Bohnsack, R. 2000. *Rekonstruktive Sozialforschung. Einführung in Methodologie und Praxis qualitativer Forschung* [Reconstructive social research. Introduction to methodology and practice of qualitative research]. 4th ed. Opladen, Germany: Leske and Budrich.

Breakwell, G. M. 2001. Social representational constraints upon identity processes. In *Representations of the social: Bridging theoretical traditions*, ed. K. Deaux and G. Philogène, 271–84. Oxford: Blackwell.

Brewer, M. B. 2001. Social identities and social representations: A question of priority? In *Representations of the social: Bridging theoretical traditions*, ed. K. Deaux and G. Philogène, 305–11. Oxford: Blackwell.

Clémence, A. 2001. Social positions and social representations. In *Representations of the social: Bridging theoretical traditions*, ed. K. Deaux and G. Philogène, 83–95. Oxford: Blackwell.

Cohen, J. J. 1996. Monster culture (seven theses). In *Monster theory. Reading culture*, ed. J. J. Cohen. London: University of Minnesota Press.

Donnellan, K. S. 1962. Necessity and criteria. *Journal of Philosophy* 59 (22): 647–58.

Durkheim, E. 1895/1982. *The rules of sociological method.* London: Macmillan.

Duveen, G. 2001. Representations, identities, resistance. In *Representations of the social: Bridging theoretical traditions*, ed. K. Deaux and G. Philogène, 257–70. Oxford: Blackwell.

Duveen, G., and B. Lloyd. 1986. The significance of social identities. *British Journal of Social Psychology* 25 (3): 219–30.

Gaskell, G., and M. W. Bauer, eds. 2001. *Biotechnology 1996–2000. The years of controversy.* London: Science Museum.

Gaskell, G., N. Allum, W. Wagner, T. H. Nielsen, E. Jelsoe, M. Kohring, and M. Bauer. 2001. In the public eye: Representations of biotechnology in Europe. In *Biotechnology 1996–2000. The years of controversy*, ed. G. Gaskell and M. Bauer, 53–79. London: Science Museum.

Grabner, P., and N. Kronberger. 2003. " . . . aber ich sage: 'das was ich esse, das bin ich,' nicht?": Widerstand gegen gentechnisch veränderte Nahrungsmittel im Kontext von Identitätsfragen [" . . . but I say: 'I am what I eat,' ain't I?": Resistance towards genetically modified food in the context of identity concerns]. *SWS-Rundschau* 43 (1): 129–52.

Habermas, J. 2001. *Die Zukunft der menschlichen Natur. Auf dem Weg zu einer liberalen Eugenik?* [The future of human nature. Towards a liberal eugenics?]. Frankfurt: Suhrkamp.

Harré, R., and L. van Langenhove. 1999. *Positioning theory.* Oxford: Blackwell.

Haslam, N. 2006. Dehumanization: An integrative review. *Personality and Social Psychology Review* 10 (3): 252–64.

Hutchby, I., and R. Wooffitt. 1998. *Conversation analysis. Principles, practices and applications.* Cambridge: Polity.

Kronberger, N. 2007. Moralities we live by: Moral focusing in the context of technological change. In *Meaning in action—construction, narratives and representations,* ed. T. Sugiman, K. Gergen, and W. Wagner. New York: Springer.

Kronberger, N., U. Dahinden, A. Allansdottir, N. Seger, U. Pfenning, G. Gaskell, N. Allum, et al. 2001. "The train departed without us"—Public perceptions of biotechnology in ten European countries. *Notizie di Politeia* 17 (62): 26–36.

Lübbe, H. 1993. Sicherheit. Risikowahrnehmung im Zivilisationsprozeß [Safety. The perception of risk in the civilization process]. In *Risiko ist ein Konstrukt. Wahrnehmungen zur Risikowahrnehmung,* ed. Bayerische Rück, 23–42. Munich: Knesebeck.

Marková, I. 2000. Amédée or how to get rid of it: Social representations from a dialogical perspective. *Culture & Psychology* 6 (4): 419–60.

Medin, D. L., and A. Ortony. 1989. Psychological essentialism. In *Similarity and analogical reasoning,* ed. S. Vosniadou and A. Ortony, 179–95. Cambridge: Cambridge University Press.

Moloney, G., and I. Walker. 2002. Talking about transplants: Social representations and the dialectical, dilemmatic nature of organ donation and transplantation. *British Journal of Social Psychology* 41 (2): 299–320.

Moscovici, S. 1984/2001. The phenomenon of social representations. In *Social representations. Explorations in social psychology,* ed. S. Moscovici and G. Duveen, 18–77. New York: New York University Press.

Moscovici, S., and G. Vignaux. 1994/2001. The concept of themata. In *Social representations. Explorations in social psychology,* ed. G. Duveen, 156–83. New York: New York University Press.

Nerlich, B., D. D. Clarke, and R. Dingwall. 2000. Clones and crops: The use of stock characters and word play in two debates about bioengineering. *Metaphor and Symbol* 15 (4): 223–39.

Quine, W. V. 1969. *Ontological relativity and other essays.* New York: Columbia University Press.

Reicher, S. 2004. The context of social identity: Domination, resistance, and change. *Political Psychology* 25 (6): 921–45.

Reicher, S., C. Cassidy, I. Wolpert, N. Hopkins, and M. Levine. 2006. Saving Bulgaria's Jews: An analysis of social identity and the mobilisation of social solidarity. *European Journal of Social Psychology* 36 (1): 49–72.

Rothbart, M., and M. Taylor. 1992. Category labels and social reality: Do we view social categories as natural kinds? In *Language, interaction and social cognition*, ed. G. R. Semin and K. Fiedler, 11–36. London: Sage.

Rozin, P. 2005. The meaning of "natural": Process more important than content. *Psychological Science* 16 (8): 652–58.

Torgersen, H., C. Egger, P. Grabner, N. Kronberger, F. Seifert, P. Weger, and W. Wagner. 2001. Austria: Narrowing the gap with Europe. In *Biotechnology 1996–2000. The years of controversy*, ed. G. Gaskell and M. Bauer, 131–44. London: Science Museum.

Torgersen, H., J. Hampel, M.-L. Bergmann-Winberg, E. Bridgman, J. Durant, E. Einsiedel, B. Fjaestad, et al. 2002. Promise, problems and proxies: Twenty-five years of debate and regulation in Europe. In *Biotechnology. The making of a global controversy*, ed. M. W. Bauer and G. Gaskell, 21–94. Cambridge: Cambridge University Press.

Wagner, W., and N. Hayes. 2005. *Everyday discourse and common sense: The theory of social representations*. Basingstoke, UK: Palgrave Macmillan.

Wagner, W., N. Kronberger, S. Berg, and H. Torgersen. 2006. The monster in the public imagination. In *Genomics & society: Legal, ethical and social dimensions*, ed. G. Gaskell and M. Bauer, 150–68. London: Earthscan.

Wagner, W., N. Kronberger, G. Gaskell, A. Allansdottir, N. Allum, S. Cheveigné, U. Dahinden, C. Diego, L. Montali, A. T. Mortensen, U. Pfenning et al. 2001. Nature in disorder: The troubled public of biotechnology. In *Biotechnology 1996–2000. The years of controversy*, ed. G. Gaskell and M. Bauer, 80–95. London: Science Museum.

Wagner, W., N. Kronberger, M. Nagata, and R. Sen. Forthcoming. *The monstrosity effect across cultures: Affective entailments of cognizing violations of animal kind essence.*

Wagner, W., N. Kronberger, and F. Seifert. 2002. Collective symbolic coping with new technology: Knowledge, images and public discourse. *British Journal of Social Psychology* 41 (3):323–43.

Wagner, W., H. Torgersen, F. Seifert, P. Grabner, and S. Lehner. 1998. Austria. In *Biotechnology in the public sphere: A European sourcebook*, ed. J. Durant, G. Gaskell, and M. Bauer, 15–28. London: Science Museum.

Zavalloni, M. 2001. E-motional memory and the identity system: Its interplay with representations of the social world. In *Representations of the social: Bridging theoretical traditions*, ed. K. Deaux and G. Philogène, 285–304. Oxford: Blackwell.

Zittoun, T., G. Duveen, A. Gillespie, G. Ivinson, and C. Psaltis. 2003. The use of symbolic resources in developmental transitions. *Culture & Psychology* 9 (4): 415–48.

CHAPTER 11

IDENTITY, SELF-CONTROL, AND RISK

Hélène Joffe

INTRODUCTION

The concept the "other" is central to a theory of identity and identity formation. Social psychology has not made sufficient use of it. Outside the discipline, "othering" is widely utilized to explain Western ways of subordinating certain peoples and thereby constructing superior identities. However, the process by which people buttress their own sense of identity by locating undesirable qualities in others is not necessarily culture-specific. For certain psychodynamic theories, such processes lie at the root of identity formation. Since social psychology is centrally concerned with issues of identity yet lacks a satisfactory theory thereof, it would do well to integrate these insights.

In this chapter I draw on my work concerning the role played by the "other" in the social representation of risk (Joffe 1999). I develop this thinking with the aim of exploring how the "other" functions in the ongoing project of identity construction. My argument is that social representations of certain groups serve identity functions. These range from self and in-group identity protection to the maintenance of power relations by sustaining the status quo at the level of values and ideologies. My concern is not only with the process of identity construction but also with the contents of identity-based representations. To this end, I integrate into a social psychological understanding aspects of psychodynamic and sociocultural theorization. The theory of identity that emerges posits that subjective, internal forces interact with external forces in the construction of identity. Cultural, societal, institutional, environmental, and symbolic factors play a part in the sense of identity and identification that individuals experience.

"Othering" as an Ongoing Process in Society

The West and the "Other"

The notion of the "other" is widely used in cultural theory. Here the "other" generally applies to those outside of, and implicitly subordinate to, the dominant group. A distinctive aspect of being "other" is that one is the object of someone else's fantasies but not a subject with agency and voice. This is illustrated by Said's (1978) claims concerning "the Orient" in which he describes it as an entity constructed by European culture. During the post-Enlightenment period, a set of political, sociological, military, ideological, and scientific discourses established "the Orient." Members of "the Orient" did not speak for themselves. They did not represent their own emotions, presence, or history. Rather, "the Orient" was filtered through the lens of European culture, which diminished the status of "Orientals." The superiority of European identity was constructed and affirmed on the basis of a set of comparisons with such non-European peoples and cultures.

This theory highlights a crucial aspect of how people forge their identities. Identity is constructed not merely by what people affiliate with, but also by their comparisons with other groups in which they emerge as the superior party. Gaining a positive sense of identity through comparison with negatively valued groups is common in modern and earlier societies alike (Said 1978). A fifth century BC Athenian was as likely to gain his sense of identity from being defined as a non-Barbarian as from positively feeling like an Athenian. In a similar line of reasoning, Stallybrass and White (1986) show that the bourgeois person continually defines the self through the exclusion of what (and who) is marked out as "low" in terms of being dirty, repulsive, noisy, or contaminating. This act of exclusion is constitutive of identity.

One might argue that Africans have provided the prototypical example of the lowly, "uncivilized" "other" for contemporary Europeans, who buttress their positive sense of identity by way of this representation. McCulloch's analysis (1995) of the written work of psychiatrists in Africa in the first sixty years of the twentieth century shows that the "African" was described in terms of everything that the "European" was not: savage, lazy, violent, and sexually promiscuous. These qualities were the very antithesis of the order, reason, moral standards, discipline, sexual continence, self-control, and altruism attributed to the European. This emphasis of the virtues of white people and the supposed vices of black people has a long history. Young's analysis (1995) of representations of black people in the West focuses on the influential nineteenth century scholar Gobineau, whose theory is believed to have had a major impact on Hitler's racial theories. He postulated that races have their own characteristics, with black races having feeble intellect, strong animal propensities, and a lack of morality. In contrast, according to Gobineau, white races have vigorous intellect, less pronounced animal propensities, and highly cultivated morals. These older and more recent writings reflect and perpetuate a representation in which culture and civilization are associated with white races, and nature with black races.

This pattern of representation reflects important aspects of Western understandings of "others." First and foremost, the "other" is construed as fundamentally different from the European. More particularly, "others" are viewed in terms of two extremes: they are highly debased but also, perhaps less obviously, extremely admirable and enviable. As a corollary of their association with "nature," they are invested with excessive sexuality, emotionality, and spirituality (for example, Said 1978); having not kept pace with the Western notions of progress, they are seen to possess animal eroticism (Fanon 1992). Finally, cultures think of themselves in terms of hierarchies in which some elements are "high" and others are "low." Bourgeois culture represents its "low" "other" not only in terms of disgust and fear, but also in terms of desire, and the two are interrelated in the following way: *Disgust always bears the imprint of desire. These low domains, apparently expelled as "Other", return as the object of nostalgia, longing and fascination. The forest, the fair, the theatre, the slum, the circus, the seaside-resort, the "savage": all these, placed at the outer limit of civil life, become symbolic contents of bourgeois desire"* (Stallybrass and White 1986, 191). Thus, "others" are imbued with, and lauded for, the very qualities that are kept underground, surrounded by taboo, in the rational climate of Western culture. These range from the supernatural to the instinctual.

While such qualities may be admired, people associated with them can, simultaneously, be the objects of debasement. The "other" can excel in those areas "at the outer limit of civil life" without threatening a sense of Western superiority. Westerners do their "identity work" (Crawford 1994)—they mark out what it is to be a good and upright citizen precisely by way of devaluing certain qualities. One core Western value is that of self-control, particularly over the body, mind, and destiny (Joffe and Staerklé 2007). Therefore, the construction of the "other" often hinges around a deficit of this valued entity. This value accounts for several categories of "others," ranging from the obese to the poor, from addicts and welfare recipients to "mad" people and refugees.

THE "OTHER" AND THE VALUING OF SELF-CONTROL

Sociological theory casts light on the history of the valorization of self-control in the West, and the role that it plays in "identity work." The taboo related to out-of-control aspects of the self has developed in Europe since the early Middle Ages, according to Elias's (1939/2000) classic *The Civilising Process*. He posits that rules about the body change through the ages, and this manifests in the development of an increasing tendency toward self-control over the body. In Europe, behaviors linked to the body (for example, when, where, and how one has sex, urinates, and so on) have become more tightly regulated. The civilizing process makes people increasingly bodily inhibited, and changes the threshold of repugnance, fostering increasing feelings of shame and disgust with the body. People clothe and screen their more "instinctual" selves, and higher levels of order and restraint are demanded of them.

This developing restraint becomes a core norm in Western society, buttressed by secular and religious forces alike. People acting in a manner deemed to be out of control—be they from foreign nations or from within the society—present a major threat to the Protestant ethic of moderation. Protestantism has helped to create a self preoccupied with discipline, and Calvinism in particular demonstrates a horror of disorder (Weber 1904/1905/1976). Thus, religious forces work alongside a secular push toward civility in the West. According to Crawford (1985), the body is the symbolic terrain upon which desire for and displays of control are enacted. In particular, the health of the body has come to act as a central metaphor for self-control, self-discipline, self-denial, and will power (Crawford 1994). "Being healthy," and the appearance of being so, has become a metaphor for being a responsible, "good" citizen. Conversely, the "others"—smokers, obese people, alcoholics, drug users, and people with AIDS—are all associated with excess and indulgence, with a loss of the West's most cherished qualities.

While cherished, there are a number of counternormative aspects that one might argue are equally characteristic of the West. Consumerist facets of Western culture are associated with a release from control (Crawford 1994). Gratification of pleasures and desires are intrinsic aspects of consumer culture. Yet, rather than accept the antithetical control-release inclinations as two sides of the same coin, Western culture expunges its association with the uncontrolled aspects—such as addictions—linking them with disparaged "others." These "others," who are blamed for bringing their bodies into disrepute and illness, are held outside the culture symbolically, so that the existing core values cannot be morally contaminated.

The chapter has shown, thus far, that in an ongoing way, a positive sense of identity is forged by values, by culture's symbolization of the facets of human existence that are laudable and, on the other hand, those that are "low." A large category of "others" is constructed from those identities that can be easily marked out as deficient in self-control over body, mind, and destiny. This has been vastly underexplored in contemporary psychology.

The "Other" and Crisis

While representations of "others'" difference, their debased and "low" qualities, form a constant feature of society, in periods of potential threat and crisis, the focus on the negative and threatening features becomes intensified. One only has to think of the amplification of anti-Semitism in the German economic crisis of the 1920s and 1930s to be reminded of the salience increasingly accorded to Jews as debased "others," or, indeed, with less severe consequences, of the escalation of antigay sentiment from the time when AIDS began to affect the West in the 1980s. A multitude of past and contemporary instances could be added to this. However, caution is called for in relation to framing the litany of "hate crimes" or acts of genocide as responses to crises. Rather, a sense of threat and imminent crisis can sometimes be engineered in order to justify the harsh treatment of "others."

In periods in which crisis is seen to loom on the horizon, when anxiety is raised, those associated with undesirable qualities move from being represented as mildly threatening, a challenge to the core values of the society, to being seen as the purveyors of chaos. Thus, while the "other" is defined in terms of difference and inferiority in relation to normative values in an ongoing sense, the representations that arise at times of crisis intensify this distinction. They reflect a powerful division between a decorous, righteous "us" and a disruptive, transgressive "them" (Douglas 1966). Representations that declare which groups and practices pollute the order and decorum of the community proliferate (Douglas 1992). Vivid representations circulate that undermine the "other" by debasing it, such as the equating of Jews to vermin, bacteria, and maggots in the key Nazi text *Mein Kampf* (see Bar-Tal 1990). This categorization is motivated by communities' impetus to maintain their safety and comfort. The decorum and positive sense of identity of "us" is sustained through imbuing "others" with devalued properties. Such representations can lead to the desire for the removal of this polluting force. The prototypical act that aims to rid a community of impure elements—those represented as the source of chaos—and thereby restore order and a positive sense of identity, utilizes scapegoats for the ritual transfer of evil from inside to outside the community (Douglas 1995). Scapegoating has its counterpart within the individual psyche in the defense termed projection. Both the more macrosocial and microsocial processes will be explored, followed by discussion of the applicability of the othering process beyond Western contexts.

THE ROOTS OF OTHERING IN INDIVIDUALS: A MICROSOCIAL FOCUS

Melanie Klein's (1946; 1952) psychodynamic theory of the affective roots of human subjectivity developed out of Freud's later writing, particularly the duality between the life and death instincts, set out in *Beyond the Pleasure Principle* (1920/1955). By tracing the building block of this developmental theory, one can augment the social psychological understanding of identity construction and its link to the "other."

The infant's early interaction with its primary caregiver (often the mother) is both gratifying and frustrating. Satisfaction depends on the ability of the caregiver to fathom and to respond to the infant's needs. At times when its needs are fulfilled, the infant experiences the caregiver as satisfying and loving. When not fulfilled, its experience is persecutory and frustrating, which elicits feelings of aggression and hate. The infant becomes anxious that forces are motivated to harm it. However, infants do not merely endure such feelings. They appear to be orientated toward maintaining their experience of nurturance, satisfaction, safety, and security. Freud attests to the primacy of the body's drive to maximize pleasure and to minimize pain in the early structuring of the psyche (see Sloan 1996). Adherence to a life force and the "spitting out" of destructive impulses provide the seeds of an explanation for the psyche's orientation toward identification with positive experiences.

The earliest of representational activity strives to protect a positive inner space. It does so by putting mechanisms to work to ward off the anxiety induced by the perceived threat of persecution. Splitting, introjection, and projection determine that loving feelings are separated from the more paranoid feelings. The more positive experiences and feelings are taken into the self, or introjected, and their negative equivalents are projected outward. Thus, in this earliest phase of life, bad experiences and objects tend to be represented as outside the self, while the infant clings to good experiences, not wanting to sully them. The goal of splitting is to keep the bad away from the good at the level of representation in the hope that the bad will not invade and destroy the good.

The roots of these processes lie in the affects present in the earliest moments of infancy. Anxiety in particular forms an organizing concept in the psychodynamic understanding of humans. The theory situates affect at the root of identity development. From birth, the infant experiences anxiety. The maturing process revolves around strengthening and organizing the self against anxiety. From the earliest stages of infancy, splitting, introjection, and projection are brought into play unconsciously to reduce anxiety, ensuring a sense of safety and security for the maturing being.

The key factor is that these mechanisms sustain a lack of integration of the opposite poles of feeling within the infant: one side of its experience is represented as all good, and the other as all bad. The two are kept separate in the infant's mind and are available only as alternatives. Thus, splitting, introjecting, and projecting are ways of viewing the world in simplistic terms: either as all good or as all bad. A middle ground or "gray area" is missing when one splits.

While subsequent psychic developments facilitate apprehension of complexity, of the "gray areas," residues of this early split representation of the world remain in the individual's pattern of representation. A key emphasis of the Kleinian outlook is that rather than passing through phases and leaving them behind, each phase of development leaves its mark on the developing human, and in later life all humans can be plunged back into operating as if they were in one of the early phases. When changes in the social environment make for insecurity, thereby raising levels of anxiety, forms of this early representational activity in which the "other" can be fantasized in terms of one's own unwanted thoughts re-emerge. The early pattern of representation, which allows the infant to handle anxiety, is thereby reproduced in adult life.

Beyond the forces of splitting, introjection, and projection, Klein and her followers developed the notion of "projective identification" (Klein 1946) to characterize a more complex dynamic that occurs in early development. This construct is particularly relevant for theories concerning the location of threat within the "other," and thus highly pertinent for theories of identity construction. Projective identification means that parts of the self that one does not want to own are not only projected onto external objects, but these external objects are also then seen to be possessed and controlled by, as well as identified with, the projected parts. Thus, the objects or humans onto which people project their aggression become feared as a source of belligerence (Frosh 1989; Moses 1989). Material placed outside the space of the self comes back to torment it, as will be demonstrated later in the chapter. One comes to fear that which one gets rid of in the project of identity construction. Rather than gaining a firm sense of safety and comfort from the projection of undesirable qualities onto others, in line with the unconscious aim, the "self" comes to experience the "other" as a threat by way of the "other's" association with polluting, contaminating qualities. The bad qualities that the "other" is left to carry threaten to "leak" back into the space of the self.

In sum, infantile representations are orientated toward protection of the self from anxiety. To accomplish this, the "other" becomes the repository of material that the individual seeks to push out from its own space. These early building blocks of what is to be associated with "others" rather than with the self leave their mark on the developing identity.

The chapter will move on to show how social representations come to augment the individual's notion of what can comfortably be associated with self and in-group identity, and what is unacceptable and must be placed outside in the service of identity protection. Since anxiety and the response to it are organizing concepts in the construction of the "other," raised levels of anxiety, as a consequence of potential danger or sense of crisis, intensify this more ongoing process of identity protection.

While psychodynamic theorization is often seen as solely concerned with the intrasubjective, I hope to have begun to show that it has social relevance. From infancy to later life, when faced with anxiety-provoking situations, there is a rearrangement in people's representations of themselves and of others. People organize their representations in accordance with the struggle for a sense of boundary between a pure inner space and a polluted, outside world. The subjective management of anxiety springs from a relational process in which the self continuously strives for protection from negative feelings evoked in it by dumping unwanted material onto "others" at the level of representation. Holding certain and not other representations in relation to threatening phenomena relates to a self-protective motivation, but, as will be further elaborated, such representations are constituted by the values and ideologies that circulate in the particular communities, cultures, and societies of which all individuals form a part.

FROM A MICROSOCIAL FOCUS TO THE BROADER SOCIAL WORLD

A psychodynamic stance theorizes the development of representations of the "other" that contain material that the self seeks to distance itself from. Yet it does not account for the contents of that material, other than it being undesirable in some way. Thus it cannot account for the specific social representations that adults hold about others. To understand the link between the "other" and identity construction, one needs to incorporate broader social forces. This can illuminate both the process of forming and the contents of identity-linked representations.

Assuming that identity contains both subjective and group-based elements, how do the representations held by individuals become permeated with group-specific expressions of affiliation and protection in the course of the life-span? Mainstream social psychology has a "toolbox" that it tends to open in relation to such questions. Social identity theory (SIT) (for example, see Tajfel and Turner 1986) provides one of the ways to make the transition between the intergroup and individual levels of thought, as does self-categorization theory (for example, see Turner *et al.* 1987). SIT provides pointers as to how group identification is likely to work, especially in relation to the relatively fixed social categories into which humans are born, such as gender.

However, such social psychological theories pay little attention to the contents of the representations that structure identity, a key focus of this chapter. Tajfel's work focuses on process in the hope that content will take care of itself (Duveen 2001). In attempting to cast greater light on content, work from beyond mainstream psychological traditions must be incorporated. One essential aspect of such work is that group membership is not regarded as the crucial feature of one's conception of who one is and how one defines oneself.

According to psychodynamically influenced sociocultural theory, representations that circulate in a particular social group prior to the individual's entry into it influence who and what the individual chooses as "other." Certain groups have already been represented as respectable and others as degenerate. Each social group has various "repositories" that it stores as potential targets for its projection of unwanted material (Sherwood 1980). Echoing and extending this, Gilman states, "Every social group has a set vocabulary of images for this externalized Other. These images are the product of history and of a culture that perpetuates them. . . . From the wide range of the potential models in any society, we select a model that best reflects the common presuppositions about the Other at any given moment in history" (1985, 20). In the ideas they pass down through the generations, groups store not only a sense of which their disfavored groups are but also what aspersions are to be linked to such groups. The groups and aspersions chosen are mutually informative of one another, and this connects with the core values in the society.

This psychodynamic or sociocultural theory is useful for the social psychological theorization of identity. Yet, the way in which individuals come to know which groups and practices constitute the "other" in their network, the transmission of knowledge between the social environment and the individual, is not operationalized by these theories. It is here that social representations theory must be drawn upon.

According to Duveen's (2001) theorization of the link between identity and social representation, individuals enter a world of existing representations from the very start of life. These representations both precede the entry of the individual into the world and impose themselves upon the growing being. Thus far, social representational ideas are very similar to those of the psychodynamic sociocultural theorists, but at this point, the former become more specific regarding identity construction. In the course of interpersonal communication, people identify individuals within certain social categories (for example, as male or female) and they thereby have an identity, and the contents associated with it, imposed upon them via the shared thinking of others. Broader communication systems, such as the mass media, also relay ongoing representations concerning certain identities, and if one is already situated within an identity—such as having been represented as female—the ongoing babble in the environment constantly constructs and reconstructs one. Having developed the notion that value violation (for example, violating the self-control value) can underpin which identities are chosen for othering (Joffe and Staerklé 2007), it must be noted that identity goes beyond the much theorized social categories of gender, race, and class. The addict, the refugee, and the "mad" person are perhaps equally salient in people's conceptions of who they are and how they define themselves. Such "others" tend to symbolize the counterpoint of desirable identity: a self in control of body, destiny, and mind.

The augmentation of a social representational theory of identity outlined earlier in this chapter provides a further, finer grain of detail for understanding how identity is constructed. A key process in the formation of social representations is objectification (Moscovici 1984/2001). It describes how abstract ideas are assimilated and come to be associated with particular entities. Objectification, which is highly analogous to symbolization, involves people making something abstract more easy to grasp by transforming it into a more concrete entity. This can occur in a number of ways (see Moscovici and Hewstone 1984), including abstract ideas being substituted with people (termed personification) or groups. This process can be used to explain how people and groups get attached to various values, such as that of self-control (or its violation). Thus, objectification of cultural values produces a set of common points of reference through which social groups are conceived. Shared thinking regarding the "other" is grounded in such common knowledge.

OTHERING BEYOND THE WEST

While there is strong evidence in Western culture for the pattern of othering laid out in this chapter, does it generalize beyond the West?
Psychodynamic theorization would see it as a more universal pattern,
though the sociocultural variants would bring into relief culture-specific
values. By touching on a few social representational studies conducted in
non-Western contexts, one can begin to build a picture of whether the
process of identity construction posited in this chapter is specific to
Western cultures or might generalize beyond them.

Despite the central role played by women in societies the world over,
to a lesser or greater degree, they continue to be denigrated. Othering and
its function as an identity-buttressing process for dominant groups is well
established in Western feminist literature. If anything, the process is more
extreme in non-Western contexts, such as many African cultures. For
example, a study of the social representation of AIDS among urban
Zambian adolescents reveals a core representation in which AIDS is
linked to the West, God, and local teenage girls (see Joffe and Bettega
2003). In the face of AIDS's alarming prevalence in Zambia, particularly
among young people, this African sample distances HIV/AIDS from its
African identity. In the teenagers' social representation, it is Western per-
versity, including scientific and sexual experimentation that allows AIDS
to come into being. Local immorality then ushers in this punishment
from God. Since the group sampled also reports very high levels of
(Catholic) church attendance (as is common in much of Zambia), its
identity is rendered distant from AIDS in terms of both its African and
spiritual facets.

While representing AIDS as linked to the West and God offers identity protection for the sample as a whole, the link to teenage girls renders
female identity unprotected. In line with the inferior status of females in
the society, they form the repository into which this unwanted disease is
lodged. Following a history of linking a range of illnesses to women in
Zambia (see Joffe and Bettega 2003), the study finds that teenage girls are
seen as the vectors of HIV in terms of their liaisons with "sugar daddies"
(older men who have sex with the girls in return for gifts or money) and
with teenage boys.

The social representation circulating among the adolescent sample renders the boys unable to take responsibility for safer sex due to the attrac-
tiveness of adolescent girls, particularly when they are clad in Western
dress, and by a range of factors including alcohol, peer pressure, and the
uncontrollable male sex drive. Thus males who are involved in unsafe sexual liaisons are not held culpable for their consequences: all responsibility

lies with the girls. The males—adolescents and "sugar daddies" alike—are threatened by the danger but do not generate it; they are not actors in the spread of the epidemic. Male identity, as well as the male superiority that characterizes the social system, is largely protected by way of the social representation of AIDS in Zambia. Conversely, the young females, onto whom the bad event is projected, are not afforded the same level of protection by the social representation. They are blamed for HIV's spread and become objects of fear in that they are represented as the dangerous vectors of threat. This speaks to the role played by projective identification in othering: a group can buttress a positive sense of identity and power via projection, but the projected material then returns to haunt it.

A growing body of AIDS research speaks to such processes. The phenomenon also extends well beyond this arena into the risk field more generally. In a study of social representations of the Hong Kong bird flu epidemic of 2001, for example, Hong Kong women linked it to mainland China and to what were regarded as undesirable practices within Hong Kong (Joffe and Lee 2004). Dirt played a major role in the women's understandings of the transmission of the flu. Unhygienic conditions in the markets where chickens were bought, as well as on the farms where they were raised, were centrally implicated in spreading, if not in generating, the epidemic.

Dirt has not been heavily emphasized in the construction of Western food scares (Miles and Frewer 2001), though it has been implicated, historically, in a range of epidemics that Westerners regard as having been brought in from outside (see Joffe 1999) and is centrally implicated in the contemporary risk of *Methicillin Resistant Staphylococcus Aureus* (MRSA) in hospitals the world over (Washer and Joffe 2006). Despite possible differences across societies and historical periods in the contents of the core values that are implicated in risks, the key points are that outsiders are seen as purveyors of risk in a number of different cultures, and risk events tend to be objectified in images of the good and the bad. In the Hong Kong study, the images were of the dirty, greedy, rule-disobeying (Chinese mainland) chicken rearers and (Hong Kong based) sellers, as opposed to the suffering, innocent chicken buyers and consumers.

Periods of heightened threat—when facing crises such as epidemics— seem to evoke defenses to counter anxieties and fears both within and outside the West. Perhaps a universalist vein of theorization is called for that draws upon sociocultural theory, as well as upon psychodynamic notions, without overlooking more localized dynamics. The psychodynamics of the projection of blame for crisis onto others appears to grapple successfully with the root cause of othering within individual psyches and to go some way to explaining the more social process of scapegoating.

DISCUSSION: A THEORETICAL INTEGRATION

In some sense, the social representations vision and psychodynamic framework are apparently incompatible. The idea of representations pre-dating the individual, and the individual merely being born into a location within them, is very different from the notion of the infant constructing a representational system that is identity protective and then slotting material in the environment into its own pre-existing system of thought. However, the two can sit together more comfortably if one differentiates between the structuring of people's representations and the contents that come to constitute their social representation. I hope to have shown that even if proclivities toward certain patterns of representation are forged in the early years, this in no way diminishes the role played by the slowly unfolding social world in constraining or exacerbating such proclivities.

The concern in this chapter is with a sedimentation of the "we" in the "I." The early social environment of the child, in which needs are, or fail to be, responded to, forms the seeds of identity: "These [seeds] are sedimented in affectively toned representations of self-in-relation-to-others" (Sloan 1996, 111). Thus identity, according to what I have developed here, is about self-other relations in which vestiges of the early, infantile representations inform later responses to ideas encountered in the social environment. Social representations concerning certain categories (ranging from traditional identity categories such as gender to other divisions in society such as those between obese and "normal" weight people) are among those ideas that circulate in this environment, and they are particularly pertinent to identity construction. The early introjective and projective processes provide the seeds of an explanation for *why* people locate threat with categories with which they do not identify, with the "other."

Both the clinical and the culturally based psychodynamic traditions drawn upon here challenge aspects of contemporary psychology, with its assumption that the individual is a self-regulating, largely rational thinker. Instead, the alternative offered in this chapter forges a vision of an essentially emotive and social being whose motivations are not easily fathomable. Even though there is increasing attention within psychology to nonconscious processing—which harks back to ideas suggested by Zajonc (1980), among others—the links between such processes and identity construction are underdeveloped. Furthermore, contemporary social psychology is reticent in relation to psychodynamic thinking for a range of reasons, including the psychodynamic idea that the patterning of adult representations can be forged within infancy, before the individual has knowledge of the macrosocial world. However, this chapter argues that patterns can be established very early on, and that social material that is subsequently encountered shapes the manifestation of particular ideas in specific groups and individuals.

There is a need to bring to light a final aspect of psychodynamic theorization as a route to showing that identity need not be solely tied in with othering. This chapter has established that ongoing tensions between "us" and "them" are intensified at moments of potential danger and crisis. At such times, the early splitting mechanism of defense reappears in adults, and the "other" becomes the target of a rich array of projections that contain those aspects of experience from which individuals seek to distance themselves. Othering is a way of protecting the self and the ingroup; it is defense by way of representation. It also serves the function of status-quo maintenance in that each society perpetuates existing values by the ways in which it responds to crises—such as expunging dirt in the Hong Kong bird flu context mentioned or tightening the reigns of control in Western contexts. The particular characteristic of the early, split state that is reinvoked at such times is that contradictory feelings cannot sit together. Were they to do so, this would constitute a rather complex orientation toward threats and toward the groups seen to embody them.

However, it is important to highlight that in the course of early development, humans tend to learn to think in this complex way, to reconcile the split parts. The first position, detailed above and termed the paranoid-schizoid position, develops the infant's capacity to order chaos by splitting good from bad objects and experiences at the level of representation. However, Klein (1952) posits that following this, infants move into the "depressive position" in which the ability to tolerate ambivalence develops. It is here that the capacity to deal with anxiety in a nonsplit way is cultivated. Within this position, the infant realizes that both nourishment and deprivation, satisfaction and persecution, derive from the same primary caregiver. It reconciles the polarization between "good" and "bad" experiences and objects when it begins to mourn the loss of the purely "good" self and the "purely good" primary object, realizing that "bad" is contained within both. If mourning takes place, the infant is said to have entered the depressive position in which it acquires an ability to tolerate ambivalence. This is central to a nonsplit way of viewing the world.

The most basic of defenses against anxiety is to be found in the paranoid position in which the infant oscillates between the unlinked experiences of hate and love. Yet when it moves into the depressive position, it begins to worry, to engage with the idea that the hate will destroy the good, and this sends the individual down a path toward nonidealized and nondenigrating representations. The newfound ambivalence allows the

infant to represent both itself and others in terms of a compl
ings. To be emotionally ambivalent is to be able to hold, sir
positively and negatively charged feelings. This is particularly difficult for
the developing psyche since it must link and reconcile states that have
previously been held apart to defend the core of the self. However, when
it achieves this, complex rather than simplistic and polarized representations become possible.

This subsequent aspect of development is often neglected in socioculturally orientated psychodynamic theories, but lends hope that splitting
is neither inevitable nor unchangeable. It has implications for identity
formation and social exclusion, and can be used in service of opposing
the notion that currently pervades social cognition—that negative
stereotyping and prejudice are "normal" and routine parts of what it is to
be human.

CONCLUDING REMARKS

This chapter has forged a social psychological framework for understanding the link between the "other" and identity construction. In a nutshell,
an aspect of how identity is constructed is by excluding or othering those
qualities that do not map onto the core values of the culture. In turn, people associated with these qualities are used to buttress a positive sense of
identity by being represented as the "low," undesirable beings in the society. Thus identity and social representation are linked insofar as social
representations construct out-groups that symbolize difference and a
lowly place in the hierarchy of values associated with different groups.

The foundations of identity formation, at least in part, lie in the
human unconscious response to anxiety. Freud's bodily metaphor for
projection of the bad outward—spitting out bad-tasting food—becomes
layered with wider social and moral connotations as the human being
becomes acculturated, and such connotations are integrated into identity.
Identity is forged, largely, by exclusion of those that one (and the culture
in which one is located) sees as associated with undesirable qualities as follows: *"If the aim of a system is to create an outside where you can put the
things you don't want, then we have to look at what that system disposes of—
its rubbish—to understand it, to get a picture of how it sees itself and wants
to be seen"* (Phillips 1995, 19). This statement complements the claim
made by cultural theorists such as Said (1978) that the way that a culture
defines the "other" discloses how the culture characterizes itself. This can
be extended to individuals. They have a tendency to introject what is seen
as "good" and project outward "the bad."

The claim that all groups have "others" whom they utilize to form a sense of positive identity needs to be tempered by reference to power differences in societies. Dominant groups exert power by controlling the process of representation; some representations gain greater currency than others, not only within certain cultures but also on the world stage. There is a silencing of certain voices, while others are more pronounced. An understanding of this is not highly developed in social psychology, other than in works such as that of Jost and Banaji (1994) that offer tremendously rich pickings for integration with a theory of identity construction. A further area that offers much potential for future integration is the interconnection between projection at the individual level and scapegoating at the community level. This project would also, inevitably, allow for the location of blame and stigma in the nexus of identity-related aspects of social psychology.

REFERENCES

Andreski, S. 1989. *Syphilis, puritanism and witch hunts.* London: Macmillan.
Bar-Tal, D. 1990. *Group beliefs.* New York: Springer.
Crawford, R. 1985. A cultural account of health—control, release and the social body. In *Issues in the political economy of health care,* ed. J. B. McKinlay, 60–103. London: Tavistock.
———. 1994. The boundaries of the self and the unhealthy other: Reflections on health, culture and AIDS. *Social Science and Medicine* 38 (10): 1347–65.
Douglas, M. 1966. *Purity and danger.* London: Routledge and Kegan Paul.
———. 1992. *Risk and blame. Essays in cultural theory.* London: Routledge.
Douglas, T. 1995. *Scapegoats: Transferring blame.* London: Routledge.
Duveen, G. 2001. Representations, identities, resistance. In *Representations of the social: Bridging theoretical traditions,* ed. K. Deaux and G. Philogène, 257–70. Malden, MA: Blackwell.
Elias, N. 1939/2000. *The civilising process.* Oxford: Blackwell.
Fanon, F. 1992. The fact of blackness. In *"Race," culture and difference,* ed. J. Donald and A. Rattansi, 220–40. London: Sage.
Freud, S. 1920/1955. *Beyond the pleasure principle.* Standard Edition. London: Hogarth Press.
Frosh, S. 1989. Psychoanalysis and racism. In *Crises of the self: Further essays on psychoanalysis and politics,* ed. B. Richards, 229–44. London: Free Association.
Gilman, S. 1985. *Difference and pathology: Stereotypes of sexuality, race and madness.* Ithaca, NY: Cornell University Press.
Joffe, H. 1999. *Risk and "the Other."* Cambridge: Cambridge University Press.
Joffe, H., and N. Bettega. 2003. Social representations of AIDS among Zambian adolescents. *Journal of Health Psychology* 85 (5): 616–31.
Joffe, H., and N. Y. L. Lee. 2004. Social representations of a food risk: The Hong Kong avian bird flu epidemic. *Journal of Health Psychology* 9 (4): 517–33.

Joffe, H., and C. Staerklé. 2007. The centrality of the self-control ethos in western aspersions regarding outgroups: A social representational analysis of stereotype content. *Culture & Psychology* 13 (4).

Jost, J, and M. R. Banaji. 1994. The role of stereotyping in system-justification and the production of false consciousness. *British Journal of Social Psychology* 33 (1): 1–27.

Klein, M. 1946. Notes on some schizoid mechanisms. *International Journal of Psycho-Analysis* 27:99–110.

———. 1952. Some theoretical conclusions regarding the emotional life of the infant. In *Developments in psycho-analysis*, ed. M. Klein, P. Hemann, S. Isaacs, and J. Riviere, 198–236. London: Hogarth Press.

McCulloch, J. 1995. *Colonial psychiatry and "The African mind."* Cambridge: Cambridge University Press.

Miles, S., and L. J. Frewer. 2001. Investigation specific concerns about different food hazards. *Food Quality and Preference* 12 (1): 47–61.

Moscovici, S. 1984. The phenomenon of social representations. In *Social representations*, ed. R. M. Farr and S. Moscovici, 3–69. Cambridge: Cambridge University Press; Paris: Maison des Sciences de l'Homme.

Moscovici, S. 1984/2001. Why a theory of social representations. In *Representations of the social, ed.* K. Deaux and G. Philogène, 8–35. Oxford: Blackwell.

Moscovici, S., and M. Hewstone. 1984. De la science au sens commun. In *Psychologie Sociale*, ed. S. Moscovici, 539–66. Paris: Presses Universitaires de France.

Moses, R. 1989. Projection, identification and projective identification: Their relation to political process. In *Projection, identification, projective identification*, ed. J. Sandler, 133–50. London: Karnac.

Phillips, A. 1995. *Terror and experts*. London: Faber and Faber.

Said, E. W. 1978. *Orientalism: Western conceptions of the Orient.* London: Penguin.

Sloan, T. 1996. *Damaged life: The crisis of the modern psyche.* London: Routledge.

Sherwood, R. 1980. *The psychodynamics of race.* Sussex: Harvester Press.

Stallybrass, P., and A. White. 1986. *The politics and poetics of transgression.* Ithaca, NY: Cornell University Press.

Tajfel, H., and J. C. Turner. 1986. The social identity theory of intergroup behavior. In *The psychology of intergroup relations*, ed. S. Worchel and W. G. Austin, 7–24. Chicago: Nelson-Hall.

Turner, J. C., M. A. Hogg, P. J. Oakes, S. Reicher, and M. S. Wetherell. 1987. *Rediscovering the social group: A self-categorization theory.* Oxford: Basil Blackwell.

Washer, P., and H. Joffe. 2006. Social representations of the "hospital superbug." *Social Science & Medicine* 63:2141–52.

Weber, M. 1904/1905/1976. *The Protestant ethic and the spirit of capitalism.* Trans. T. Parsons. 2nd ed. London: Allen and Unwin.

Young, R. J. C. 1995. *Colonial desire: Hybridity in theory, culture and race.* London: Routledge.

Zajonc, R. 1980. Feeling and thinking: Preferences need no inferences. *American Psychologist* 35:151–75.

SOCIAL IDENTITIES AND SOCIAL REPRESENTATIONS

HOW ARE THEY RELATED?

Ivana Marková

THE CONCEPTS OF "IDENTITY" AND "REPRESENTATION" have had a long history both in mundane and philosophical thought; over aeons of time, they have both retained some stable characteristics, but they have also changed. Questions like "who am I?" "who are we?" and "who are they?" as well as "what do we know about the world and how do we represent it?" have been everlasting. However, answers to these questions have been continuously changing throughout history.

The theory of social identity and the theory of social representations are among the major theories that have influenced generations of social psychologists since the 1960s. These two theories are concerned with the understanding of complex social phenomena that turn the contemporary society upside down. Research based on these two theories is inquiring into basic human conditions that have led to the world-shaking tragedies, conflicts, and dramas of the twentieth century, including Nazism, Stalinism, AIDS, and environmental disasters, to mention but a few. The theory of social identity and the theory of social representations have both responded to the compelling challenge with which social psychology has been faced as a discipline: they have brought into focus the study of inter-actions and interdependencies between groups, individuals, and institutions shaped not only by contemporary events but also by collective memories and forgetting, as well as future visions.

It is therefore not surprising that researchers have been interested in searching for and specifying links between these two theories, and that numerous publications have brought this issue into focus. Breakwell

(2001) calls the subject matter of their relations "a fundamental question" (271) and one can find a number of sections in volumes as well as journal articles (for example, Duveen and Lloyd 1986, 1990; Breakwell 1993; Deaux and Philogène 2001) substantiating Breakwell's claim. Wagner and Hayes point out that social representations and social identity "appear to define each other" (2005, 311), while others refer to the fact that the two phenomena are always in mutual exchange (see Brewer 2001; Duveen 2001; Breakwell 2001).

Yet despite much effort to find a satisfactory answer, the question of the relationship between these two theories cannot be easily resolved. There are a number of reasons for that. Both theories are concerned with group and intergroup conflict and relations, phenomena with which humankind has wrestled throughout all its history. Each theory views these phenomena from a specific theoretical perspective that does not easily merge with that of the other perspective. The two theories play a fundamental role in all the chapters of this volume, and I am proposing to discuss here some theoretical issues with regard to their relations. This will necessarily draw on practical implications of this subject matter.

A Chicken-Egg Problem

Claims and phrases like "identity is a representation," "there is an exchange relationship between social representations and identity" or "identity representation," which all closely link the two theories, one can suppose, might have led to the query as to what comes first—social representations or social identity. The question of the priority of one phenomenon over the other has been debated in literature on a number of occasions (see Brewer 2001), and it keeps reappearing. "What comes first?" is an old philosophical and psychological question with respect to other issues as well, including, for example, whether thought is prior to language, whether acts are prior to words, and whether language is prior to communication.

But one cannot answer such big questions once and for all because an answer to each of them depends on the problem that the researcher is trying to solve or understand. It cannot be settled by arguing or providing evidence that researcher "X" is correct in claiming the priority of social representations, or that the researcher "Y" is right in prioritizing social identity. The question of the priority of one phenomenon over the other has one meaning if the researcher is concerned with, say, the social development of the individual, another meaning if she explores the sociocultural development of a nation or groups, and still another one if she questions the relations between the self, others, and an object (Ego-Alter-Object) (Moscovici 1984; Marková 2003), among many other topics.

With respect to ontogenetic development, the question of priority should not really arise. It is self-evident that the individual is born into the world that has existed before he comes into it. This includes not only social realities like families, tables, chairs, television sets, and mobile telephones, but also commonsense knowledge, social representations, and biological classifications (which are sometimes called social identities)—like male or female, blue-eyed or brown-eyed, people born with a genetic disease like hemophilia versus those born without it, and so on. One might also include here classifications of people defined by fixed societal structures like castes or hierarchical orders in premodern European societies, nationalities, and so on. Such social realities into which each of us is born involve both social representations and social identities. They are, to use Duveen's term, obligatory. Subsequently, of course, the individual chooses membership in social groups, takes on contractual identities (Duveen 2001), and acquires new forms of knowledge and representations.

In a different kind of problem, however, the question of what comes first could be of interest. Consider, for example, the formation of new social or national identities in postcommunist Estonia (see Raudsepp, Heidmets, and Kruusvall, forthcoming). These cannot be properly understood without considering collective memories, national identities, and loyalties to the interwar independent state of Estonia. Estonians may view Russian minorities as having been involved in the persecution of Estonians during the totalitarian Soviet regime and thus hold specific social representations of them. These representations might in turn influence relations between Estonians and non-Estonians today and affect their attitudes with respect to who is considered to be "in" and who is "out" of various national groups. In this case, in order to answer the question "what comes first?" one would need to assess the weight of past social representations and identities, their transformation, and the future vision of Estonian citizens.

But the question of what comes first could also be formulated as an ontological and epistemological issue in terms of the relations between the Ego and the Alter, or the self and others. If one adopts the hypothesis according to which humans have an innate capacity of sociality, that is, of openness toward others, one may follow it by another hypothesis, namely that the Ego/Alter–relation is basic to humanity. Anthropological studies show that the idea of the self desiring to fuse, merge, or identify with certain others, or, in contrast, to separate from others, has been implicit in history since the beginning of humankind.

This idea has been viewed as coming from the mystic search for one-ness, from the search for unity with nature, the cosmos, and gods, and it has been part of rudimentary and primitive religions. In mimetic religious ceremonies, humans represented sacred beings or they acted a rebirth through imitation or identification with gods (Hastings 1908–26). The idea of an intimate relation with gods was already present in Etruscan mythology, and it is also part of the mystic transformation in many religions; it is rooted in emotions, activity, and the primordial human experience of the world. Symbolic merging of the self and others has been realized probably in all societies throughout the history of mankind through music, dance, and rhythm. This primordial and unconscious search for belonging has become, since the seventeenth century, part of the theories of the unconscious mind (Whyte 1962). One could argue of course that such "irrational" and mystic identifications have nothing in common with rational social science, and that they should not be associated with possible precursors of modern identities. Yet one cannot avoid noticing the idea of semiconscious and unconscious search of the self or groups for identification with others in modern social theories like those of charisma, leadership, propaganda, and persuasion (Moscovici 1993). The idea of identification goes hand-in-hand with that of separation from dark powers and with witch-hunting. Could this ontological search for identification therefore be excluded from modern theories of social identity and social representations?

Another form of the self's desire for identification with others takes on various patterns of intersubjectivity (see Coelho and Figueiredo 2003), primarily in ontogenetic development, but also in traumatic intersubjective experiences. While in the former it has been explored in child development and in close interpersonal relations, in the latter, traumatic intersubjective experiences could result from the existential desire of the Ego for identity (e.g., the Freudian identification with the father figure). In contrast, and following the view of Levinas (1974/1981), traumatic experiences could result from the self's conflict: to be for the "other" means that the self is left without identity. Still other researchers wish to argue that the emphasis on intersubjectivity needs to be balanced by attention to interobjectivity: rather than focusing on individuals, researchers should explore minority and majority contacts within and between groups (Moghaddam 2003).

For the theory of social representations, the Ego and Alter interaction is crucial in several respects. First, the Ego and Alter relations are at the basis of most social phenomena with which the theory is concerned because it is these that turn society upside down. Social phenomena that involve, say, justice or injustice, equality or inequality, and morality or immorality are phenomena in which the Ego and Alter relations play a crucial role. For example, they focus on social recognition and its denial, on the discriminated and the privileged, and on trust and conspiracy. It is these struggles involving the Ego and Alter relations in their multitude forms, both in their histories and contemporary appearances, that provide rich resources for social representations.

In yet another sense, the Ego and Alter interdependence is the point of departure in the original theory of social representations in which Moscovici places the major emphasis on communication. In the preface to the second edition of *La Psychanalyse* (1976), he points to the funda-mental characteristic of a social representation: representation is always directed at others. It speaks through pointing out something to someone, and more generally, through expressing something to someone with whom it communicates. Social representations are formed in and through dialogues.

This kaleidoscope of the Ego and Alter relations points to their oblig-atory presence both in the theory of social identity and in the theory of social representations. One cannot meaningfully ask the question about identity without posing the question about the self and others. And one cannot talk about social representations as a theory of social knowledge without examining public discourses in which different dialogues between the Ego and Alter take place and through which they generate representations. But each of these relations presents itself as part of a spe-cific problem, and in each of them, therefore, the question of the priority of identity or representation must be answered in its specific way.

WHICH SOCIAL IDENTITIES AND WHICH SOCIAL REPRESENTATIONS?

We now must ask a more specific question: which theory of social repre-sentations and which theory of social identity are we speaking about? There are numerous approaches within both theories. They offer diversi-fied concepts, they are based on various analytical assumptions, and they are applied to a wide range of phenomena. For example, within the theory of social representations, some approaches are concerned primarily with the structured content of representations, others are based on organizing principles, still others emphasize the sociocultural nature of representa-tions, and some view social representations as forms of communication and dialogue. Equally, the notion of "social identity" has become widely diversified. Some notions of social identities are cognitively based, while others emphasize the sociocultural perspective; some social identities refer to demographic or biological classifications that are relatively stable, while others base social identity on belonging to a dynamic social group in which the members share the "interdependence of fate"; social identities may refer to political, national, social, or group-related similarities; and so on.

This diversity presents yet another reason why it is not easy to answer the question about the relationship between these two significant approaches without further clarification. All one can do is to select a particular approach from this multitude. In the present volume, the notion of "category" occupies a crucial place with respect to the study of relations between social identity and social representations. This relation is clearly expressed in the claim that "category is a representation" (Augoustinos 2001, 205), and in view of this, I propose to explore the meaning of this claim.

SOCIAL CATEGORIES AND SOCIAL PHENOMENA

The identity approach based on the theory of social categorization has shown over many years an enormous research output that comes from laboratory and field research. It has also attracted many critics who, above all, have been disappointed with its individualistic, mechanistic, and cognitivist character (see Krech and Crutchfield 1948; Newcomb 1951; Greenwood 2004).

In his scholarly article on the context of social identity, Reicher (2004) makes two important contributions. First, he presents, in a very comprehensive manner, the fundamental features of the social identity theory based on social categorization and self-categorization. Second, he challenges "the various reductionist treatments of the social identity tradition" (922). His paper therefore will help me to illuminate some conceptual differences regarding social categorization and social representations.

In the classical Aristotelian view, categories are discrete entities characterized by a set of properties shared by their members. They should be clearly defined, mutually exclusive, and collectively exhaustive. Any entity of the given universe of classification must unequivocally belong to one and only one of the proposed categories. In view of this, categorization is usually defined as a process by which our environment is simplified by clustering objects into groups. In social identity theory, this process refers to categorizing people on the basis of some kind of similarity that differentiates them; in other words, due to the presence or absence of their specific similarity, they become members of an in-group or an out-group.

Reicher (2004) insists that social identity theory aims to explain how individuals define themselves with respect to cultural contents, relations with others, and pursuing the group's goals. Social categories are context sensitive and events can be construed in different ways. Accordingly, the same individuals can be categorized as an immigrant, as poor, as working in a low-paid industry, as being of a specific ethnic background, and so on. In whatever ways categories are formed, they turn the researchers toward the social world and require them to bring out from analyses of data their specific contents. Social categories are not stable but are rather in constant motion: not only their meanings, contexts, expectations, and relations but also their boundaries change over time. Yet despite all these changes, categories must be seen as fixed at specific points in time.

Reicher points out that the group members do not only define themselves in terms of specific categories but also act on the basis of beliefs, norms, and values associated with that self-definition—or self-categorization. Moreover, social identities based on categorization should be seen as future-orientated projects of flexible collective actions: "flexibility is a function of varying social categories and is achieved through differing category constructions" (Reicher 2004, 936). In addition to flexibility of categorization, social identity theory studies how members of a group compare themselves to the out-group, how they understand the relations of the out-group and the in-group, and whether they feel empowered to act against the out-group. The self, Reicher points out, is not unitary but is instead a complex system. We define ourselves as persons both in terms of what makes us unique as well as different from others; we are members of a variety of groups. The minimal-group paradigm brings into focus social identification with one's own group, and comparison with and differentiation from the other group. This however, as Reicher points out, was no more than a starting point of research for Tajfel (1978). The theory is concerned not only with discrimination but also with resistance, "not with the inevitability of domination but with the possibility of change" (Reicher 2004, 931). The members of subordinated groups may act individually or collectively, collective self-definition will challenge the dominant group if it is perceived as illegitimate and amenable to cognitive alternatives, and the nature of collective action will depend on contextual factors such as power and domination, among others.

One can get an impression that Reicher's thoroughgoing exposition of the social identity theory, and his response to various challenges with respect to social categorization, brings the theory of social identity and the theory of social representations closer together. In particular, like the theory of social representations, social identity, according to Reicher, places emphasis on the dynamics, change, context, and content of social categories, and on the role of culture and history in constructing social categories.

Nevertheless, Reicher's exposition guides us to recognize, above all, some fundamental epistemological differences between social categorization (including self-categorization) and social representations. These differences could be analytically approached in different ways, and it would be impossible to discuss them fully in this chapter. Therefore, I shall follow up with only two issues. One concerns the difference between similarity and interaction as criteria of the group membership, and, following from this, the other issue concerns the meaning of "content" in these two theories.

SIMILARITY AND INTERACTION

Throughout the last sixty years or so, a number of social psychologists have drawn attention to controversial definitions of a group (for an early review, see Gibb 1954). Among these, and of particular interest in the context of this chapter, are two definitions of a group. One defines group members by similarity—for example, they are immigrants, they have a particular ethnic origin, they are disabled, and so on—and the other definition privileges the interdependence or interaction of its members as a criterion of group membership. These two definitions bring us immediately to the center of controversy. A number of researchers have argued that in the former definition, group members form an aggregate, that is, their membership in a group is based on some kind of similarity, and that such a group must be distinguished from genuine social groups (see Krech and Crutchfield 1948; Newcomb 1951; Gibb 1954; Greenwood 2004; Lewin 1940/1948).

Among the most vociferous critics of aggregate groups was Kurt Lewin. Originally, Lewin developed the field theory as a dynamic approach, examining interdependencies between the individual's behavior and her life space or psychological environment. Equally, his ecological psychology emphasizes the notion of "interdependence." Later, he studied the factors that determine the actions of individuals in a group dynamic. In this context, he drew attention to the difference between static concepts, such as similarity or dissimilarity on the one hand, and dynamic concepts based on interdependencies on the other hand. This explains why concepts like tension, the level of aspiration, motivation, and conflict played such an important role in Lewin's group dynamic (Moscovici and Marková 2006). With respect to groups, "it is not similarity or dissimilarity that decides whether two individuals belong to the same or different groups, but social interaction or other types of interdependence. A group is best defined as a dynamic whole based on interdependence rather than on similarity" (Lewin 1940/1948, 184).

For Lewin, "the main criterion of belongingness is *interdependence of fate*" (184; emphasis original). He returns to the notion of "interdependence of fate" on a number of occasions in his work, and sometimes he also talks about the "common fate," noting, for example, that "the common fate of all Jews makes them a group in reality" (166). Thus, while he vehemently argues for interaction and interdependence as the defining features of the group, Lewin, at the same time, unwittingly opens the door for diverse interpretations of the "interdependence of fate."

Lewin's notion of the "interdependence of fate" has been adopted both by those who study social identity and prejudice as well as those who work within the minority and majority paradigm and in social representations. However, here we come to the problem, because "interdependence of fate" means different things in these two research approaches. For the former, "interdependence of fate" means, above all, "the common fate." For example, passengers travelling on the airplane do not constitute a group, but once the plane becomes hijacked, they suddenly share a common fate that increases their interdependence and welds them into a cohesive group (Brown 2000). This interpretation of "the common fate" fits very well with the theory of social categorization: the hijacked passengers are all in the same boat—they are similar to each other because they face the same danger. When the danger passes, they disperse, again, as individuals into their homes. There is an important consequence of this interpretation. If members of a group are defined by a common or similar fate as a category—for example, they are all hijacked, are all immigrants, are of the same ethnic origin, or are all disabled—it implies that because they face the same problem, there should be a general solution to their problem, such as being released from the hijacked plane, being granted human rights, and so on.

The minority and majority paradigm and the theory of social representations take on a totally different interpretation of Lewin's "interdependence of fate." When Lewin speaks about the danger of Jews in the face of Nazism, and when he claims that "the common fate of all Jews makes them a group in reality" (Lewin 1940/1948, 166), his emphasis on "interdependence of fate" refers to the "organic life of a minority group" (165). Our hijacked passengers are kept together merely by outside pressure. Instead, Lewin maintains, "there is one more characteristic peculiar to minority groups kept together merely by outside pressure as contrasted with the members of a minority who have a positive attitude towards their own group. The latter will have an organic life of its own. It will show organization and inner strength. A minority kept together only from outside is in itself chaotic. It is composed of a mass of individuals without inner relations with each other, a group unorganized and weak" (Lewin 1948, 165).

It is this essential characteristic of a minority group, "having organic life," that constitutes the meaning of Lewin's position that "interdependence of fate" has constituted itself historically. Its inner cohesiveness manifests itself in and through interaction among members. Members are ready to accept dissimilarities and a variety of opinions and beliefs as something organic to the group. They may even dislike members of their group and they may oppose traditions imposed on them as members; nevertheless, inner cohesive forces make them part of the group although they are dispersed all over the world. Belonging or not belonging to a group is not a matter of similarity and dissimilarity.

This difference in the interpretation of "interdependence of fate" is by no means a minor one. It is a major epistemological difference between the two theoretical approaches that cannot be glossed over. True, a common danger surely can instigate a common action. However, it would be trivial to reduce "interdependence of fate" to a temporary task of hijacked passengers. And it is highly questionable whether one can make generalizations from such an arbitrarily composed group and their "common fate" to those minority groups that have established their "interdependence of fate" through long historical and cultural traditions. This is why any attempts to bring the theory of social categorization and the theory of social representations together will need a careful consideration.

THE QUESTION OF CONTENT

Social categories have content, and as Reicher (2004) maintains, their content changes *over* time. While he does not particularly elaborate on what counts as content, one can assume that content might refer to the way a category is described, or that it could contain stereotypical statements and judgements of an out-group, or self-descriptions and self-judgements of an in-group. The social categorization theory emphasizes the role of culture and the dynamics of change, although categories are fixed *at* the time. This fixedness enables the treatment of data in terms of stable dependent and independent variables, in particular in the laboratory.

The meaning of content in social representations is different in nature from that in social categories. Above all, social representations are complex social phenomena, for example, of a disability, whether physical, mental, or otherwise, and their content is structured, with some features being embedded in common sense and unconsciously transmitted from generation to generation. Others might be thematized in public discourses, yet interdependent with unverbalized ideas that are part of traditions and habits of thought. What this means is that the content of social representations is underlain by *theories* penetrating and explaining the group members' beliefs, norms, and actions. In order to understand the content of social representations, the researcher attempts to uncover these mundane theories so that she can create social scientific theories about such phenomena.

Social representations can be formed and maintained in diverse ways, for example, through anchoring and objectification—and they can be also generated from themata. Themata—for example, men versus women— are not independent social categories, but are instead relational oppositions. Themata (Moscovici and Vignaux 2000) are usually very basic relational oppositions, often of a very long cultural duration. They could be personally and collectively relevant (for instance, male versus female, good versus bad, or equal versus unequal), could have an epistemic significance (for example, stability versus change, or old versus new). Importantly, they are not independent categories, but are instead a constellation of interdependent and interacting constituents, one defining the other, like a figure-ground setup. We could call them meaning potentialities in waiting because, while they may be unconsciously part of mundane thinking and speaking, they could be transmitted without awareness from generation to generation through commonsense knowledge. Only when for some reason—whether political, affective, religious, or otherwise—they are brought to awareness will they start generating concrete contents in specific conditions and activate the formation of more complex forms of socially shared knowledge, or of social representations.

Themata are accompanied by various kinds of social and ideological tensions and conflicts that, in and through thematization, are explicitly or implicitly brought into language and communication. Communicative processes, through which these changes in meanings are usually achieved, carry symbolic rituals and images, power relations and interactions, some of which are explicit, while others are implicitly shared. For example, the themata man/woman has become filled with particular kinds of content in specific cultures and regions of the world due to sociocultural circumstances, such as the division of labor, the roles that have resulted from biological differences between males and females. A social representation of a woman is likely to be generated from a number of interdependent components in which the themata of male/female plays an important role, such as equality and inequality between sexes, beauty, power relations, and so on. Some themata endure throughout generations and continue engagement in the thematization of difficult discourses over aeons of time. Others, when established, transformed, and legitimized, may become stabilized and lose their temporary significance; they may fall again into implicitness and oblivion.

But in addition to such descriptions, which superficially can be similar to those in social categorization, there are theories behind such contents. Contents not only circulate in public discourses but also organize and generate discourses, shape common thinking, language, and behavior, and provide grounds for the formation of new social representations. Their meanings have been thematized in infinite private and public discourses throughout the history of mankind. It is thematization and theories that are generated from themata that enable one to say, without contradiction, that "this man is a woman" and equally that "this woman is a man." But this is also why for interactions and interdependences that feed into theories of social representations, there is no collective solution to discrimination that would be acceptable to all members of a minority. For some women, in the era of emphasis on human rights and political correctness, a positive discrimination as a solution to their problem could be seen as an offense. These characteristics mean that the *content* of a social representation cannot be decomposed into fixed and independent variables because meanings are always relational (and not independent).

All in all, this suggests that while one can claim that "categories are representations," one cannot claim that "representations are categories." Attempts to discover theories hiding behind the content of social representations could be of the order of detective stories in which the researcher, like an archaeologist, may be searching for pieces fitting together. One of the pieces in this complex puzzle is the question and here, again, we shall see that the question plays a very different theoretical role in social categorization and in the theory of social representations.

THE TABOO OF CONTACT

Since the publication of Allport's (1954) *The Nature of Prejudice*, research in social psychology has devoted much effort to show that prejudice and discrimination can be reduced by improving intergroup contact. Social identity theory, specifically, attempts to provide a theoretical insight into how, by bringing together members from in-groups and out-groups, conflict and discrimination can be diminished. For example, using correlational data from random sample surveys in religiously divided Northern

Ireland, Hewstone et al. (2006) have found that the amount of inter-group contact was positively related to out-group attitudes, perspective taking, and trust. Based on their findings, the authors express a firm belief that in "deeply segregated societies, contact is an essential part of any solution" (116).

Contact, whether spiritual or physical, is indeed a very important concept in the theory of social representations. But what is contact? It is one thing for members of in-groups and out-groups to mix together in public, to sit next to each other on a train, or in a café, or to play games together. It is another thing, however, to mix privately and have intimate physical contact like touching, drinking from the same cup, or having sex. While some kinds of contact can be examined using attitude scales and opinion surveys, others cannot be accessed in this way. They may not be the subject of opinions and attitudes, but rather of the conscious and the unconscious, symbolic and subtle interactions, and communications that have established themselves through culture, collective memories, and through implicit and explicit prohibitions of contact (for example, Douglas 1966; Brandt 1985; Moscovici 1972). It is these prohibitions and their explanations that are part of the study of social representations.

HEMOPHILIA

My first example of the taboo of contact comes from social representations of hemophilia, the oldest known genetic disorder of blood clotting. The patient with hemophilia may bleed excessively after a physical or an emotional trauma, either externally or into internal organs. People with hemophilia do not form a homogeneous group. There are different types of hemophilia, the commonest of which is a sex-linked recessive disorder in which the disorder affects males and the gene is passed by females. There are mild, moderate, and severe forms; some hemophiliacs have additional health problems like hepatitis C, and some have chronic liver disease and inhibitors to treatment. In addition to the stress of possible HIV infection, psychological problems in young men include the fear of stigma and rejection by female partners, which militates against disclosing that one suffers from the disorder. In some people, hemophilia is a visible disorder, while in others, it is invisible. Some hemophiliacs might categorize themselves as hemophiliacs, and others might reject this categorization.

Hemophilia affects people all over the world. It was already known in ancient Europe, and the first references can be found in Talmudic writings in the second century. Rabbinical rulings prohibited circumcision in the third boy in a family if the first and the second child died as a result of bleeding following circumcision.(Katzenelson 1958). Throughout history, cases of this mysterious family bleeding have been described. Hemophilia became known as "the royal disease" in Europe when, as it seems, Queen Victoria was a carrier through spontaneous mutation and the disease affected several members of the royalty throughout Europe.

The general public holds representations about hemophilia. The blood mysticism, prevalent in religions and in mythologies, and implicit fears of blood impurity and of the disease all contribute to the formation of social representations of hemophilia in the general public. There is a widespread belief among people that hemophiliacs will bleed to death from superficial cuts of the skin and that, therefore, hemophiliacs are untouchable.

Equally, hemophiliacs have representations of others' representations. Analyzing views of people with hemophilia on their employment prospects, we have found that because of fears of rejection, adult men attempt to conceal hemophilia (Forbes et al. 1982; Marková 1997; Marková, Lockyer, and Forbes 1980; Marková and Forbes 1984; Marková et al. 1990). For many, whether "to tell or not to tell" others and employers, specifically, remains a dilemma, as our postal surveys (Forbes et al. 1982) have shown:

> First of all say nothing to employers that you suffer from haemophilia. They think you can bleed to death from a pin prick.
> Lie like hell when interviewed and pray you have enough time between bleeds to prove you can do the job as well as the next person when you are fit.

And so while people with hemophilia live in society like anybody else and have contact with others, in some ways they are separated by an invisible screen.

In his autobiography *Touch Me Who Dares*, Shelley (1985), a hemophiliac, describes how, from his childhood, he had to cope with the ignorance of others and with their fear that he would bleed to death from superficial injuries. Another author, Robert Massie (1985), in his childhood reflection, describes an unforgettable event when his schoolmaster announced that no one was to touch Bobby Massie, under threat of punishment. He states that his sudden transformation into an untouchable, although the headmaster did that with good intentions, filled him with a sense of powerlessness and stinging humiliation.

While these cases refer to clearly verbalized events, many beliefs about illnesses and disabilities are not stated explicitly. Rather, they are implicit and operate under the level of awareness. People often shy away from those with chronic diseases for unconscious fears of contamination, whether physical or moral (Douglas 1966; Brandt 1985).

MENTAL ILLNESS

Another example is that of Denise Jodelet's (1989/1991) research of madness and social representations in Ainay-le-Château, France. Although psychiatric patients are medically and administratively cared for by the establishment, which is called the Family Colony, they are not shut there; rather, they live with villagers' families in their homes. Villagers have taken them voluntarily as paying guests into their homes, allowing for a great deal of contact. Yet behind this closeness of contact between patients and nonpatients, Jodelet finds hidden secrets in the village that on the one hand is open toward the mentally ill, but at the same time rejects them. Interactions between the in-group and out-group are controlled by concrete and symbolic measures. The families define a permissible threshold of interaction, and whatever falls outside the threshold is not permitted. They have created partitions and protected areas as defenses against intrusion into their privacy.

The fundamental feature of Jodelet's research is that she not only describes contacts between patients and villagers by which these barriers have been erected, but she also searches for the exact meanings and explanations that are hidden behind these interactions. On the one hand, most villagers do not believe in medical dangers coming from mental patients. They know that mental illness is not contagious and that the lodger does not transmit germs or microbes, as would be the case with sufferers of tuberculosis, yet at the same time, they believe in an unarticulated contamination. There are folk-beliefs, superstition, and perhaps beliefs in magic power in operation here that have been unconsciously transmitted for generations, therefore any risk of contamination must be avoided. Villagers are preoccupied with hygiene—they wash their laundry, dishes, and cutlery separately from those of their lodgers and they eat separately from them. Intimate physical contact, and, above all, any sexual contact, is strictly prohibited. Although in-groups and out-groups mix in public spaces like streets and cinemas, and in semipublic places like festivals and dances, strict rules about contact in these places and spaces are kept to uphold the established social division. Social representations become "self-fulfilling prophesies," for people act on the basis of these prophesies. As Jodelet says,

> In this network of multiple signifiers which is provided by the acting out of a conception of madness, contact and illness are associated with magic

power and pollution on the one hand and with the otherness and impurity
which give rise to social differentiation on the other. . . . The pollutant
power of the illness, a magic force transmitted by the contact with living
secretions, becomes in the sign of otherness proper to his nature as a bearer
of insanity whose impurity threatens the integrity of others. The avoidance
of this contact, a measure of hygiene adopted to protect the human body
from contamination, becomes a social division established to protect the
social body from mixture. (Jodelet 1989/1991, 261–62)

IN-GROUPS, OUT-GROUPS, AND DIALOGICAL TRIADS

There is an essential point in Jodelet's analysis: social categorization is
based on perception, the formation of stereotypes and prejudice, and on
the study of relations between groups, including comparison and discrimination. These theoretical positions that systematically separate the
in-group and out-group use a cognitive model that supposedly organizes
and interprets groups' physical and social environments. However, the
theory of social categorization ignores, Jodelet points out, that in-groups
and out-groups are not the only participants in this social game. There is,
in addition, a "third party" who takes the role of an active participant in
this communicative enterprise.

Groups do not live in a vacuum but are rather part of a broader community with which they interact. Outsiders are not neutral onlookers,
but they communicate with in-groups and out-groups and can make flat-
tering as well as damaging judgments of either of them. What it means in
the context of Jodelet's research is that the third party—for example, visitors to Ainay-le-Château or any outsiders of the village—can evaluate
and judge this "incredible" contact between villagers and mental patients.
As a result, villagers become anxious about their social recognition by
others. A close association with mentally ill patients could downgrade, in
the eyes of others, the villagers' social identity. This communicative
aspect that the third party brings into the interaction between in-groups
and out-groups, is, however, totally missing from the theory of social categorization. Jodelet refers in this context to the important theoretical
contribution that the triadic conception of the Ego-Alter-Object
(Moscovici 1984) introduces into the study of social influence as an
organizer of minority and majority interactions.

The triadic conception of the Ego-Alter-Object has a very broad significance. It constitutes an epistemological unit in the theory of social representations. Communication between the Ego and the Alter is always about
something: the Ego and the Alter generate social representations of objects
of knowledge (or belief) jointly, that is, dialogically. I have previously

characterized dialogicality as the capacity of the human mind to conceive, create, and communicate about social realities in terms of, or in opposition to, otherness (Marková 2003). The dialogical triadic conception is multifaceted. The object of representation in the triadic conception does not have to be a "thing"; it can also be another person, a group, a self-representation, or a representation of another.

Self- or other-representations are expressed by names. Villagers in Jodelet's research represent the mentally ill as being of different types: innocent, crazy, epileptic, mentally disabled, insane, or neurotic. The names that mentally ill patients are given hide implicit theories of morality and immorality, of danger and violence, and of purity and impurity; or they may indicate a passive and insufficient mental functioning of patients. The names control what kinds of interactions, such as physical contact, villagers of Ainay-le-Château and mentally ill patients are permitted or at least recommended to have. They also imply what kinds of contact are advisable to protect members of the family, in particular children and daughters, and what kind of care patients of different types may need in order to be safe.

Taxonomies, however, can also express contents of social representations explicitly without shame or embarrassment. While taxonomies in Jodelet's (1989/1991) research implicitly control interactions between villagers and mentally ill patients, other taxonomies express contents of social representations explicitly without shame or embarrassment. For example literature on the history of representation of people with learning disabilities shows that at the beginning of the twentieth century, people with learning difficulties were categorized and defined as follows: "Low grade: . . . temperament bestial [to] High grade: . . . with a genius for evil (Barr 1904, 1; quoted by Jahoda 1995).

The interaction between the *Ego* and *Alter* is never solely an exchange of words in a dialogue involving participants who are copresent. It always involves third parties who are not present, including the "third person," "virtual others," "other others" (like friends, peers, and institutions), or the "positioning" of the self with respect to physically or symbolically copresent "others." One can refer in this sense to George Herbert Mead and Sigmund Freud, who introduced the terms "generalized other" and "superego," respectively. Although the underlying concepts of these terms are theoretically different, they both function as a societal "super-addressee," sanctioning and reprimanding individuals who dissent from socially imposed norms. They are part of individuals' consciousness (e.g., "the people," science, and tradition), unconscious (e.g., Freud's superego), or conscience (e.g., Mead's "the generalized other"). In addition to the here and now, every communication has roots in the past, as well as an orientation toward the future. Anticipations of future judgments and evaluations of an unknown third party, too, play a communicative role.

But one does not need to have an external judge as the third party. There is also an internal judge in the self. Traditions, institutions, friends and colleagues, political parties, and so on speak, just like the present dialogical participants, through "the inner *Alter.*" What I mean here is a symbolically and socially represented *Alter* that is in an *internal dialogue* with the Ego. Such an inner third party, just like the external third party, organizes topics, ideas, and even positions from which the self speaks.

The research on hemophilia and on madness shows that in-groups and out-groups are in contact. What is important in both cases, however, is that the taboo of contact imposes the control on the kind of contact that is permitted and forbidden. Control can be imposed in and through behavior, language, and communication, through the rules of politeness, and through a forbidden trespassing into the private space. Control in communication, in particular, can be very powerful: we say things to each other, but we may not communicate. This means that although people are spoken to, and words are used, these are just labels or signals rather than meaningful signifiers of any trustworthy relations. They may be "politically correct" expressions, safe kinds of things that are expected to be said, but they leave the common space empty, and are so isolating interlocutors in a ghetto. And so despite being in contact, controlled non-communicative words and gestures appear as forms of "communication."

TOWARD INTERGROUP TOLERANCE

It has often been presupposed in the history of humankind that progress in society can be achieved through education, enlightenment, and through the pursuit of knowledge. Likewise, rationalistic models in social psychology assume that social contact, interaction, and a better knowledge of others can remove barriers between groups. For example, if we transform belief-based social representations that engender discrimination and prejudice into knowledge-based social representations, and if we promote more contact between groups, we would challenge discrimination and improve intergroup relations. This is why people with hemophilia often make considerable educational efforts to change belief-based social representations of the general public into knowledge-based social representations. And this is why governments, in order to eliminate the spread of AIDS, run educational campaigns under slogans like "don't die of ignorance."

These attempts to transform beliefs into knowledge, despite their good intentions, usually ignore that the hardness of a belief lies in its attachment to other beliefs. For example, the belief that people with hemophilia are "untouchable" may be connected with another belief, such as the thought that a person with hemophilia will bleed to death from a needle prick, or even an unexpressed belief that has something to do with the impurity of blood, and so on. People who hold belief-based social representations of hemophilia do not try to find proof for their beliefs or facts about the disease. Instead, their representations perpetuate and reinforce themselves through discourse with others.

Moreover, beliefs live in the community and may be transmitted unconsciously from generation to generation through collective memory and through commonsense knowledge. They may not even be activated for generations, and they rely primarily on consensus with others, exerting an irresistible pressure to conform. Also, since we are unaware of these beliefs, this pressure is very powerful.

In their research on social representations of Gypsies, Pérez, Moscovici, and Chulvi (2007) draw attention to concealed aspects of discrimination that can hardly be removed by the rationalistic models in which society would like to believe. These researchers explore the taboo against group contact. Their experiments show that the Gypsy minority is more discriminated against when the context of that minority constitutes a threat to the anthropological differentiation from the majority. Referring to contemporary changes with respect to the discrimination of minorities that are now viewed more positively than in the past, the authors claim, "Gypsies, similar to other minorities, benefit from this change in the 'spirit of the times,' as our research indicates. Yet we wonder all the same whether prejudices or the taboo against contact are receding as much as would be expected, in this heyday of human rights" (Pérez et al. 2007, 269).

The contact hypothesis, in contrast, does not tell us anything either about hidden theories transmitted among the general public or about the nature of communication or interaction between in-groups and out-groups. One would certainly like to believe the finding of Hewstone et al. (2006, 100) that the contact hypothesis contributes "to the fact that psychology is now in its best position ever to make a contribution to the advancement of world peace by actively promoting intergroup tolerance." But is "promoting intergroup tolerance" not something that mankind has been attempting to do throughout its long history? Have religions of all kinds, political regimes, and humanistic associations not tried to do that either peacefully or through the most intolerant means? Can social psychology claim such an easy solution to the most difficult social phenomena that are still poorly understood?

The research to which I have referred in this chapter indicates that before we really can find solutions to how to promote intergroup tolerance, social psychology must pay attention to the complex nature of the human mind, its history, its unconscious, and its implicitly shared social representations. This may take some time, but this desirable outcome can be the goal of the theory of social representations and of social identity.

REFERENCES

Allport, G. W. 1954. *The nature of prejudice*. Reading, MA: Addison-Wesley.
Augoustinos, M. 2001. Social categorization: Towards theoretical integration. In *Representations of the social: Bridging theoretical traditions*, ed. K. Deaux and G. Philogène, 201–16. Oxford: Blackwell.
Barr, M. W. 1904. *Mental defectives: Their history, treatment and training*. Philadelphia: Blakinston's Sons.
Brandt, A. M. 1985. *No magic bullet*. New York: Oxford University Press.
Breakwell, G. M. 1993. Integrating paradigms, methodological implications. In *Empirical approaches to social representations*, ed. G. M. Breakwell and D. V. Canter, 180–201.Oxford: Oxford University Press.
————. 2001. Social representational constraints upon identity. In *Representations of the Social: Bridging theoretical traditions*, ed. K. Deaux and G. Philogène, 271–84. Oxford: Blackwell.
Brewer, M. B. 2001. Social identities and social representations: A question of priority? In *Representations of the social: Bridging theoretical traditions*, ed. K. Deaux and G. Philogène, 305–11. Oxford: Blackwell.
Brown, R. 2000. *Group processes: Dynamics within and between groups*. 2nd ed. Oxford: Blackwell.
Coelho, N. E., Jr., and L. C. Figueiredo. 2003. Patterns of intersubjectivity in the constitution of subjectivity: Dimensions of otherness. *Culture & Psychology* 9:193–208.
Deaux, K., and G. Philogène eds. 2001. *Representations of the social: Bridging theoretical traditions*. Oxford: Blackwell.
Douglas, M. 1966. *Purity and danger*. London: Routledge; Henley: Kegan Paul.
Duveen, G. 2001. Representations, identities, resistance. In *Representations of the social: Bridging theoretical traditions*, ed. K. Deaux and G. Philogène, 257–70. Oxford: Blackwell.
Duveen, G., and B. Lloyd. 1986. The significance of social identities. *The British Journal of Social Psychology* 25:219–30.
————, eds. 1990. *Social representations and the development of knowledge*. Cambridge: Cambridge University Press.
Forbes, C. D., I. Marková, J. Stuart, P. Jones. 1982. To tell or not to tell: Haemophiliacs' views on their employment prospects. *International Journal of Rehabilitation Research* 5:13–18.

Gibb, C. A. 1954. Leadership. In *The handbook of social psychology*, vol. 4, ed. G. Lindsay and E. Aronson, 205–82. Reading, MA: Addison-Wesley.

Greenwood, J. D. 2004. *The disappearance of the social in American social psychology*. Cambridge: Cambridge University Press.

Hastings, J., ed. 1908–26. *Encyclopaedia of religion and ethics (1908–1926)*. Vols. 10, 12. New York: Charles Scribner's Sons.

Hewstone, M., E. Cairns, A. Voci, J. Hamberger, and U. Niens. 2006. Intergroup contact, forgiveness, and experience of "the troubles" in Northern Ireland. *Journal of Social Issues* 62:99–120.

Jahoda, A. 1995. Quality of life: Hope for the future or an echo from the distant past. In *Representations of health, illness and handicap*, ed. I. Marková and R. Farr, 205–24. Amsterdam: Harwood.

Jodelet, D. 1989/1991. *Madness and social representations*. Trans. T. Pownall. Ed. G. Duveen. London: Harvester Wheatsheaf.

Katzenelson, J. L. 1958. Hemophilia with special reference to the Talmud. *Hebrew Medical Journal* 1:165–78.

Krech, D., and R. S. Crutchfield. 1948. *Theory and problems of social psychology*. New York: McGraw Hill.

Levinas, E. 1974/1981. *Otherwise than being, or beyond essence*. Trans. A. Lingis. The Hague: Martinus Nijhoff.

Lewin, K. 1940/1948. Bringing up the Jewish child. In *Resolving social conflicts*, by K. Lewin, ed. G. Weis Lewin, 169–85. New York: Harper and Row.

Marková, I. 1997. The family and haemophilia. In *Textbook of haemophilia*, ed. F. Forbes, L. Aledort, and R. Madhok, 335–46. Malden, MA: Blackwell.

———. 2003. *Dialogicality and social representations*. Cambridge: Cambridge University Press.

Marková, I., and Forbes, C. 1984. Coping with haemophilia. *International Review of Applied Psychology* 33:457–77.

Marková, I., R. Lockyer, and C. Forbes. 1980. Self-perception of employed and unemployed haemophiliacs. *Psychological Medicine* 10:559–65.

Marková, I., P. A. Wilkie, S. A. Naji, and C. D. Forbes. 1990. Knowledge of HIV/AIDS and behavioural change of people with haemophilia. *Psychology and Health* 4:125–33.

Massie, R. K. 1985. The constant shadow. Reflections on the life of a chronically ill child. In *Issues in the care of children with chronic illness*, ed. N. Hobbs and J. M. Perrin, 13–22. San Francisco: Jossey-Bass.

Moghaddam, F. M. 2003. Moghaddam, F. M. 2003. Interobjectivity and culture. *Culture & Psychology* 9:221–32.

Moscovici, S. 1972. *La société contre nature*. Paris: Plon.

———. 1976. *La Psychanalyse: Son image et son public*. 2nd ed. Paris: Presses Universitaires de France.

———. 1984. Introduction: Le domaine de la psychologie sociale. In *Psychologie sociale, ed.* S. Moscovici, 5–22. Paris: Presses Universitaires de France.

———. 1993. The return of the unconscious. *Social Research* 60:39–93.

Moscovici, S., and I. Marková. 2006. *The making of modern social psychology.* Cambridge: Polity.

Moscovici, S., and G. Vignaux. 1994. Le Concept de Thêmata. In *Structures et transformations des représentations sociales,* ed. Guimelli, 25–72. Neuchatel: Delachaux et Niestlé.

Newcomb, T. M. 1951. Social psychological theory: Integrating individual and social approaches. In *Social psychology at the crossroads,* ed. J. M. Rohrer and M. Sherif. New York: Harper.

Pérez, J. A., S. Moscovici, and B. Chulvi. 2007. The taboo against group contact: Hypothesis of Gypsy ontologization. *British Journal of Social Psychology* 46: 249–72.

Raudsepp M., M. Heidmets, and J. Kruusvall. Forthcoming. Changing patterns of trust: The Estonian case. In *Trust and distrust: Sociocultural perspectives,* ed. I. Marková and A. Gillespie. Greenwich: Information Age.

Reicher, S. 2004. The context of social identity: Domination, resistance, and change. *Political Psychology* 25:921–45.

Shelley, L. F. 1985. *Touch me who dares.* Llandsyul, Wales: Gomer Press.

Tajfel, H. 1978. Social categorization, social identity and social comparison. In *Differentiation between social groups,* ed. H. Tajfel, 61–76. London: Academic Press.

Wagner, W., and N. Hayes. 2005. *Everyday discourse and common sense. The theory of social representations.* Basingstoke, UK: Palgrave.

Whyte, L. L. 1962. *The unconscious before Freud.* New York: Doubleday.

INDEX